Intelligent LAN Management with Novell® NetWare®

Intelligent LAN Management with Novell® NetWare®

Elenore M. Amon

Novell Certified NetWare Engineer™

Annette N. Heatherington

Novell Certified NetWare Engineer™

Douglas D. Henderson

Prentice Hall

Englewood Cliffs, New Jersey 07632

Library of Congress Cataloging-in-Publication Data

AMON, ELENORE M.
Intelligent LAN management with Novell NetWare / Elenore M. Amon, Annette N. Heatherington, Douglas D. Henderson.
p. cm.
Includes index.
ISBN 0-13-472259-0
1. Local area networks (Computer networks) 2. NewWare (Computer operating system) I. Heatherington, Annette N. II. Henderson, Douglas D. III. Title.
TK5105.7.A48 1991
004.6—dc20 90-44605
CIP

Cover design: *Diana Hartland*
Manufacturing buyer: *Kelly Behr*

A Division of Simon & Schuster
Englewood Cliffs, New Jersey 07632

The publisher offers discounts on this book when ordered in bulk quantities. For more information, write:

Special Sales/College Marketing
Prentice-Hall, Inc.
College Technical and Reference Division
Englewood Cliffs, New Jersey 07632

Printed in the United States of America

10 9 8 7 6 5 4 3

ISBN 0-13-472259-0

PRENTICE-HALL INTERNATIONAL (UK) LIMITED, *London*
PRENTICE-HALL OF AUSTRALIA PTY. LIMITED, *Sydney*
PRENTICE-HALL CANADA INC., *Toronto*
PRENTICE-HALL HISPANOAMERICANA, S.A., *Mexico*
PRENTICE-HALL OF INDIA PRIVATE LIMITED, *New Delhi*
PRENTICE-HALL OF JAPAN, INC., *Tokyo*
SIMON & SCHUSTER ASIA PTE. LTD., *Singapore*
EDITORA PRENTICE-HALL DO BRASIL, LTDA., *Rio de Janeiro*

CONTENTS

7 NETWARE 386

PART 2 REFERENCE

8 INSTALLATION OVERVIEW

9 DIRECTORY STRUCTURES

INTRODUCTION

Business has come to depend on networks, which provide efficient and inexpensive computing power. Insuring that these systems operate effectively has become the management challenge of the 90's. Intelligent LAN Management has been designed to help you meet that challenge.

Making management decisions involving networks and computers requires information. It also requires a technical level of understanding, essential to interpret that information. There are literally hundreds of necessary decisions that must be made with networks, whether its in the initial network setup and configuration, or in the day to day network operation.

This text has collected the information you need to make informed management decisions about Novell networks in one volume. It has been designed to provide technical information required by management to understand the network, from the basics of stand-alone computers, to the most complex network concepts. Great care has been taken to ensure that it is written in English, not any one of the varieties of "techspeak."

Intelligent LAN Management has been designed to fill the gap between basic understanding, and highly-technical manuals, which explain NetWare in exhaustive detail, but do not simply explain common problems such as

- **"Our printers do not seem to work, why?"** This is one of the most common and frustrating problems facing network managers. Printers are deceptively simple, that is why printer basics have been explained in part 1 CONCEPTS, in the hardware chapter under basics for stand-alone personal computers, in section 2.1.5. "Printing with NetWare" (part 2 REFERENCE) builds on the base of understanding established by the CONCEPTS section, and explains network printing.

- **"Users want things to be automatic, how is that done?"** A network should be "transparent" to end users. Proper installation and setup is the key to using NetWares features such as installation options (chapter 8), login scripts (chapter 12), or search drives (chapter 9).

- **"Can we establish menus for users, to keep it simple?"** Chapter 13 clearly explains how to set up NetWares menu system for your users, with fully detailed examples.

Correctly structured menus provide a management tool to make network operation simple for the end user, saving time, money, and frustration. This simplicity will reduce the need for extensive training.

- **"We have some very sensitive data, how do we protect it?"** NetWare offers an incredible variety of effective security measures, however few of them are set up by default. Chapter 10 explains the security options available, and details their implementation, from a management perspective.

- **"Why does our network go down so often?"** Networks must be managed, if they are not you run the risk of inefficient operation and excessive down time. To insure efficient and secure operation, the network must be properly installed (chapters 8 and 9), security must be established (chapter 10), and it must be effectively maintained (chapter 5) and managed using concepts, ideas and management options explained throughout the text.

- **"What will NetWare 386 do for me?"** NetWare 386 is dealt with in detail in Chapter 7, at the end of the PART 1, **CONCEPTS**. Chapter 7 will provide you with the information to understand 386, or to evaluate its features if you are planning to upgrade. In keeping with the management information focus of PART 1, **CONCEPTS**, chapter 7 concentrates on what is new, and what has been changed from previous NetWare versions.

Recognizing the opportunities available with a network is a little like moving to a foreign country. You must learn a new language, adopt new customs or standards, and be able to mold your thinking to this new adventure. Novell's Local area networks (LANs) have terms that at first will seem foreign, such as BINDFIX, FCONSOLE, FILER and NetWare. A glossary has been included, with concise explanations for all of the terms you will need to understand a Novell network. This text will enable you to understand computer and network concepts and speak "network language".

Intelligent LAN Management has been designed as the complete managers handbook for Novell networks. It is a management tool, to help you make informed management decisions encompassing the capabilities of this technology. To fully understand those capabilities, we have taken the time to establish a good foundation of computer basics, and then built on that base. We explain each piece of the puzzle, to an understanding of "the big picture"

New computer technology has swept over us with amazing speed. Computer literacy once a unique skill, is now an essential management requirement. Literacy requires information, and there is no lack of that in today's marketplace. In assembling this text our biggest hurdle was to reduce the volume of material to a manageable level. Unfortunately much of the information available is written with the assumption that you are already familiar with the material, and you only require a few reference items. This makes learning about the NetWare operating system a little like learning english from a dictionary, possible but extremely frustrating. If you have ever tried to find a simple explanation (in English), of anything technical you will know about frustration. In this text, we have collected information from the many technical sources available, and organized it in a simple logical way. Novell's naming conventions are used throughout for ease of understanding, and consistency with other NetWare documentation.

This text has been organized to fully explain networks, as well as both the hardware and software components they require to function. The material has been divided into these parts

PART 1 CONCEPTS

PART 2 REFERENCE

PART 3 DATA COMMUNICATIONS

GLOSSARY

APPENDICES

Intelligent LAN Management is unique because it recognizes that before you can understand networks, you must first have a grasp of computer basics, or an understanding of a single computer (often referred to as a stand-alone microcomputer). That has been the focus of PART 1, **CONCEPTS**.

PART 2, **REFERENCE** explains how you establish your network, and how it can be best maintained. This is important, for without proper implementation your LAN can become a black hole into which you throw time and money. We have taken great pains to ensure that unlike other publications, we do not get caught up in the keystrokes, but rather we emphasize the overall descriptions of the processes involved. Our guiding rule for this entire text has been: "Concepts first-keystrokes second." After many years in the computer industry we feel that if you have a good grasp of the concepts, you can easily understand the keystrokes required using the logic inherent in most computer applications. If on the other hand you focus on the keystrokes, and never get a clear overview, you will never be able to make any changes, updates, or provide the kind of informed decisions required to perform routine maintenance, and to provide management direction.

PART 3, **DATA COMMUNICATIONS** outlines the information you will need to understand your NetWare communications options. This part discusses the products available from Novell that will enable you to connect remote PCs, LAN to LAN, LAN to asynchronous host, PCs to synchronous host, and LAN to synchronous host. Part three has been logically written, to reduce this rather complex subject to its simplest terms.

The **GLOSSARY** has been included to give you the reader a valuable information resource. In keeping with the theme of the rest of the text of providing the tools for informed management decisions, it has been written to insure that you can quickly grasp the meaning of the terms used with computers, communications, and with Novell's network operating system called NetWare.

In the **APPENDIX** we have provided a list of common file extensions, and a checklist for a working system to give you the information you need, in a format you can easily access.

Good Luck with your network and thank you for choosing "Intelligent LAN Management".

DEDICATIONS

My heartfelt thanks to Jerry and Margot Hodgson, my parents, who freed me to fulfill my potential. To my daughters, Katherine and Stacy, thank you. Also a special thank you to Taito Software Inc., for their encouragement.

Elenore Amon

Kelly, thank you for helping me live through the creation of this text, and for your love and faith in my abilities. Mom, William, Brenda and Sheila, I thank you for your love and support.

Annette Heatherington

I wish to thank Roberta, who had faith in my ability, and my friend Bill who helped in his own special way. A historical thank you for Burton Thompson, who taught me word economy twenty years ago. Also, a special appreciation to fellow broadcaster Frank Thompson, who convinced me to take rest breaks in the country, and helped to maintain my level of enthusiasm.

Doug Henderson

ACKNOWLEDGEMENTS

We wish to thank our reviewers Steve Fairbairn, Doug Bailey, and John Campbell, for their dedication, support and encouragement. They reviewed the text of this text as a favor, and without their generous contribution, this text would not have been possible. A special thank you to Peter Whitelaw of Novell Canada, for providing essential research material. We wish to thank Computer Associates for supplying their invaluable assistance in the preparation of the ACCPAC install section. Darlene Robinson freely assisted us in the difficult area of personnel concepts, and has earned our eternal gratitude. Taito Software Inc., has generously supported and encouraged our efforts, and we sincerely appreciate their contribution. Gary Mitchell of Main Computers Inc., for over a decade, has provided us with the benefits of his practical hardware and software experience. The computer-generated graphics in this text were made possible with the invaluable assistance of Karen Featherston of Art Right Software Corporation, who went the extra mile to supply us with the graphics we required.

DESKTOP PUBLISHING

This manuscript was prepared using WordPerfect 5.0, and 5.1, products of WordPerfect Corporation. Graphics were accomplished using Corel Draw, Pagemaker and Art Right Clip Art Images.

DISCLAIMER

Readers of this text are advised that

1. Compliance with software licenses and licensing agreement, copyright, and all laws and regulations pertaining to computers, and software are the sole responsibility of the reader.

2. Nothing contained in this text should be interpreted as counseling or promoting the reader to violate software licenses and licensing agreements, and copyright law.

3. Manufacturer's recommendations and directions for the use of computer software are to be followed at all times, and the reader must ensure that they take all necessary precautions, and liability remains the sole responsibility of the reader.

4. The authors and publisher accept no responsibility for any loss or damage suffered by the reader or any other individuals as a result of their failure to observe the contents of this disclaimer.

5. Readers are cautioned that individual applications of the NetWare operating system, and applications software programs vary greatly. It is the reader's responsibility to consult with the manufacturer or an authorized representative of the applicable product, to ensure compatibility.

6. Every effort has been made to ensure the accuracy of the directions, procedures and information in this text. The purpose of this text, however, is to give management direction and information on the NetWare operating system, and computers. Therefore, the authors can accept no responsibility for any loss or damage suffered by any reader or other individual as the result of any error or omission contained in this text, or as a result of the application by the reader of any information contained in this text.

TRADEMARKS

The corporate trademarks listed below are for the company names, products and services mentioned in this text. Every effort has been made to ensure that this list is complete.

286A and 286B are trademarks of Novell, Inc.
3COM is a trademark of 3COM Corp.
3COM 3C501 ETHERLINK, 3COM 3C505 ETHERLINK Plus, and ETHERLINK are trademarks of 3COM Corporation.
ACCPAC is a registered trademark of Computer Associates International, Inc.
Acer 910 and Acer 1100 are trademarks of Acer Corporation.
Adaptec is a trademark of Adaptec, Inc.
ADIC is a registered trademark of Advanced Digital Information Corporation.
ALLEN-BRADLEY VISTALAN/PC is a trademark of ALLEN-BRADLEY Company, Inc.
Apple Imagewriter II and Apple Laserwriter I/PLUS are registered trademarks of Apple Computer, Inc.
APPLETALK is a registered trademark of Apple Computer, Inc.
ARCNET is a registered trademark of Datapoint Corporation.
AST is a trademark of AST Research, Inc.
AT&T is a trademark of AT&T.
AT&T STARLAN is a trademark of AT&T.
Btrieve is a registered trademark of Novell, Inc.
CableTamer is a trademark of 3COM Corporation.
CDC WREN III is a trademark of Control Data Corporation.
Chips and Technologies is a registered trademark of Chips and Technologies, Inc.
CITOH 310/315 and CITOH 600 are trademarks of CITOH Corporation.
CMI is a trademark of Computer Memories, Inc.
COMPAQ is a registered trademark of Compaq Computer Corporation.
Compact Disk is a trademark of Sony Corporation.
Corona is a trademark of Corona Data Systems, Inc.
Corvus Omninet is a trademark of Corvus Systems.
DBASE III is a registered trademark of ASHTON-TATE Corporation.
DEC is a registered trademark of Digital Equipment Corporation.
Diablo is a registered trademark of Xerox Corporation.
Diablo is a trademark of Diablo Systems, Inc.

DISK MANAGER is a trademark of ONTRACK Computer Systems, Inc.
Epson is a trademark of Epson America, Inc.
Ethernet is a registered trademark of Digital Equipment Corporation, Intel Corporation, and Xerox Corporation.
EXCEL is a registered trademark of Microsoft Corporation
File Shuttle is a trademark of Getc Software Inc.
Fujitsu is a trademark of Fujitsu America, Inc.
Gateway and G/NET are registered trademarks of Gateway Communications, Inc.
Gemini is a registered trademark of Star Micronics America, Inc.
Hayes is a registered trademark of Hayes Microcomputer Products, Inc.
Hayes Smartmodem 1200 and Hayes Smartmodem 2400 are trademarks of Hayes Microcomputer Products, Inc.
HEWLETT-PACKARD is a trademark of HEWLETT-PACKARD Company.
Honda is a trademark of the Honda Corporation.
Hot Fix is a trademark of Novell, Inc.
HP LASERJET is a registered trademark of HEWLETT-PACKARD Company.
IBM is a registered trademark of International Business Machines Corporation.
IBM PC AT, IBM PC XT, IBM PS/2, IBM PS/2, and Micro Channel are trademarks of IBM.
IBM PC Network is a registered trademark of International Business Machines Corporation.
IBM PROPRINTER is a registered trademark of International Business Machines Corporation.
IBM TOKEN-RING is a trademark of International Business Machines Corporation.
IMAGEWRITER is a registered trademark of Apple Computer, Inc.
Intel is a registered trademark of Intel Corporation.
Internetwork Packet Protocol is a trademark of Xerox Corporation.
Internetwork Packet Exchange (IPX) is a trademark of Novell, Inc.
LanScanner is a trademark of 3COM Corporation.
LANSWER is a trademark of Novell, Inc.
LANSpool is a registered trademark of LAN Systems Inc.
Lap-Link is a trademark of Travelling Software Inc.
Laserline is a registered trademark of Oki America, Inc.
LASERWRITER is a registered trademark of Apple Computer, Inc.
LOCALTALK is a trademark of Apple Computer, Inc.
LOMAX Utilities is a product of J.A. Lomax Associates
Lotus, Lotus 1-2-3, and Symphony are trademarks of Lotus Development Corporation.
LT Stat is a trademark of Blue Lance
Macintosh is a registered trademark of Apple Computer, Inc.
Maxtor is a trademark of Maxtor Corporation.
Mercedes is a trademark of the Mercedes Benz Corporation.
MBA Accounting Software is a registered trademark of Micro Business Applications, Inc.
METAFILE is a registered trademark of METAFILE Information Systems, Inc.
MICOM Interlan is a trademark of MICOM Corporation.
MICOM is a trademark of MICOM Systems, Inc.

Micro Channel is a trademark of International Business Machines Corporation.
Microline is a registered trademark of Oki America, Inc.
MINISCRIBE is a trademark of MINISCRIBE Corporation.
MS-DOS is a trademark of Microsoft Corporation.
Multiport Repeater is a trademark of 3COM Corporation.
NETWARE is a registered trademark of Novell, Inc.
NETWARE Requester is a trademark of Novell, Inc.
NETWIRE is a registered trademark of Novell, Inc.
Novell is a registered trademark of Novell, Inc.
Office Writer is a trademark of Office Solutions, Inc.
Okidata is a registered trademark of Oki America, Inc. Marque Deposee de Oki America, Inc.
OMTI is a trademark of Scientific Micro Systems, Inc.
Operating System/2 and OS/2 are trademarks of International Business Machines Corporation.
Pagemaker is a trademark of Aldous Corporation
PairTamer is a trademark of 3COM Corporation.
PAL is a registered trademark of Monolithic Memories Inc.
Panasonic is a registered trademark of Matsushita Electric Industrial Co., Ltd.
Paradox is a registered trademark of Borland International, Inc.
PC-DOS is a trademark of International Business Machines Corporation.
PDI508 is a trademark of Pure Data Ltd.
Pinwriter is a registered trademark of NEC Corporation.
Postscript is a trademark of Adobe Systems Inc.
Porsche is a registered trademark of the Porsche Corporation.
Proteon and PRONET-10 with Checksum are trademarks of Proteon, Inc.
Pyxis is a trademark of Ampex Corporation.
QEdit is a trademark of Applied Systems Technologies, Inc.
Quantum is a trademark of Quantum Corporation.
R:Base 5000 is a trademark of MICRORIM, Inc.
Revelation is a registered trademark of COSMOS, Inc.
Rodime is a trademark of Rodime PLC.
RX-NET is a trademark of Novell, Inc.
S-NET is a trademark of Novell, Inc.
Santa Clara Systems is a trademark of Novell, Inc.
SFT is a trademark of Novell, Inc.
SIDEKICK is a registered trademark of Borland International Inc.
Spinwriter is a registered trademark of NEC Corporation.
SQ and Syquest are trademarks of SYQUEST Technology.
SuperCalc is a trademark of Computer Associates International Inc.
Standard Microsystems and Standard Microsystems ARCNET are trademarks of Standard Microsystems Corporation.
Star is a registered trademark of Star Micronics America, Inc.
STREAMS is a trademark of AT&T Bell Laboratories.

Superkey is a trademark of Borland International, Inc.
Taito is a trademark of Taito America Corporation.
The Coordinator is a registered trademark of Action Techologies, Inc.
TI is a trademark of Texas Instruments, Inc.
TOKEN-RING is a trademark of International Business Machines Corporation.
Toshiba is a registered trademark of Toshiba America, Inc.
Transaction Tracking System and TTS are trademarks of Novell, Inc.
UNIX is a trademark of AT&T Bell Laboratories.
Ventura is a trademark of the Xerox Corporation.
Vertex is a trademark of Priam Corporation.
VMS is a registered trademark of Digital Equipment Corporation.
Wangtek is a trademark of Wangtek, Inc.
Western Digital is a trademark of Western Digital Corporation.
WINDOWS is a product of Microsoft Corporation.
WORDPERFECT is a trademark of Wordperfect Corporation.
WORDSTAR is a registered trademark of MICROPRO Corporation.
WYSE is a trademark of Wyse Technology.
Xebec is a trademark of Xebec.
Zenith Z300 is a trademark of Zenith Corporation.
Zenith Z300 is a trademark of Zenith Data Systems.

PART 1 CONCEPTS

1 LOCAL AREA NETWORK CONCEPTS

In this chapter

What is a LAN, LAN Defined, Network Components, Centralized versus Distributed Processing, Network Operating System, Types and Versions of NetWare, Why Install a LAN, LAN Planning and Design, LAN Security, System Fault Tolerance (SFT), File Allocation Table (FAT) Corruption Protection, Hot Fix (Protecting Data Against Hard Drive Defects), Disk Mirroring, Disk Drive Duplexing, The Uninterruptable Power Supply (UPS) Monitoring System), Transaction Tracking System (TTS), and NetWare Security Levels

1.1 WHAT IS A LAN?

A Local Area Network (LAN) links personal computers (workstations) together so they can communicate and share resource, such as hard drives, printers, application software, and datafiles. All workstations and resources are connected to a file server. Your network may consist of one or more file servers and workstations, depending on your type and NetWare version. Data communication capabilities are available to allow you to connect to a remote PC, another LAN, or a mainframe. Figure 1.1 illustrates a sample network displaying some of the possible components.

1.1.1 Network Components

Network components consist of file, print or communications server(s), workstations, network interface cards (NIC), connectors, cables, wiring boxes, and any other required hardware, for the chosen topology (cabling).

Figure 1.1 A network ties resources together physically and logically.

- The file server is usually a high-performance PC which can be installed to function as a file server only (dedicated), or as a combination file server/workstation (nondedicated). File server means "serving" files to users as requested. It also handles the sharing of resources (e.g., hard drives and printers) and security. NetWare is the operating system that operates this system. In other words the file server, utilizing NetWare acts the same as a network traffic police, which controls the workstation file requests (reads and writes to network drives), printer output, and communications between users and file servers attached to the network.

- When a microcomputer is attached to a network, it is commonly referred to as a workstation. Workstations can be either a low- or high-performance machine. Keep in mind that using a low-performance machine can create a slower response time. Some application software packages require a specific CPU type and therefore will only operate in a high performance machine.

- A network interface card (NIC) is required for any workstation communication. A NIC must be present in the file server and all workstations. These cards form and transmit packets of data within the network. Your network cabling connects these cards. You will also hear the term LAN boards in reference to NICs. Network interface cards are available in various types, that is Arcnet, Ethernet, Token Ring, and so on.

- Cabling, Transceivers, Hubs, Wiring Boxes, Connectors, and so on, are the possible components that connect all of the workstations and file servers together (see Part 1 CONCEPTS, Chap. 2 Hardware, Sec. 2.2.3. Cabling.)

1.1.2 Centralized versus Distributed Processing

Centralized Processing is utilized by mini computers. In this process, all applications are executed at the central controlling device. As a result, adding more terminals to the system directly impacts the overall system performance.

Distributed Processing is utilized by LANs. This is the process of loading an application program into a workstation's memory where it will be run. This is efficient because you are utilizing the central processing unit (CPU) of the individual workstation and therefore not reducing the file server performance.

1.1.3 Network Operating System

Many stand-alone microcomputers utilize the disk operating system (DOS). This can be either MSDOS (from Microsoft), or PCDOS (from IBM). The operating system which is installed in and runs on the file server is called NetWare.

One confusing concept is the relationship between NetWare and DOS. NetWare runs in the file server. DOS runs in the workstation. They communicate across the network using programs referred to as the SHELL. The SHELL acts as a translator between the two operating systems. The SHELL which runs in the workstation consists of two programs, IPX.COM and NET3.COM. Depending on the DOS version running at your workstation, the SHELL may also be generated as a NET2 or NET4.COM. These files are generated as part of your installation.

1.1.4 Types and Versions of NetWare

Each type of NetWare can have several versions. The number of users that can be supported by the file server varies according to the NetWare Operating System type, (see table 1.1.)

Table 1.1

CPU	Type	Number of Users
386	386 NetWare 3.1	1000
386	386 NetWare 3.0	250
286/386	System Fault Tolerant NetWare	100
286/386	Advance NetWare	100
286	Entry Level System I	4
286	Entry Level System II	8

1.2 WHY INSTALL A LAN?

Networks have been designed to allow you to share data and program files and peripherals such as printers and modems. In addition there are many features that can be utilized with NetWare. They include:

- electronic mail,
- sharing application software packages,
- central backup of files and application software,
- security,
- charging and tracking for resources used,
- communication to remote workstation, LAN, and mini/mainframe connectivity.

  For example:

  - a doctor's office can easily access the records on a poison control database maintained on a network as close as next door, or halfway around the world,
  - a salesman can phone in to the network utilizing a microcomputer equipped with a modem from a remote location to place orders, for immediate access to inventory information,
  - data can be transferred between networks,
  - files can be created at a corporate national office, and transferred electronically to each location and printed out, especially important when timing is a factor.

LANs are essential to remain competitive in an increasingly electronic business environment.

For more information about connectivity (See Part 3 DATA COMMUNICATIONS.)

1.3 LAN PLANNING AND DESIGN

LANs offer incredible computing power. Planning is vital to fully utilize that power without creating a handicapped system.

Once the decision has been made to purchase a LAN, plan and design your system before purchasing any equipment. Of course only computers live in a totally logical environment, but if possible there are some considerations to take into account when planning a new system. If you are dealing with an existing LAN, this process can be used to upgrade or reorganize the system. If necessary,

- attempt to define a budget range for funding available for the new LAN,
- total the current number of users, and if possible project future network use for one or two years,
- determine what application software packages your firm will need, and which are currently supported by NetWare,
- make a drawing of the physical layout, with dimensions using an office blueprint if available. This will be required for upgrades or system changes,
- choose the cabling and network interface cards best suited for your needs and available budget,
- determine connectivity requirements for current and projected communications,
- determine the type and speed of file server, hard drive size, printers, peripherals, and required file server memory,
- update the budget to reflect your requirements identified in this planning stage,
- plan the installation of cabling, and all network components,
- design datafile (hard drive) storage. This is the same as designing a "filing system" for your firm. It consists of volume(s) and directory structures for the storage of application software, and datafiles,
- design your security system. The design should include the following: user access to directories, documentation of your installation. It is far easier to do this while installing your system, and login and password restrictions (See Part 1 CONCEPTS, Chap. 1 Local Area Network Concepts, Sec. 1.4 LAN Security.)

NOTE: After a successful installation, a preventive maintenance plan should be formulated (See Part 1 CONCEPTS, Chap. 5 System Maintenance, Sec. 5.1 Preventative.)

1.4 LAN SECURITY

Network Security can be examined from two different aspects

- system fault tolerance (SFT),
- NetWare security levels.

1.4.1 System Fault Tolerance (SFT)

System Fault Tolerance (SFT) is the process of protecting the system against faults.

Advanced NetWare contains the protection for the File Allocation Table (FAT), bad blocks, and an additional module called Transaction Tracking System (TTS) which can be purchased to maintain database integrity, if required.

SFT NetWare provides the following protective measures for your data:

- file allocation table (FAT) corruption protection,
- hot fix,
- disk mirroring,
- disk duplexing,
- uninterruptable power supply (UPS) monitoring system,
- transaction tracking system (TTS).

1.4.2 File Allocation Table (FAT) Corruption Protection (occurs on all 2.1x NetWare versions)

A hard drive's directory entry table (DET) and file allocation table (FAT) are extremely important because they contain the physical address information the operating system needs to determine where to read or write data.

NetWare maintains duplicate copies of both the DETs and the FATs on separate physical areas of the file server hard drive.

If one of the entries in the original table is damaged, the operating system automatically switches to the duplicate table to get the data it requires. The faulty sector is then listed in the drive's "bad block table," and the data it contained is moved to a safe location elsewhere on the drive.

1.4.3 Hot Fix (Protecting Data Against Hard Drive Defects) (occurs with all 2.1x NetWare versions)

When the Hot Fix feature is activated on a file server hard drive (during installation), a small portion of the hard drive storage space is reserved as the "Hot Fix Redirection Area." This area is set up as an area to hold data blocks that are "redirected" there from faulty areas on the drive. An area of 2 percent of the hard drive is reserved for this process. Hot Fix occurs automatically once activated through installation. You can modify the 2 percent redirection table requirement to increase or decrease the size, however this is not recommended under normal usage.

During read-after-write verification, a block of data is written to a file server hard drive, and the data is immediately read back from the drive and compared to the original that is still in the file server's memory (RAM). If the data from the drive matches the data in RAM, the write operation is considered successful. The data in memory is released, and the next file server operation takes place.

> **NOTE:** NetWare stores data in 4096-byte blocks on the file server hard drive(s).

If the data from the drive does not match the data in memory, NetWare determines (after making appropriate retries) that the drive storage block is defective. If this happens, the Hot Fix feature redirects the original block of data (which is still in memory) to the Hot Fix redirection area, where the data will be stored correctly. NetWare records the address of the defective block in a section of the Hot Fix area reserved for that purpose and the file server will not attempt to store data in that block again. The redirection area is also protected by Hot Fix.
Your Hot Fix area status can be monitored through the FCONSOLE Utility, file server Statistics option.

> **NOTE:** Monitoring is essential, particularly on networks that have been up and running for some time, with the same Hard Drive. If the 2 percent allocated (by default) is used up your system will likely crash!

1.4.4 Disk Mirroring (SFT NetWare Only)

With disk mirroring, two disk drives on the same controller card (channel) are paired together. Blocks of data written to the original (primary) drive are also written sequentially to the duplicate (secondary) drive. The two drives operate in tandem, constantly storing and updating the same files. Should one of the drives fail, the other drive in the pair can continue to operate on its own, without data loss or interruption. The operating system sends a warning message to the file server console to indicate the failure so that the mirroring protection can be restored as soon as possible.

Disk mirroring pairs drives on the same channel (controller card), therefore it does not protect against failures that may occur along this channel between the drives and the file server.

Once an error has occurred on a failed drive, use the UNMIRROR console command. This will terminate the mirroring process of that particular pair. When you have purchased a replacement drive and are ready to install, you must first DOWN the file server. Next you will need to replace the failed drive, with a new drive that has been initialized for NetWare. Bring the server back up and execute the REMIRROR console command after re-booting the file server, with the new drive in place.

> **NOTE:** Ensure that your drive sizes and types are the same as NetWare looks for an exact match to mirror a pair.

1.4.5 Disk Drive Duplexing (SFT NetWare Only)

Whereas drive mirroring protects data only from the failure of a hard drive, disk duplexing protects against failure of either a hard drive or of the channel between the drive and the file server. This channel includes the hard drive controller, power supply, and interface cable.

SFT NetWare 286 provides the capability to mirror a drive on one channel with a drive on another channel.

With disk duplexing, as with disk mirroring, the same data is written to both drives. However, since the hard disk drives are on different channels, data is written to the two drives simultaneously, making data transfer faster.

Another advantage of drive duplexing is "split seeks." This feature sends read requests to whichever drive in the pair can respond the fastest.

1.4.6 The Uninterruptable Power Supply (UPS) Monitoring System

It is strongly recommended that every file server be attached to an uninterruptable power supply (UPS) to protect it against data loss caused by power failure or power surges. A line-surge suppressor will also help to protect the microcomputer and the network interface cards in the network from power surges.

> **NOTE:** UPS Monitoring will only occur in systems that have installed a UPS monitoring board or SS Key Card, Disk Co-processor Board (DCB) or Microchannel Mouse port. Without monitoring, the UPS will sustain the file server until the UPS battery is drained. Then the system will crash with absolutely no warning!

Since the life of the UPS battery is limited, the file server must be DOWNed if power is not restored within a predetermined length of time. When the file server switches to UPS power, NetWare sends a message to any workstations that are still operational, either from a separate power source or their own UPS units, informing them that the server is running on UPS power. The message also states how much time they have to logout before the file server shuts itself down. This message is taken from the CONFIG.UPS file set up by the system manager.

If power has not been restored before the specified time (set up in the CONFIG.UPS file) has elapsed, the file server closes all open files, writes all data in the file server memory to the hard drive, and shuts itself down.

1.4.7 Transaction Tracking System (TTS)

Transaction Tracking System (TTS) prevents *database* corruption if the system fails while data is being written to database files. TTS is designed to work with sequential databases.

TTS views an entire sequence of database changes as a single "transaction" that must be fully completed or fully "backed out" (no changes made at all). Only after all files have been correctly updated will the transaction be completed and released.

If the system fails during a transaction, TTS performs an "automatic roll back." That is, TTS will undo all database changes made during the transaction and returns the database to its original state. The database files and underlying system information are left as they were before the transaction began. The lost transaction will have to be re-entered, but all files and system information will be intact and consistent. For more information on TTS (See Part 2 REFERENCE, Chap. 16 Transaction Tracking System (TTS).)

1.4.8 NetWare Security Levels

Network security is handled by a structure of rights which specifies users access to data. This can be particularly important, for example, for a company's personnel and payroll files which should not be available to employees. Datafile security is an extremely serious matter, and most business data should be regarded as sensitive unless management indicates otherwise. For example, imagine if private corporate accounting data ended up in the wrong hands and this resulted in a takeover. There are many possibilities such as this which can have insider trading possibilities, and all the resulting legal implications. Input from your legal department, or your legal counsel might be worth considering. This should include both the file server data and all printed output.

With the 2.1x series of NetWare, you have the ability to restrict the date, time, and physical location from which a user can login. In addition, an option known as Intruder Detection Lockout can be utilized to notify supervisors of any attempted unauthorized login. Many password restrictions have now been added as options to provide greater security. These options include: required password, length and encryption, forced periodic changes and required unique passwords. (See Part 2 REFERENCE, Chap. 10 Network Security (SYSCON and FILER), Sec. 10.2 NetWare's Security System.)

Another security option worth considering is the installation of diskless workstations (no floppy disk drives) on the network. This means that it will be impossible to physically remove an electronic copy of a file at a diskless workstation.

> **NOTE:** The determined thief can still take a printout, or use a workstation with a floppy disk drive for files to which they have access (trustee rights).

There are four levels of NetWare security:

1. LOGIN / PASSWORD: access to the file server

2. TRUSTEE (user/group):controls what a user can access in a specified directory

3. DIRECTORY: controls what a directory will allow any user to do providing they also have the appropriate trustee access

4. FILE ATTRIBUTES: controls how you can manipulate files, a file level security

> **NOTE:** For more details on each of these security features of NetWare (See Part 2 REFERENCE, Chap. 10 Network Security (SYSCON and FILER), Sec. 10.2 NetWare's Security System.)

With Novell NetWare, if a user does not have the right of access, they cannot even determine if the file exists. Often there is no error message indicating "access denied," they simply find an empty directory. It's the same as having a bag of money in a locked car. If the money is strewn all over the seats, the incentive is to break in and steal the visible funds. If the money is wrapped in a garbage bag and hidden under the seat, there is less incentive. There is an old cliche that fits this situation, "out of sight, out of mind." That's exactly how NetWare operates with the effective rights of a user. For specifics of rights use and implementation (See Part 2 REFERENCE, Chap. 10 Network Security (SYSCON and FILER), Sec. 10.3 Effective Rights.)

2 HARDWARE

In this chapter

Hardware Basics for Stand-alone Personal Computers (PCs), Central Processing Units (CPUs), Memory, Video Types (Graphics), Drives, Printers, Modems, LAN Hardware basics, LFile Server (Memory and Drives), Workstations (Memory), Cabling (Topologies, NIC Cards, and Bridging), Network Printers.

2.1 HARDWARE BASICS FOR Stand-alone PERSONAL COMPUTERS (PCs)

2.1.1 Central Processing Units (CPUs)

In microcomputers, the Central Processing Unit (CPU) is a set of microprocessor chips. They are located on a board often referred to as either a motherboard, or system board, which contains the components required to make the computer work. They include the microprocessor, support chips, the expansion bus, and memory chips.

The CPU is the brains of a computer. The CPU clock determines speed, and a result is a major factor in determining the speed at which your database, wordprocessor or spreadsheet will run.

CPU Microprocessor Chips

The CPU is a tiny silicon chip, usually located on the "motherboard" of a computer. Originally IBM and compatible PCs used an 8088 chip. Current higher speed machines use 80386 and 80486 chips.

CPU Clock Speed

CPU processing speed can be called internal cycle time, clock time, clock speed, or simply cycle time. This CPU speed of processing information is measured in Megahertz (MHz). A clock speed of 1 MHz would mean that the CPU is capable of handling information at the rate of one million cycles per second. A cycle is more difficult to explain. All computer information must be processed in the binary state, that is, the circuit is either on or off. Simply, cycle time is the time required to change a set of CPU registers.

Bits

Each CPU chip has a certain number of bits. A bit, the smallest unit of information, is the basic unit of measurement used in computer systems. All microprocessor chips are identified by both speed and bits.

The analogy of cars on a freeway explains the relation of microprocessors, bits, and speed.

- Microprocessors, are like automobiles with different performance capabilities, such as a Mercedes, a Porsche, and a Honda. Each vehicle will get there, but at a vastly different speed and performance,
- Bits are equivalent to the number of lanes or width of the highway (or the *bus*, see Glossary), and how many cars it can handle at one time. The number of bits is the same as the number of lanes, with 8 bits equivalent to eight lanes, with eight cars all going in one direction side by side at the same time, or 32 bits, 32 cars,
- In this example of the freeway, megahertz (MHz) is equivalent to the speed limit.

Ideally, the bit sizes of the various components should match for the best performance. For example a 32-bit 80386 microprocessor should be matched with a 32-bit bus. Mixing the bit sizes is possible but usually at a sacrifice of performance. Normally a 16-bit motherboard will have a combination of 16-bit and 8-bit slots, to accommodate 8-bit cards. Another example would be a low priced 386, which may have a 32-bit CPU installed on a 16-bit motherboard. This will mean that you can never add 32-bit boards to this lower priced machine.

The Bus Architecture

The individual chips such as the CPU, RAM, and ROM are connected together by conductor lines called busses. The bus links all internal components by use of a shared set of electrical paths. These busses are etched onto the motherboard and are connected to the slots in which you install add-on boards. Also, the pins on the sides of the chips installed on the motherboard are a part of this circuitry. Data travels along these circuits from one component to another.

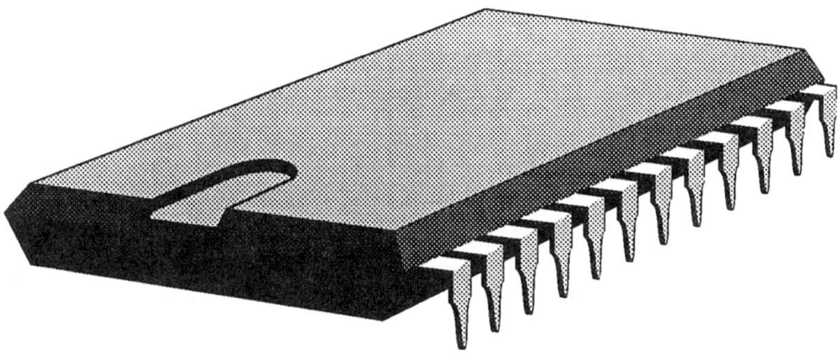

Figure 2.1 The pins on a computer chip are an integral part of the circuitry.

These circuits consist of data, power, and control lines. Data lines carry data. Power lines distribute electrical power. Control lines send timing and interrupt signals to other components connected to the bus. An address bus selects the components that control data or information. This is all determined by the CPU chip in use.

All of these busses follow a set of industry guidelines for design. This design is known as an architecture. The three most common architectures are: ISA, EISA, and MCA. A brief description for each follows:

ISA (Industry Standard Architecture): This is a standard 8 (XT) or 16 (AT) bit bus architecture used by standard AT compatible and clone manufacturers.

EISA (Extended Industry Standard Architecture): This architecture was devised as an extension of the standard AT bus (ISA) to provide upward compatibility and also the performance capability of the MCA bus. Support for this 32 bit bus standard is growing in popularity.

MCA (Micro Channel): The Micro Channel introduced by IBM is a relatively new standard. MCA promises certain benefits for the future, including allowing more than one CPU to occupy the same bus, but at present the microcomputer world is in factions. It is also a 32-bit bus structure. Micro Channel cards are used in Micro Channel machines.

Throughput and Pipelined Architecture

An automobile analogy best explains this concept. A small one-lane bridge will allow one car at a time to travel in one direction. A larger bridge will allow several cars to travel in both directions, simultaneously.

The 8086 and 8088 chips are the same as the one-lane bridge. A complete sequence including fetching, decoding, and execution of an instruction must be completed before another can be processed. The 80286 and above are like the larger bridge, they perform these sequences in parallel, greatly increasing the throughput.

Choosing a Microprocessor Chip

A fast CPU chip matched with a fast hard drive, will load your software applications faster, and process them more efficiently. This can be particularly important for large wordprocessing files, database applications, spreadsheets, and Computer Aided Design (CAD) software packages. While the higher speed chips have higher performance, you many not need the more expensive processors. A list of the most common processors, their bit size and speed, and some suggested uses follows.

8086 and 8088, Clock Speeds of 4.77 to 10 MHz, Addressing Up to 640k of Memory: These 8-bit chips have sufficient capacity for word processing. They can handle larger documents, however, you will notice a slowdown in performance. An 8-bit chip will easily process small spreadsheets and databases (with files up to 100,000 bytes), simple graphics, small accounting systems, and desktop publishing. In many cases these chips are adequate for your users, but for large files, and more complex manipulations speed can be a major concern. If you're paying someone by the hour to watch a message such as "processing information, please wait" their hourly cost of waiting, can soon pay for a more expensive processor.

80286, Clock Speeds of 8 to 20 MHz, Addressing Up to 16 Megabytes of Memory: These 16-bit chips will process application software much faster than 8-bit chips. The 16-bit chips will work with larger wordprocessing, database and spreadsheet applications, as well as modest size graphics and computer-aided design applications.

80386, Clock Speeds of From 16 to 33 MHz, Addressing Up to 4 Gigabytes of Memory: The 80386 chips have a 32-bit architecture but may have different bus sizes, to suit different requirements. For comparison purposes, two 80386 chips made by Intel are discussed. There are other manufacturers, and other chips, however, these two should readily demonstrate the options available. Memory management is one of the major advantages of 386, allowing for true multitasking.

Intel's 80386SX: This chip has a 32-bit internal architecture, but has only a 16-bit bus. Operating at 16 to 20 MHz it is lower in price than the 32-80386DX. While this chip represents a compromise in performance, it allows access to a much wider application software base.

Intel's 32-80386DX 16-33MHz: This chip has a 32-bit internal architecture, and also a 32-bit bus. The DX model is the same chip as the SX, however the wider bus makes it faster.

Intel's 32-80486, with Clock Speeds of From 25 to 33 MHz.: Intel describes their 486 processor as "a 32-bit architecture with on-chip memory management, floating point, and cache memory units. On-chip cache memory allows frequently used data and code to be stored on-chip reducing accesses to the external bus." The features of the 486 "lead to performance greater than twice that of a 386 microprocessor," according to Intel. The 486 is basically a 386 with a math coprocessor and cache controller.

Math coprocessor: As the name implies a math coprocessor is another processor in addition to the CPU. The math coprocessor has been specifically designed to do arithmetic calculations, and is only called on when the software is capable of utilizing a math coprocessor to perform calculations more effectively.

2.1.2 Memory

The same as the human brain, computers also have a memory. Memory is used to store programs and data for fast access. Computer memory comes in many forms: ROM, RAM, PROM, EPROM, and EEPROM.

ROM

The read only memory (ROM) chips are used to store a set of instructions provided by the manufacturer. These instructions are known as firmware, and can include program routines, and machine language interpreters. ROMs exist to provide the computer with instantaneous instructions required for its operation. This information is burned into the chip providing permanent storage even when the power is turned off. This is referred to as nonvolatile storage. ROM can only be read or accessed, never written to.

RAM

The random access memory (RAM) chips are used to store application software programs and data. It can be read from and written to. If the power is turned off, the contents are lost, as a result, RAM is known as volatile. Therefore, required programs and data must be loaded into RAM when the computer is powered up.

PROM

Programmable read only memory (PROM) is a ROM chip that is programmed with a device called a PROM burner or a programmer. These special purpose chips can be used to store application software, graphics, and computer games.

EPROM

Erasable programmable read only memory (EPROM) chips are the same as PROM chips, except they can be erased and reprogrammed multiple times. Erasing is accomplished by exposing the chip to ultraviolet light.

EEPROM

Electrically erasable programmable read only memory (EEPROM) chips are the same as EPROM, however they can be reprogrammed while installed in the computer, from the keyboard - often referred to as Nonvolatile RAM.

Expanded versus Extended

As computers have advanced so have application software packages. As thesc packages have added new features and complexity, they have required more and more memory to function. This has forced hardware and software manufacturers to find ways to increase the amount of memory that is available.

RAM memory can be accessed in two ways, it can be extended, or expanded. The basic difference between these two memory types is the way the CPU sees them, and therefore, how applications use them.

The 8088/86 CPU limits the memory it can address to 1MB. Of that 1MB, 384K is reserved for memory on the ROM, VIDEO RAM, and Scratch pad RAM, leaving a maximum of 640K available for DOS and DOS applications (known as conventional memory).

The 80286 CPU allows addressable memory up to 16MB. To maintain compatibility with existing DOS applications, the 80286 provides an 8088 emulation mode (known as real mode) which limits memory access to 640K. This real mode is dependant on the operating system running, DOS has a 640K limitation.

As users demand more of their programs which will require more memory, the 640K limit becomes a performance liability. To get around this problem, Lotus, Intel, and Microsoft jointly designed a way to fool the CPU into seeing more memory. They came up with a memory paging scheme called the Lotus-Intel-Microsoft Expanded Memory Specification (LIM/EMS).

The LIM/EMS provided a standard for swapping 64KB chunks or pages of memory in and out of the reserved memory space. DOS still only addresses its 640K limit, but applications written to access EMS see it as additional memory. This is what is known as EXPANDED MEMORY.

> **NOTE:** DOS 4.x has drivers available to address expanded memory.

EXTENDED MEMORY is only available on 80286 CPUs and above. This term refers to memory addressed above the 1MB 8088/86 limit that the 80286 can see in normal mode (known as protected mode). Extended memory is directly accessible by non-DOS operating systems such as OS2, NetWare, Unix, and so on. DOS applications cannot use extended memory, except with specialized software such as a RAM disk.

2.1.3 Video Types (Graphics)

Video cards (boards) are best understood when their role as an integral part of a functioning computer is fully comprehended.

Video cards are required to enable a monitor to display everything from wordprocessing and spreadsheets to complex graphic images. Some computer and application software will run without a monitor, however operating "blind" can be a unique challenge. This is an important fact, for sometimes you may want to disconnect the monitor and have the computer continue to function. For example in a network, you can have multiple file servers sharing one monitor.

How a Monitor Works

When you type in characters at the keyboard, the display on the monitor seems to be instantaneous. A lot happens however, between the keystroke and the display, in a process that is completely transparent to the end user. The monitor screen usually consists of a Cathode Ray Tube (CRT) the same as an ordinary television set (See Fig. 2.2.)

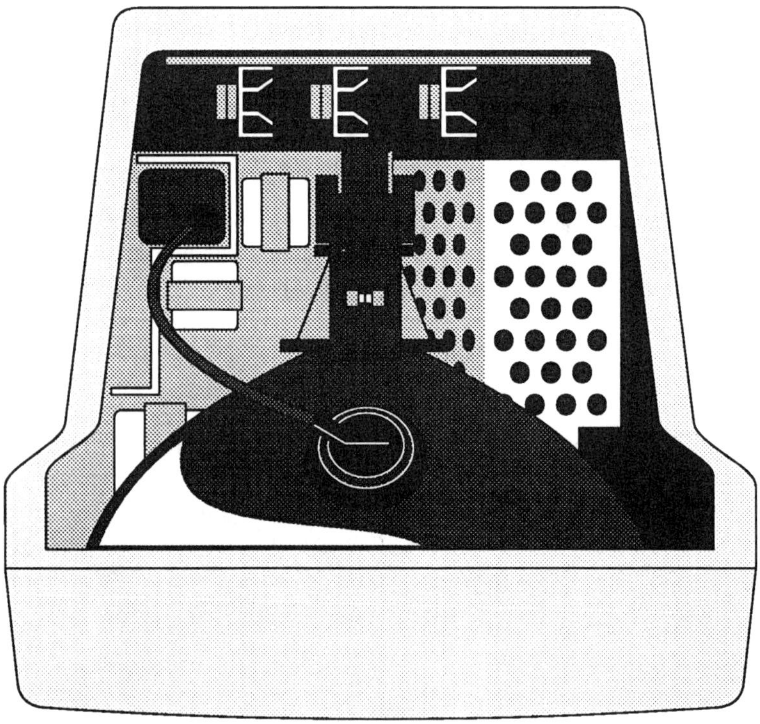

Figure 2.2 Viewed from above, the inside of a monitor resembles a TV.

The inside of a monitor is coated with phosphor salts creating a phosphorescent surface of small squares or dots called pixels. An electron "gun" fires a beam which leaves a glowing pixel wherever it hits. Four deflection plates direct the beam in a pattern similar to the one used by a dot matrix printer, only many times faster. The beam is turned on and off to produce glowing pixels, and blank spaces on the screen. Each pixel glows for a fraction of a second, long enough for the scan to return to the same spot. A letter or character formed from many pixels "glows" because it is continuously re-energized by the electron gun.

The video signals received by the electron gun begin at the keyboard and must pass through the video circuitry to determine the type of display. Some computers such as IBM's PS/2's have the video circuitry included on the motherboard. Most computers require the addition of a video card to add the circuitry for the desired display.

Monochrome and Color Display

Single color display is called monochrome, while multiple color display is simply called color. With a cable television signal, you can connect either a black and white TV or a color TV and both will produce a picture according to their capabilities. Computer monitors however require a special video signal, and these are generated by Video Cards. Video card signals are not the same as the Cable TV signal, where one message suits all.

When choosing video monitors, there are compatibilities to be considered. For example a Variable Graphics Adapter (VGA) color monitor will not physically plug into a Color Graphics Adapter (CGA) card. Newer graphics cards automatically check to determine what type of monitor is attached and change the output signal to accommodate the monitor found. On older cards, these are physical dip switches that have to be physically changed, in accordance with instructions given in the manuals supplied with all cards.

Application software must know what type of video card it is talking to, which is accomplished by the use of screen drivers. The code sent to the video card by the application software should create a comprehensible display. If the code is wrong, the screen will be blank, or filled with a variety of curious symbols.

> **NOTE:** In some cases a monitor can be physically damaged by connecting it to the wrong video adapter.

Video Card and Monitor Resolution

Resolution is a measure of the density of pixels (screen dots) per unit of area of a digitized image on a screen. This resolution is governed by the signal that is sent by the graphics card, and the monitor receiving and displaying the signal. A video card that produces a higher resolution utilizes more screen pixels per unit area creating a clearer sharper image on the screen. Card resolution, for example, for a Hercules Graphics card is expressed as "dot addressable to 720 by

348" which measures 720 dots horizontally, by 348 dots vertically which the card is capable of activating. As a guide, higher card resolution usually means higher cost, and a crisper display. Figure 2.3 illustrates various types of monitors.

Video Cards (boards)

There are many types of IBM video cards available, among the most popular are

MDA (Monochrome Display Adapter): This card made by IBM has absolutely no graphic capabilities other than standard ANSI characters.

HGA (Hercules Graphics Adapter), also MGA (Mono Graphics Adapter): Originally invented by the Hercules Graphics Company, this card has been copied by almost every other display adapter manufacturer in the world. Hercules Graphics cards may well be the most common adapter in use today. This versatile card which enables the display of graphic images, will also emulate CGA graphics with Emulator programs, even when on a monochrome screen.

CGA (Color Graphics Adapter): The original color graphics adapter comes complete with four colors (changeable) and 320 by 200 dot addressable graphics.

EGA (Extended Graphics Adapter): This card allows 12 to 16 colors which can be selected from a set of 64. Some cards have greater dot addressable graphics, (640 by 200) but only 2 colors available at this density.

VGA (Video Graphics Array): This graphic adapter card, the VGA allows up to 800 by 600 dot addressable graphics in 16 color mode. It also allows 320 by 200 dot addressable graphics with a selection of 256 colors. Most VGA cards are capable of emulating all of the previously outlined cards.

Figure 2.3 Various types and models of monitors are available.

Monitor and Card Connectivity

Monochrome	Color
HGA cards are the usual standard with monochrome monitors, which display graphics and allow shading toning.	Use CGA, EGA, or VGA cards with color.

2.1.4 Drives

Tracks and Sectors

A number of different IBM or compatible formats are used for 3.5" and 5.25" diskettes. The terms tracks and sectors are often used in conjunction with diskettes and drives. Disks are subdivided into sides, tracks and sectors referred to as the "format." Tracks are the circular areas on a disk and can be compared to the grooves on a record, except they are concentric rings, instead of one continuous spiral groove such as on an LP. You can also consider tracks as concentric cylinders. A cylinder simply refers to the same track on both sides of a disk, or the same number on all disks on a hard drive. Sectors are pie shaped segments that divide tracks. Each sector contains data fields and address fields which store the users programs and data, and tells the computer the location of this information. When a diskette or hard drive is formatted, all this is created automatically.

Floppy Diskettes and Drives

Most microcomputers sold today have at least one floppy disk drive (See Fig. 2.4). Diskless workstations are an exception to this.

Originally floppies were the primary storage devices for IBM PCs, which were single sided and stored 160KB of data on 5.25" low-density diskettes using only one side. Today their main use is for file exchange between microcomputers and for loading programs or data onto hard drive drives. The original non-IBM compatible PCs had single-sided single density 5.25", 80KB drives. The 8" drives preceded 5.25" ones, and held as little as 250KB.

As hardware developed, DOS was modified to utilize the new technology providing higher capacity storage. One advance in technology allowed both sides of a double density diskette to be used, which increased the capacity to 160KB by 2 = 320KB. With version 1.1 of DOS, formatting provided 320KB of usable space on diskettes. DOS 2.0 introduced 360KB disks by adding an extra sector to each track.

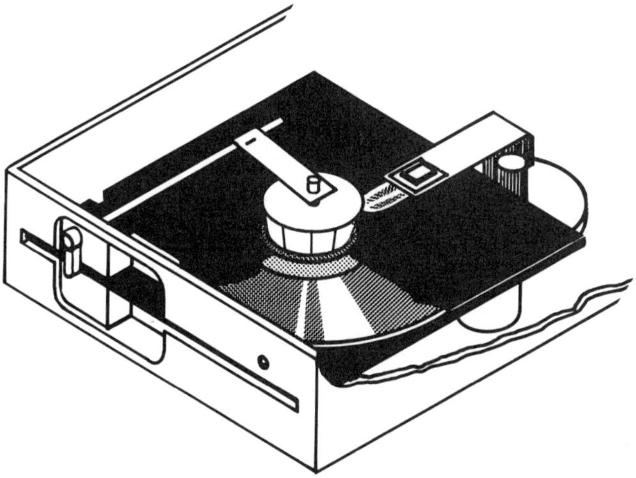

Figure 2.4 Floppy disk drives are useful for transferring data.

Since then, 5.25" diskettes known as high density have become available and have a storage capacity of 1.2 megabytes.

The newer 3.5" diskettes come in two types, a 1 megabyte size, and a 2 megabyte size.

- IBM's model 25 machines use the low density 1MB diskette which formats to provide 720KB of usable diskette space.

- Machines with a "1.44 MB drive" use the high density 2 megabyte diskettes which formats to provide 1.44 usable space.

The 360KB 5.25 low density diskette and the 720KB 3.5 low density diskette represent the lowest common denominator, therefore, all machines that have a 3.5" or a 5.25" drive can read these formats.

Hard Drives

Originally microcomputers did not have a hard drive. The PC XT changed all that, it had a 10 megabyte full height hard drive with an average access time of 105 milliseconds (see Glossary). Figures 2.5 and 2.6 illustrate how the read/write heads store data on the platters inside the hard drive casing.

Figure 2.5 Hard drives have "platters" which store data.

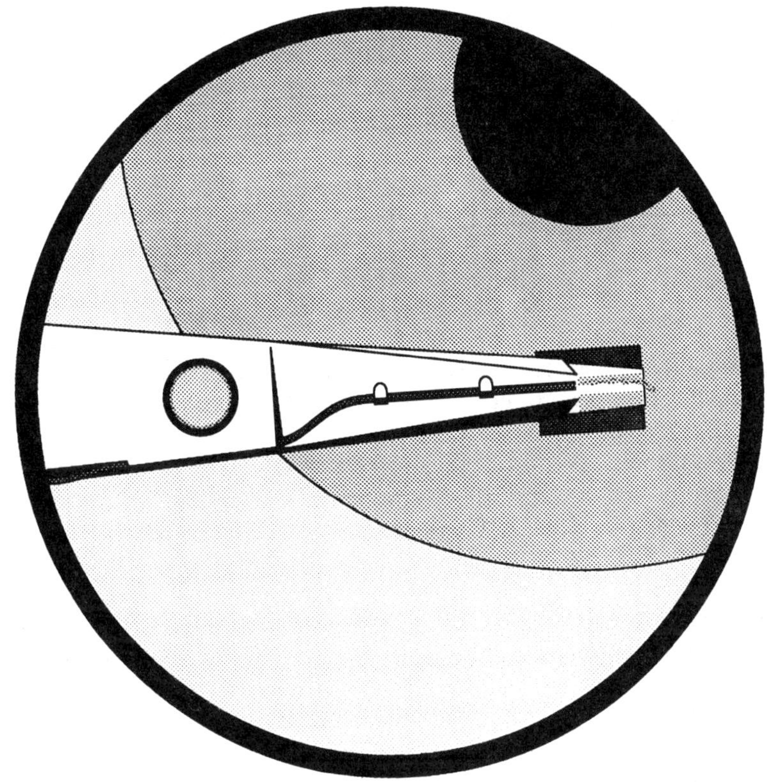

Figure 2.6 Read/write heads transfer data to and from the platters.

Formatting

All disks whether hard drive or floppy need to have their surface prepared for data storage, a process called "Formatting."

Floppy Diskettes

The FORMAT command is used to do the most basic preparation for use of a diskette. It actually does two important things with a diskette

- it writes the information to the tracks which in turn is sent to the appropriate sector making it possible for DOS to work with the diskette,
- it checks for any defects in the diskette.

See your DOS manual for further details and syntax.

> **NOTE:** It is possible to format a diskette as 360KB using a 1.2MB floppy drive but not the other way around, however this is not a recommended practice.

Hard Drives

When you first install your hard drive, you will need to boot your computer with a diskette copy of DOS, and then run a low-level format on your drive. A low-level format lays down the tracks and sectors and boot records on your drive. There are a number of low-level format utilities to choose from on the market. We have had success with ONTRACK's Disk Manager.

> **NOTE:** The high-level or DOS format recreates the File Allocation Tables (FAT).

Next you will need to run the FDISK command to partition the drive. This is a DOS command. All drives need a partition. Very often the dealer from whom you purchase your equipment will set up your hard drives before delivery for you. Because of this dealer service, many microcomputer hard drive users never learn about low-level and high-level formatting or the FDISK command. Hard drives are often divided into separate sections called partitions which can have different information in each partition.

The only reason you will need two partitions is if you are using an operating system that relied on a DOS version 3.3 and below. These older DOS versions could only work with 32 megabytes of drive space. Starting with DOS 4.0, this limitation has been eliminated.

After you create a partition, use the FORMAT command to format the partition and place a copy of DOS on the bootable partition (using the /S option of FORMAT).

Once this is completed, your hard drive will be ready to use, and you'll be able to boot up DOS from the hard drive without having to use a floppy diskette.

Hard Drive Controllers

A hard drive controller is a card or board that is installed in a slot in the computer for communication between the hard drive and the CPU.

Controller cards come in many varieties, each with specialized uses. Some of the most common ones are

MFM (Modified Frequency Modulation): This card and its encoding system was used by the first PC Hard Drives.

RLL (Run Length Limited): An RLL Card is basically an enhancement of an MFM Controller, providing for 50 percent more data on a drive than MFM.

SCSI (Small Computer System Interface): Pronounced "Scuzzy" this card allows peripheral devices including higher speed hard drives, scanners, CD ROMs and so on, to be connected to a computer. These devices are "intelligent." They also allows for hard drives of higher capacity than can be supported by conventional MFM or RLL. MFM and RLL are data encoding schemes that are used by both SCSI and ESDI drives. The actual SCSI interface is also called ST412.

ESDI (Enhanced Small Device Interface): This card is most often used for large hard drives with a fast access time.

IDE (Independent Drive Electronics): This is a host adapter to a drive which is essentially a SCSI drive with built in electronics.

Interleave

The design and speed of both hard drives and controller cards has improved as the technology has developed. The controller card communicates with the hard drives to read and write data. The controller then passes this information on to the CPU. Slow controllers are unable to facilitate both reading from the drive and passing the information along to the CPU simultaneously. This means that only one sector at a time can be read. However, the drive continues to rotate, while the controller is passing information along. After this is completed, it then reads the second sector. By reading every second sector it will take two revolutions to read a track. Two rotations of the drive to one read operation, is a 2:1 ratio. This ratio is known as the *interleave*.

New controllers usually have a 2:1 or 1:1 interleave. A 1:1 controller will read twice as fast as a 2:1 controller. It is extremely important that you specify the correct interleave when you run a low level-format, if you do not, your hard drive will run slow.

CD ROM and WORM Drives

The term CD ROM is short for compact disk read only memory. A CD ROM external or internal drive is basically just like a compact disk audio player except it's capable of reading data. One of its most attractive features is the 552 megabytes of storage available on the CD disc. In a stand-alone system, the CD ROM can be given a drive designation such as drive D:, allowing easy access, and the ability to copy files from the CD ROM. CD ROM disks cannot be written to. There is an exception, and that is the Write Once Read Many (WORM) drives. These are optical disks that can be written to but not erased, and therefore read many times. They can provide an incredible amount of storage for commonly used information. New data can be added to up to the physical capacity of the disk (See Fig. 2.7).

Figure 2.7 CD ROM and WORM drives use optical laser disks visually the same as standard CD audio disks.

For example a medical facility may have a compact disk with pharmaceutical listings of available drugs or medical information. This allows immediate electronic information access, bringing all the advantages of searching for specific words or phrases to find information quickly and efficiently. There are many CD information database publishers, and the electronic information is kept current with the delivery of the latest CD to subscribers.

The CD ROM is a natural for electronic bulletin boards. Bulletin Board Systems (BBS) can use the huge storage capacity of a CD ROM at a relatively low cost for "shareware" software programs that can be downloaded by subscribers to the bulletin boards, accessing them by modem. Many companies have developed shareware CD ROM's. Shareware is regarded by these companies as being a distribution method which allows a program author to make their product available to a wide variety of users.

One of the most exciting technological frontiers is the possibility of a CD ROM drive that can operate in the same way as a conventional hard drive, with the ability to add, change, and delete files as required.

CD ROMs are relatively expensive, however this initial cost is easily offset by the advantages for situations where access to large volumes of consistent information is necessary.

Tape Drives

Tape drives can be either the reel to reel style usually associated with mainframes, or multiple cassette styles. Tape drives are used primarily for backup purposes as opposed to on-line mass storage devices.

Some tape drives may be hooked up as a drive or DOS device, and assigned a drive letter designation. Files are backed up in much the same way as you copy data from one drive to another. Today, however, most tape drives are accessed through special software because they are no longer DOS devices.

Tape backup drives if used for backup media, require the installation of a dedicated adapter card. Configuration is complex, however the tape is much faster, and generally more reliable than floppy diskettes.

2.1.5 Printers

The Printer

When the printer receives data character codes from the computer, it simply converts each string in the code sent by the computer into the corresponding letter, number or graphics character, and then prints the symbol on paper. The ability to reproduce graphics depends on the printer firmware and setup. Plotters are printers that have been specifically designed to reproduce graphics and designs on paper using pens or pencils.

The Printer Buffer

When you send a file to the printer, the application program sends a set of codes to the printer. These codes are often configured by the software for specific printers using "printer device drivers" which come with most application software packages. The code string is then stored in the printer in an area called the buffer. This operates the same as the memory of your computer, and often printers will be sold with the buffer size stipulated. Depending on the size of the file being sent, the entire file may be sent at once, or in pieces to the buffer. The printer then prints from this buffer work space.

Parallel and Serial Ports

Computers can send data to printers in parallel or serial form. When the printer and the computer are connected by a serial interface, the bits of data are transmitted one at a time. Computers usually process information faster than the printer can print, therefore both devices must agree on the speed at which data is transmitted (the baud rate). Microcomputers generally have one parallel port, with an option for serial ports.

Microcomputers can use either parallel or serial ports to communicate with printers. Ports are located on the back panel of the microcomputer (See Fig. 2.8)

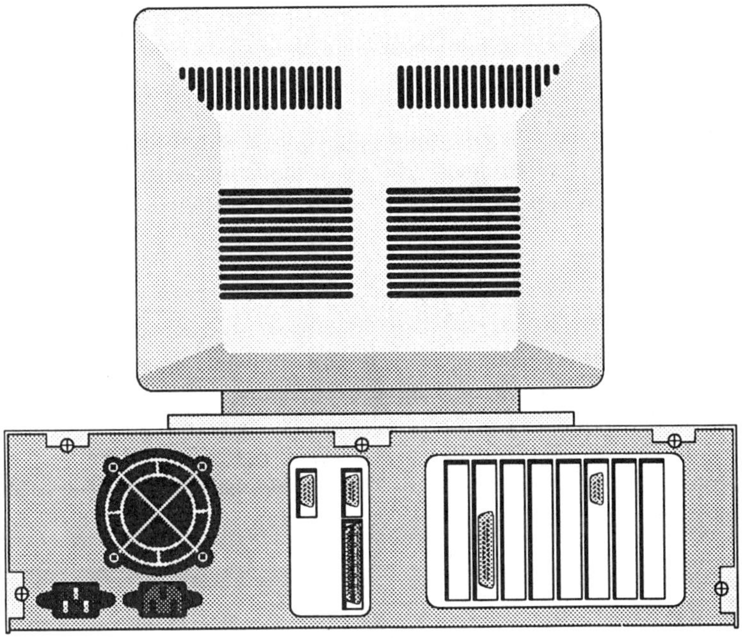

Figure 2.8 The ports on the back of the computer (on the right in the illustration) allow for the connection of the monitor, printers and other devices.

If the interface is a parallel one, the character codes are sent to the printer in groups of 8 bits at a time. Many systems also have additional ports often used to add a mouse or a joy stick. Additional ports can be added, up to existing hardware limits, depending on the type of computer.

Parallel Port (usually LPTx)

This port has almost become a standard for operating printers located short distances from the computer. For parallel port operation, 10 feet is the centronics standard, anything over 20 feet may produce "slipped bits". Longer runs can work with the addition of a line driver.

The parallel interface allows the simultaneous transmission of all 8 bits of a byte simultaneously over eight parallel wires. The distance limitation stems from the difficulty in noise induced by other wires, the longer the cable, the more susceptible to noise.

Parallel ports are desirable because they are easy to connect and can move data much faster than serial ports. For this reason some specialized software products such as LAP-LINK and FILE SHUTTLE have evolved to take advantage of the port.

Serial Port (usually COMx)

Serial ports transmit data 1 bit after another on a single wire using an industry standard method. This insures that bit order cannot be confused. It also offers simplified cabling and much greater distance, possibly up to 100 feet without repeaters or modems. Serial ports are usually used for printers, modems, or as a mouse port or for a variety of serial devices.

Dot Matrix Printers

Dot matrix printers form each character out of a pattern of dots. These printers type characters or graphics on paper using a print head that has a series of pins, usually from 9 to 24 (See Fig. 2.9). To print, the required pin strikes the ink ribbon. The pattern of pins produces the requested symbols (See Fig. 2.10). A print head can make several passes to either fill in the blank spaces with more dots, or to print over the same dots again. The Near Letter Quality (NLQ) setting on some printers uses this fill-in process.

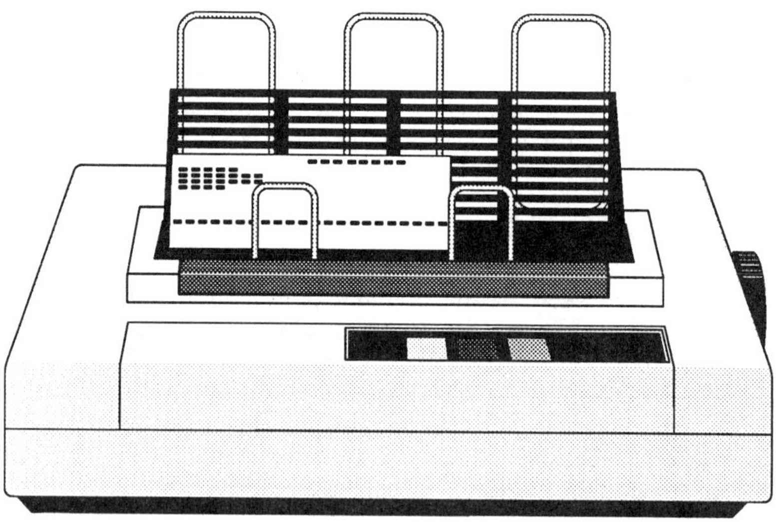

Figure 2.9 Twenty four pin printers usually have a higher speed and quality output than 9 pin printers.

Dot Matrix printers are much more economical than laser printers. They are useful to produce continuous printouts, when set up to print labels, checks, invoices, or even rolodex cards using the appropriate application software.

Laser Printers

These printers use photocopier technology to produce letter quality output from the data sent by the computer. Most Laser printers use a laser beam as a part of the printing process, hence the name. These printers produce high quality printouts on bond paper, photocopy paper, legal paper, letterhead, transparencies, labels, or envelopes (See Fig. 2.11).

Plotters

Plotters, used to print graphics, give the advantage of producing a print in a visually superior drawn form. They have a mechanical arm and a set of colored pens or in some cases, pencils. First, the arm picks one of the colored pens. Then, motors controlling the horizontal and vertical movements of the arm move the pen on the paper so that it can draw. When it requires the next color, the arm replaces the pen in use, and selects another pen of the appropriate color. Plotters are available in two different styles: flatbed and drum.

Flatbed

This plotter has a flat working surface slightly larger than the maximum output size. It can be laid flat on the working surface or tilted on an angle to conserve counter space. Most small plotters are the flatbed type (See Fig. 2.12.)

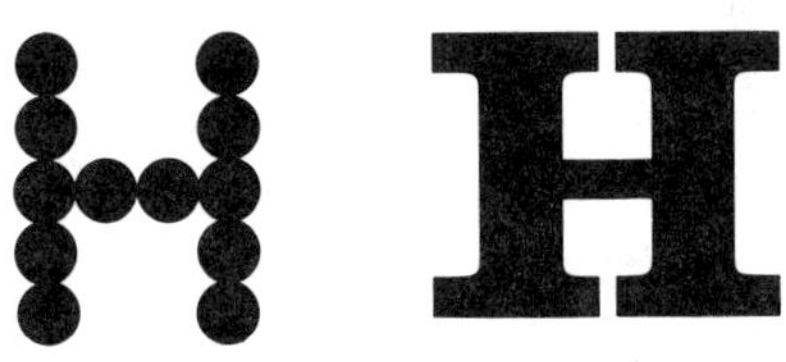

Figure 2.10 The origin of the name dot matrix is obvious from this illustration.

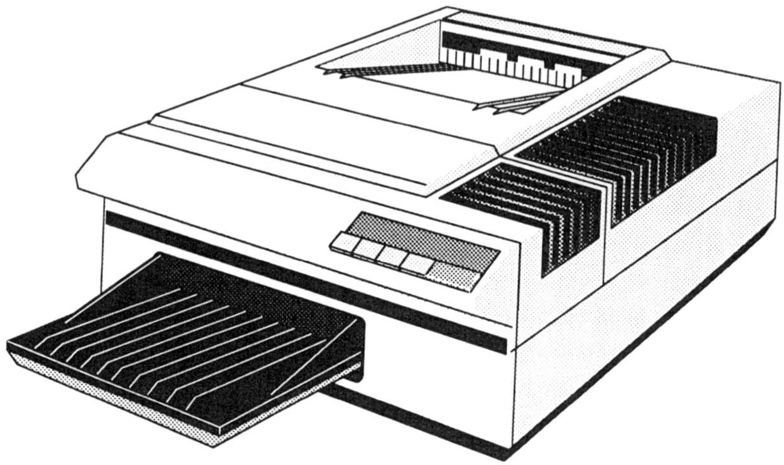

Figure 2.11 Laser printers can print four to 12 pages per minute.

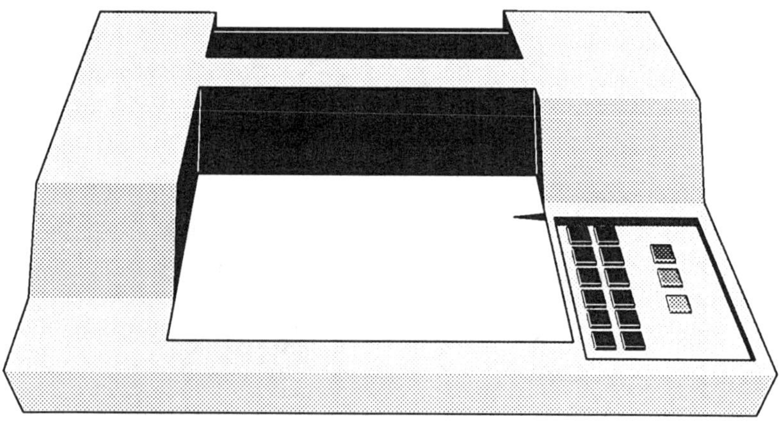

Figure 2.12 A flatbed plotter converts data to machine readable format.

Drum

A drum plotter is more common with larger page sizes. The plotter consists of a horizontal bar with the drawing pen(s) and a pair of wheels which grip the edge of the paper. The paper is moved in one direction while the pens move at right angles to the paper (See Fig. 2.13).

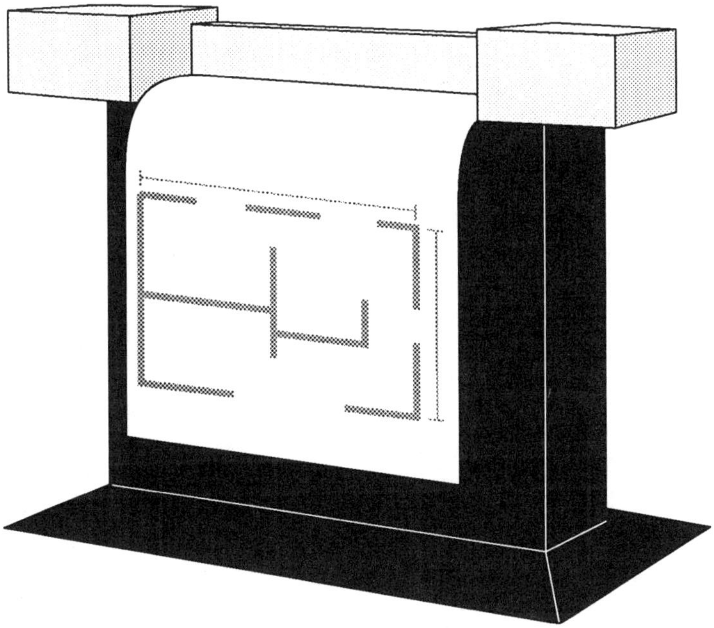

Figure 2.13 Drum plotter.

Dot Matrix Printer Settings

These printers typically have physical switches (called dip switches) that are either on or off. For proper settings refer to your printer manual, or your application software documentation.

Laser Printer Settings

One of the advantages of laser printers is their ability to support a number of type styles, type pitch, a large variety of special characters, plus some graphics. Both the software and the printer settings must be compatible for this to work. These settings can be configured from the software or by physical settings on the printer. Most newer laser printers have a menu (usually on the front panel), which can allow you to specify options such as

- the software interface such as the type of printer emulation desired, the characters per inch, the pitch, and the fonts,
- the hardware interface such as the port, baud rate, data bits, stop bits, and parity,
- yes or no for such options as "do start page," "set wait time."

> **NOTE:** In many cases a laser printer will have a default (or factory) setting. Depending on what these settings are, this can be the simplest and most consistent setup to use.

Most application software provides "printer device drivers" which interpret software output for a specific printer. Typically the software settings such as page size and fonts (type styles) will override those set on the printer, however, not in every case. If a printer will not support a font choice, it will print the default font for the printer which is usually 12-point Courier. If it cannot print a specific character, often it will leave the character blank.

Fonts

To enhance the choices you have with a printer, both for characters and type styles, you can add hardware font cartridges or downloadable software fonts available from your printer supplier. For more information on fonts and wordprocessors (See Part 2 REFERENCE, Chap. 17 Application Installations, Sec. 17.1 Wordprocessors.)

2.1.6 Modems

Modems are a vital piece of hardware allowing your computer to talk with another computer over telephone lines. This makes it possible to link microcomputers, Networks, minis or mainframes, and to exchange files regardless of their physical distance. The computer's digital language of 1s and 0s or on and off is translated by the modem to analog signals or tones of different frequency which can be transmitted over phone lines. This is known as signal **MOD**ulation. At the receiving end, the process is reversed, with the tones being converted back to computer digital code. This is known as signal **DEM**odulation, hence the term **MODEM**. Modems can be either external or internal models (See Fig. 2.14.)

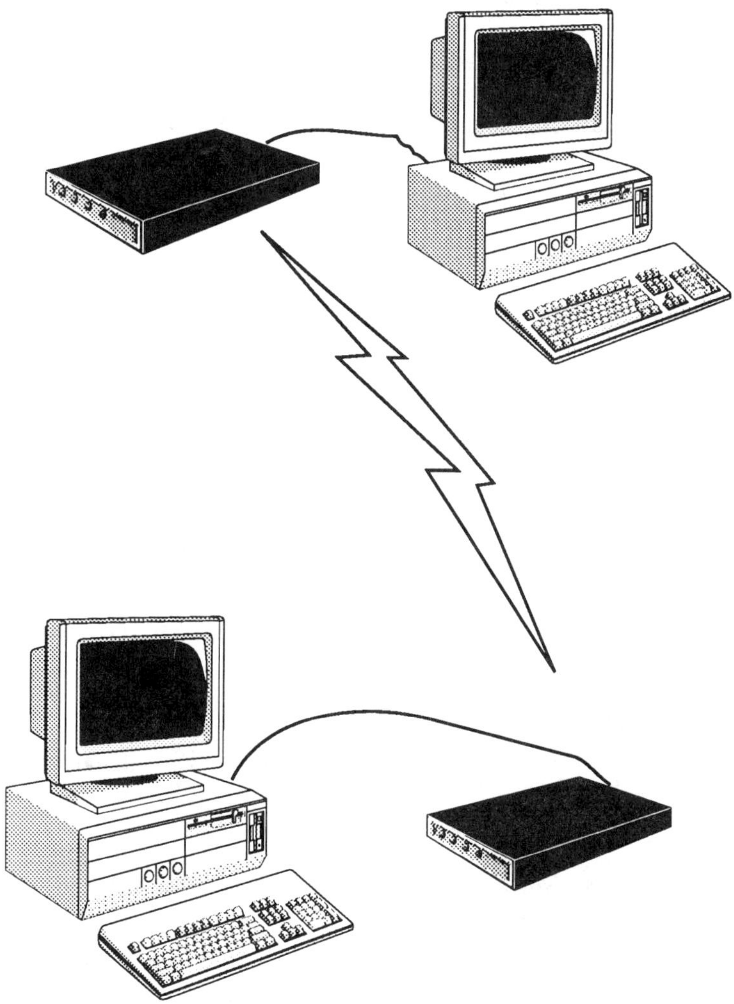

Figure 2.14 Modems make it possible to transmit data over telephone lines.

The external modem is in a self-contained case with a separate power supply, and has a variety of status lights useful for rapid fault isolation, plus a line for power, a telephone jack to access the phone lines, and a serial cable. An internal modem is basically a board which is placed in a free slot inside your computer, and is attached to the phone lines with a telephone jack.

In the previous figure 2.14, the computer at the top is transmitting, the one at the bottom is receiving. Digital signals from the first computer are converted to analog signals by the first modem. The second modem converts analog back to digital.

Software is required to translate your data into a protocol. This communication software should be setup when you install your modem. You will have to specify the modem setup, XModem (or other protocol) setup, terminal setup, general setup, host mode setup, and ascii transfer setup. Each of these selections will have a number of parameters that you will be required to specify. See your modem and communications software documentation for more details.

2.2 LAN HARDWARE BASICS

2.2.1 File Server (Memory and Drives)

File Server

The operating system for a IBM compatible computer is usually DOS. The operating system for the network called NetWare is loaded on the file server.

The file server gets its name from the fact that it actually "serves" users files and application software in response to requests. Processing of data by application software packages is done at the workstation, a process that is called distributed processing.

All of the devices on the network are connected with cabling (See Part 1 CONCEPTS, Chap. 2 Hardware, Sec. 2.2.3 Cabling) which attaches all printers, modems, disk subsystems, and any other shareable devices to the file server.

In a network the central file server "serves" files between workstations, and coordinates printing to attached printers (See Fig. 2.15).

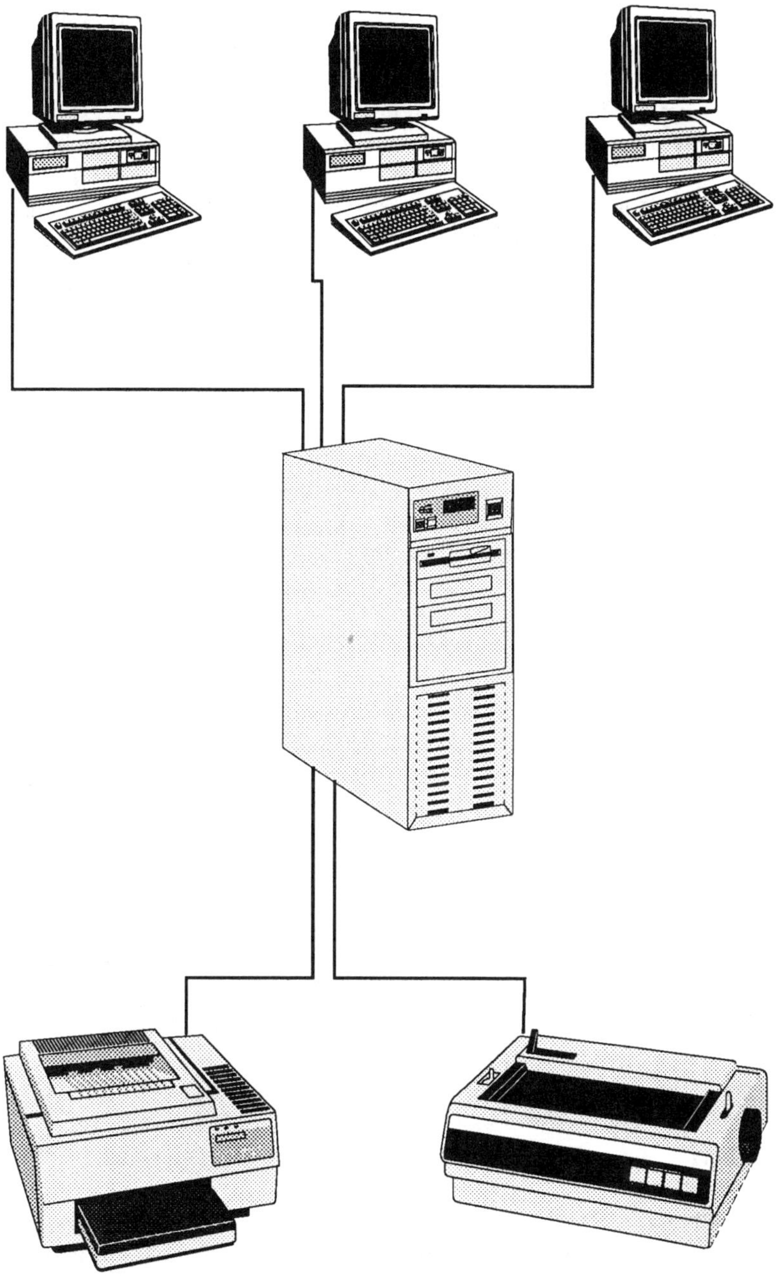

Figure 2.15 The file server is usually a high performance microcomputer.

Any 286/386 computer with at least a minimum 1 megabyte of memory will boot a file server. A better performing computer used as a file server, results in a better performing network. The server usually has a large hard drive, which is used to store data saved by all the network users, and the multiuser application software programs. NetWare controls access to the data and the application software programs through a set of rights which are part of its security structure.

A dedicated file server is one that functions only as a file server, while a nondedicated server works as both a server and a workstation. With a nondedicated file server, a failure in the workstation mode can "hang" the server. For security, and fault prevention the dedicated server is the best option.

File Server Memory

The file server memory is the heart of the network. Once NetWare has been installed on the file server, memory usage is dynamically controlled by the NetWare operating system. NetWare utilizes the following features to enhance performance (all of which use memory): directory caching, directory hashing, FAT caching, file caching, and communication (router) buffers.

Directory Caching

Directory caching is similar to a library card file system. The cards give you the address (location) of the book in the library. NetWare accomplishes the same function with a directory entry table (DET). The directory entry table contains the file name, file extension, file attributes, last update time and date, the starting cluster number (the physical location on the hard drive), and file size. Directory caching is the process of copying the entire directory entry table into the file server's memory. This allows NetWare to find files quickly, reading the file's exact location from the table in Random Access Memory (RAM), instead of reading the file server hard drive. If you run out of the specified number of entries in this table you will get a "disk full" error message, even though you have space left on your hard drive. If this occurs, run NETGEN, Miscellaneous Maintenance, and increase the directory entries. This means reinstalling your NetWare (although you will not have to change your other parameters).

Directory Hashing

If you went to a library in search of entries about networks, you would not search through every card in the card file, you would only look up the cards filed under "N" for networks. Similarly, NetWare minimizes the time required to find a file by organizing the information. NetWare creates an index (in RAM) of the directory entry table so it only needs to examine a few entries to find a file. This means that the system only has to search through a portion of the table to find the request, thus reducing the input and output to the hard drive by 30 percent.

File Allocation Table (FAT) Caching

The File Allocation Table (FAT) lists the physical location of all clusters of a file. This is used to find file locations on drives. Along with the directory entry table, NetWare stores the FAT for all disk drives in the file server's RAM. This speeds up file access, as the server determines beforehand exactly where a file's data will be found on the disk.

NetWare keeps a copy of the FAT table in memory, and two copies on the file server hard drive to prevent serious corruption of the FAT table. If an error occurs, you may have to down the server and bring it back up several times. This process compares the copy to the original. If this does not solve the problem, it is recommended that you run the VREPAIR Utility found on NetWare's diagnostic diskette, or available from the Netwire electronic bulletin board, or from an authorized Novell dealer.

File Caching

Once a file has been read from the file server drive, NetWare stores the file or the most used parts of the file in RAM. The next time that part of the file is accessed, it is retrieved at RAM speed, hundreds of times faster than disk speed. The file cache is refreshed every few seconds, with the most recently accessed files overwriting the oldest file copy in RAM. File caching only occurs if the file server has enough available memory.

File Server Memory Definitions

Cache Block: Cache Block is the area in memory where a file or portion of the file will be stored. A cache block can be one of four sizes: 512, 1024, 2048, or 4096 bytes.

Communication Buffers: This is also known as routing buffers. It is the area in memory that is set aside to hold packets of data arriving from users, and bridges. This figure is changeable through NETGEN. The minimum is 20, the default 40, and the maximum is 150 buffers. The recommended setting is to start with 40 and add one buffer for each workstation.

Directory Caching: This is the area in memory where the records of the directory entry table are stored. If you do not have enough memory in your file server to handle this, you will receive a message on server boot up, "Not enough memory to cache directories." Operating without enough memory will slow down your system.

Directory Entry: Each entry in the directory entry table is 32 bytes long. These entries can be for directories, files, and directory trustees.

Directory Hashing: Directory hashing means indexing the directory entry table. NetWare requires 8 bytes per directory entry for this process.

File Allocation Table (FAT): The FAT is a table that lists and points to the disk location of datafile blocks. It also lists parts of the disk that are not being used. Every item in the list is assigned a sequence number and a pointer (for the location of the next file). The FAT is stored in memory, utilizing 1KB of RAM for each megabyte of hard drive storage.

File Caching: This is the process of storing files or portions of files in the file server's memory, for quick access. File caching uses whatever memory is left over after all else is calculated.

File Handles: File handles is the process used by NetWare to track information on any opened files. Each file handle requires 56 bytes. The maximum number of open files is 1000. Keep in mind that each user can open between 5 to 25 files depending on the application software used, menus and batch files, and so on.

File Locking: NetWare uses 20 bytes of file server memory to handle file locking for each workstation, and the remainder for locked files. The maximum memory usage for file locking is 64K.

Worksheet for SFT NetWare 2.1

This worksheet will enable you to estimate the amount of memory required for your file server. The total you will get will be a minimum and will not include any memory for file caching. Therefore you will want to add memory to allow your most frequently accessed files to be stored in memory. There is a direct relationship between the speed of your network and the amount of memory available for file caching.

Directory Entries: First you will need to calculate the number of directory entries for your hard drive. This figure will then be used in the worksheet following. You must make the decision of either applying the general rule or the maximum. The general rule is 100 entries per user. The maximum entry is 128 per MB of hard drive.

Directory Hashing (8 bytes times the number of directory entries)	_____
Directory Caching (32 bytes times the number of directory entries)	_____
File Caching (Minimum of 8 cache blocks (4096 bytes per cache block)	32K
Caching FAT (1K RAM per MB of hard drive)	_____
File Handle (Support 1000 potentially open files)	56K
File Locking (Support 100 connections and 620 potentially locked files)	64K
Operating System (NET$OS.exe approximate size)	400K
Communication (routing) Buffers (Start with 40 and add 1 buffer per workstation) (Size of each buffer is 64 bytes (IPX and NetWare header) + 42 bytes (ECB header) + Max. Packet size in bytes.) That is, 1 buffer = 64 + 42 + 1024 = 1130 bytes 20 buffers = 22,600 (22.6K)	_____
TOTAL	_____

You can monitor how NetWare is using the file server memory through its utility, FCONSOLE (See Fig. 2.16.) Look in Cache Statistics and Summary screens.

```
NetWare File Server Console  V1.00b              Tuesday  May 29, 1990  8:26 pm
              User EAMONS On File Server TAITO_DB Connection 15

                        File Server Statistics Summary

File Server Up Time:   7 Days 17 Hours 22 Minutes  0 Seconds
Number Of File Service Processes:     3  Current Server Utilization:      29%
Disk Requests Serviced From Cache:  90%  Packets Routed:                    0
Total Packets Received:      19,326,153  File Service Packets:             67
Total Number Of Cache Buffers:      217  Dirty Cache Buffers:               1
Total Server Memory:          4,193,280  Unused Server Memory:          5,120

                           Maximum      Peak Used   Currently In Use
Routing Buffers:               150             21                  0
Open Files:                  1,000             94                 25
Indexed Files:                   0              0                  0
Transactions:                   90             25                  0
Bindery Objects:               N/A            N/A                N/A
Connections:                   100             17                  3
Dynamic Memory 1:           18,238          3,502                914
Dynamic Memory 2:           65,436          7,996              5,086
Dynamic Memory 3:           47,104          1,210                446
```

Figure 2.16 FCONSOLE Menu Utility, File Server Statistics Summary Screen

2.2.2 Workstations (Memory)

The Workstation

All microcomputers with at least one drive have the ability to function in the "stand-alone" mode. When they are connected to the network, they become a workstation. Mainframe computers utilize "dumb terminals" that cannot function in the stand-alone mode, therefore it is technically incorrect to refer to a workstation as a "terminal."

A workstation can be diskless, or it can have both floppy and hard drives. The boot files can be on the floppy or the hard drive, or for diskless workstations on the Programmable Read Only Memory (PROM) on the network interface card.

Expanded versus Extended Memory

The basic difference between these two memory types is in how the CPU sees them, and therefore, how applications use them.

The 8088 CPU limits the memory it can address to 1MB. Of that 1MB, 384K is reserved for video memory and bios ROM or interface boards, leaving a maximum of 640K available for DOS and DOS applications. This process is known as conventional memory.

The 80286 CPU allows addressable memory up to 16MB. However, in order to maintain compatibility with existing DOS applications, the 80286 provides an 8088 emulation mode (known as real mode) which limits memory access to 640K.

As programs continue to use more memory, the 640K limit becomes a performance liability. To get around this problem, Lotus, Intel, and Microsoft jointly designed a way to fool the CPU into seeing more memory. They came up with a memory paging scheme called the Lotus-Intel-Microsoft Expanded Memory Specification (LIM/EMS).

The LIM/EMS provided a standard for swapping 16KB or 64KB chunks or pages of memory in and out of the 384 reserved address section. DOS still only addresses its 640K limit, but applications written to access EMS see the 384 as additional memory. This is what is known as Expanded Memory.

Extended Memory is directly available on 80286 and above CPUs. This term refers to continuously addressed memory above the 1MB 8088 limit that the 80286 can see in normal mode (known as protected mode). Extended memory is accessible by non-DOS operating systems such as NetWare, Unix, and so on. DOS applications cannot use extended memory, except as a RAM disk.

> **NOTE:** NetWare cannot use expanded memory.

The Workstation's Memory

Shortage of available conventional memory in the workstation has become a reality with today's networks. Keep in mind that you will be loading the network shell into base 640KB memory, as well as command.com, and any applications that you are working with. Therefore, Terminate and Stay Resident (TSR) programs are not supported. You will find that some TSRs will work in conjunction with NetWare, but you may run out of memory.

Typically a workstations 640kb conventional memory will contain

Required

- 42KB minimum for the NetWare shell
  (Any shell customization will increase the size),
- approximately 3KB for the COMMAND.COM and hidden files,
- 22KB for the CONFIG.SYS file
  (this size will vary according to file contents).

Software Applications

- 460KB for a typical wordprocessor (i.e., Wordperfect)
  (this size will vary according to the application loaded).

Optional

- 1KB (or more) for utilities such as Screen Save, and so on.

In this example, 528KB of memory is in use, with 112KB free (640 - 528 = 112).

NetWare Shell

The NetWare shell consists of two files: IPX.COM and NET3.COM. The IPX.COM file is the communication software required to establish the network connection. Once the IPX program is run, a workstation can communicate with the network. Without the IPX file in the workstation memory, there is no communication with the network. The NET3.COM file is the translator between DOS and NetWare. If you are using DOS 4.x the file will be called NET4.COM.

The shell directs requests made by application software or user to either the DOS (Operating System) or NetWare (Network Operating System). It accomplishes this through function calls 21h.

2.2.3 Cabling (Topologies, NIC Cards, and Bridging)

Cabling Topologies and Protocol

Topology is the cabling schematic which includes components which make up the design of the LAN.

The protocol is the method in which the network interface cards communicate over the topology. Protocols are essentially electronic rules of behavior that allow the network interface cards to initiate and maintain communication. These rules are controlled by the protocol engine.

The protocol engine

- accepts raw data from the sending source,
- assembles and addresses packets,
- attaches any necessary information such as internet routing,
- places the packets onto the cable.

The three most widely used network interface cards are Ethernet, Arcnet, and Token Ring. Ethernet was developed by Xerox. Arcnet was developed by Datapoint, and Token Ring by IBM. The network interface cards are connected using linear, logical ring, and distributed star topologies.

Linear (Bus) Topology

This topology consists of several workstations (nodes) and a file server, which are attached to a common cable. This cable is referred to as a bus or trunk. The nodes are attached to the cable using either t-connectors or taps and drop cables. The cable ends cannot be left open, they must be terminated with a terminating resistor device matching the impedance of the cable. This terminator absorbs the signal, preventing it from echoing back on the line which will cause serious signal scrambling, and bring the network down.

Advantages

- uses the least amount of cable,
- can be the least expensive,
- conforms to industry standards,
- is easy to install.

Disadvantages

- least fault-tolerant topology,
- a break in the cable, or an open end (no terminator) can bring down the entire network,
- locating the break can be difficult when the entire network is down and little indication is given as to where the cable break occurred.

Examples of Linear (Bus) Topology (See Fig. 2.17) are Ethernet, Arcnet and G-Net.

Linear (Bus) Topology Protocol, CSMA/CD (Carrier Sense Multiple Access Collision Detection) (IEEE 802.3)

With the linear topology, each node is constantly monitoring (listening) to the cable. The node can only transmit data when the cable is idle, so it waits for the first opportunity. If two or more nodes attempt to transmit data simultaneously, the network interface card (NIC) recognizes a potential collision and transmits a jamming signal which halts the data transmissions for a predetermined length of time, generally 51.2 microseconds. The random wait feature prevents an endless cycle of collisions from nodes transmitting simultaneously. This is handled through a 64-bit preamble. The preamble is part of the header that precedes all packets of information sent. If during the transmission of the preamble the transmitting receiver receives back "exactly" what it has sent, this is a non-collision and transmission of data will follow. "Unmatched" data transmissions received back represent a collision and a back off and random restart will occur.

Collisions are handled very quickly in contention schemes such as Ethernet (51.2 microseconds). Problems occurring on the network usually occur because of lost packets caused by improperly laid cable. Available throughput depends on total network traffic, which changes from environment to environment depending on factors such as server I/O intensity, rather than on the number of nodes on the network.

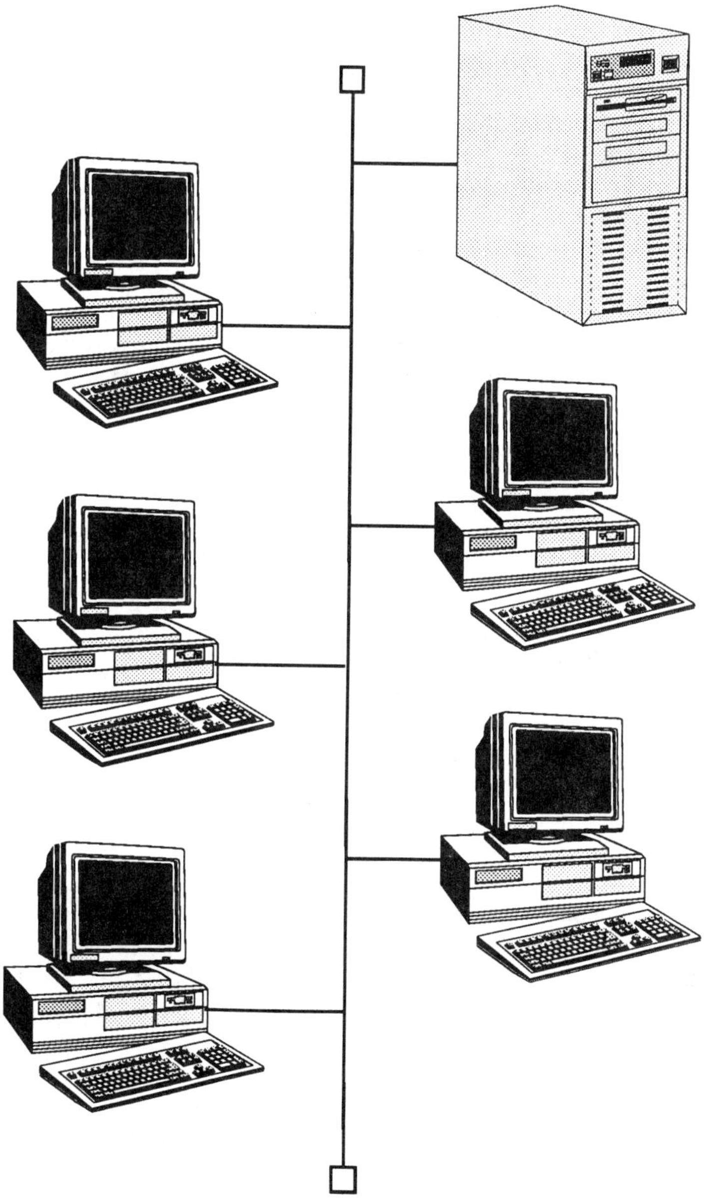

Figure 2.17 A linear bus network topology.

Distributed Star Topology

Star-wiring is not a new idea, nor is it unique to Token Ring or 802.3 LANs. It has long been used with telephone systems. Typically it involves the use of a centralized wiring closet to which all surrounding offices or nodes are cabled. This is now standard practice for all LAN cabling types except broadband. With this topology, the nodes are connected to a central device called a hub, multiport repeater, wire center, and so on. Hubs are used to split or amplify network transmission signals. In an Arcnet environment they come in active or passive types. Active hubs regenerate the signal and are connected to an electrical wall outlet. Passive hubs have no power, they merely split the signal. These hubs are called multiport repeaters if you are cabling an Ethernet network, as a star. When cabling with twisted pair cables, the hubs will have special devices located in the wiring closets. Because each concentration of nodes has its own hub, a new node or hub can be added to the network very easily. This makes the system extremely flexible for future growth considerations. As well, the system becomes easy to troubleshoot as a broken cable does not bring down the entire network (See Fig. 2.18.)

Advantages

- defective cables are easily identified,
- it is easy to add workstations to the network cabling, and
- it is easy to modify the cable layout.

Disadvantages

- uses a lot of cable, therefore, it can be more expensive,
- requires additional equipment such as hubs and multiport repeaters, therefore, more expensive.

Examples of distributed star topology are S-Net, Arcnet and Ethernet.

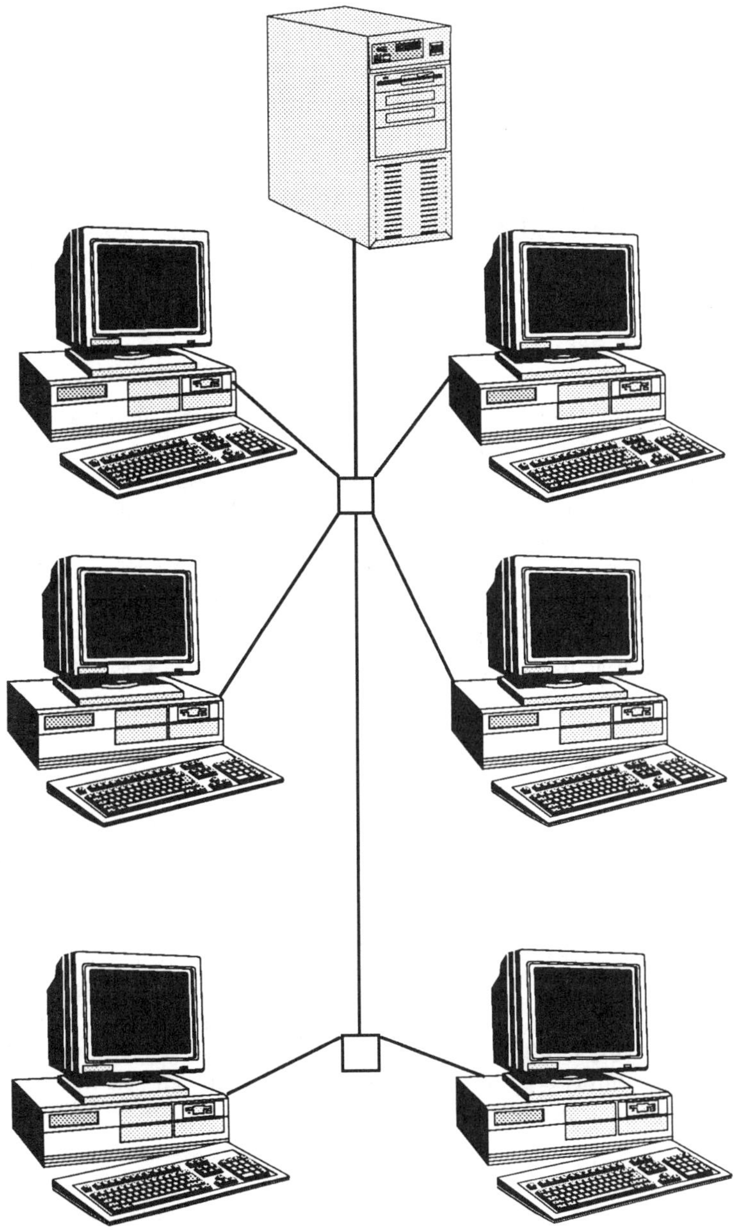

Figure 2.18 Distributed Star topology.

Polling Protocol

True star systems used to be the same as Novell's old S-Net, which incorporated a polling protocol. Here the central controlling device (file server) polls each node in a predefined sequence, querying for a request for network access. If a node makes a request, the message is transmitted. If no request is made, then the server moves on to the next node.

> **NOTE:** Distributed Star refers more to how you cable a system than to the actual form of communication. For example Ethernet still uses CSMA/CD when cabled as a distributed star.

Logical Ring Topology

In a physical ring topology, the cable runs from node to node with the last node connecting back to the first. In a logical ring the nodes are actually cabled in a distributed star (star-wired ring) or linear (token-bus) topology. A token is passed from node to node in a logical ring. A token is a combination of special recognizable bits which grant permission to the network interface card in possession of the token to transmit data. If a token is lost or a node is added to the network, all nodes stop and count down from their respective node addresses until the ring is re-established. Each node recognizes the address of the node it receives from, and the address of the node it sends to, as well as its own address creating the ring (See Fig. 2.19.).

Advantages

- uses a very efficient method of communication,
- token ring systems have a large install base, therefore, it has been well tested,
- it is easy to add workstations.

Disadvantages

- network configuration parameters are often more technical than others,
- depending on the type of cabling used, the system can become quite expensive,
- cable problems are difficult to locate.

Examples of logical ring are IBM's Token Ring and Arcnet

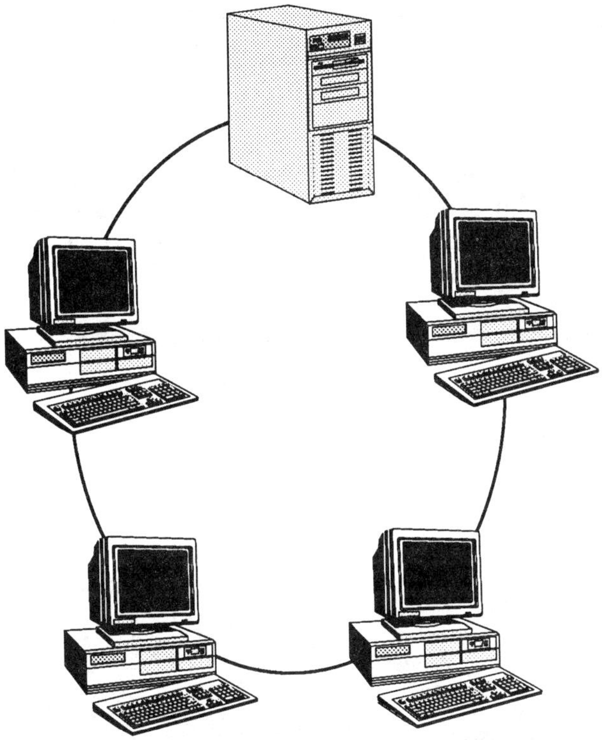

Figure 2.19 Logical Ring topology.

Token Passing Protocol

The token itself is a special broadcast with a node address attached. A node must see its address (frame) on the token in order for it to send a packet. Collisions do not occur on a token-passing network since only one node has the token at any given time. Every node handles the token on each cycle. When its address is not on the token, the workstation NIC responds by sending the token to the next node.

A token-passing scheme is called deterministic: The number of active nodes on the network rather than the network traffic determine available throughput.

Physical Cable Classes

Four classes of cable are commonly used in networks. The first three use copper, to conduct their electrical signal and the fourth conducts light through glass (fibre optic). These types are: Coaxial, Unshielded Twisted Pair (UTP), Shielded Twisted Pair (STP), and Fiber Optic.

Coaxial (Coax)

When laying coax cable, care must be taken to avoid sharp bends in cable runs. Coax's stiff property makes it ideal for pulling through conduits but not as flexible to bending as twisted pair. A conduit is a plastic or metal tube that has been installed by the builder to accommodate the installation of 110-volt electrical and phone wiring. Figure 2.20 illustrates a coaxial cable.

> **NOTE:** A crease in the cable will result in intermittent network errors which can be hard to detect or solve.

Figure 2.20 Coaxial cable is one of the common cable types used in network cabling schemes.

Coax cable comes in both solid core (RG-58/U, 53.5 ohm) or stranded core (RG-58A/U, 50 ohm). Solid core tends to give you a better connection with the center pin in a Bayonet Nut Connector (BNC). BNC is the name given to the connector used with coaxial cable. To connect the cable to the BNC connector you have a choice of solder, crimping, or twisting the cable ends. Soldering will provide you with the best connection but it can be very time consuming. Crimping is probably the most popular method used because it is easy to do and provides reasonable reliability. The twist-on method is the least attractive method as it does not provide a very reliable connection if done improperly. This is especially true if the cables are being moved around at all.

Twisted Pair

Twisted-pair cabling is popular because it is inexpensive and can be used for voice or data networks. Most networks (Arcnet, Ethernet, Token Ring, etc.), will run on twisted pair.

Twisted pair cabling uses RG11 jacks (standard phone jacks), patch panels and punch-down blocks. The RG11 jack is the same to twisted pair as the BNC connector is to Coax. A patch panel is a concentration box that acts as a distribution point that allows you to group and distribute wire so that you can move the workstations around. The punch-down block is the DIX connector that attaches the cabling to the patch panel.

Care must be taken when crimping shielded or unshielded twisted pair. The process is fairly simple, however you must ensure that the order of the pairs is correct or shorting will occur.

Unshielded Twisted Pair

Unshielded twisted pair (UTP) is more flexible, and has all of the same advantages of shielded cable. UTP can provide a single cabling solution through the use of adapters to connect coax and twinax or Apple-talk baluns, Ethernet transceivers, and IBM type 3 filters. A transceiver is a device that transmits and receives data on the local area network. It is used to connect the workstation to the backbone cable covered elsewhere in this chapter. Some network interface cards have a built-in transceiver on the card. A balun is an impedance matching device that allows the connection of coax to UTP cable.

When cabling a UTP network, your main concern is the correct distances between workstations and patch panels. Make sure you follow the manufacturers specifications.

Fiber Optic

Fiber optic cable offers many advantages over broadband or coax cable. The primary disadvantage of installing fiber is the difficulty in attaching connectors to the cable. The many advantages of fiber optics over other media are

- noise immunity,
- security, which forces snoopers to cut the cable to tap into the signal, causing the light level to fluctuate, which will be detected by a monitoring system,
- increased signal distance, with fiber extending your Ethernet network to a maximum distance of 4.5 kilometers (from 3.5). Token Ring can be increased from 100 meters to 4 kilometers using fiber,
- increased bandwidth which unlike coax cabling, measures its bandwidth in megahertz, fiber is measured in gigahertz. As a result fiber can transfer large amounts of data at high speed. For example, the FDDI standard has defined fiber optics speed at 100 megabits per second. Compared to the standards for coax this is incredibly fast.

Three Main Baseband Systems

The three main baseband systems are: Ethernet, Arcnet, and Token Ring.

Ethernet

Ethernet can be cabled as a linear system although it performs best in a distributed star, accomplished using an Ethernet repeater like Cabletron's Multiport Repeater or 3COM's MultiConnect. Cabling Ethernet in a distributed star topology will also decrease the number of collisions occurring and make it easier to troubleshoot. A break in a linear bus topology can bring the entire network down. If you are cabling Ethernet in a linear topology be sure to ground one of the terminators. Improper grounding can cause problems which can be extremely difficult to diagnose. (See Part 1 CONCEPTS, Chap. 2 Hardware, Sec. 2.2.3 Cabling (Topologies, NIC Cards, and Bridging.)

The main advantage of Ethernet is that it is FAST, with transmissions occurring at 10 megabits per second.

Ethernet runs on RG-58A cable. If you decide to run Ethernet on other types of cable, extra devices will be necessary, such as 3COM's Cable tamer (See Fig. 2.24.) Ethernet can be run on twisted-pair, broadband, or fiber optic cable. If you are using twisted-pair (10Base2) wiring it is not necessary for the workstation to utilize an external transceiver or transceiver cable. This costs savings will offset the cost of the repeater.

Table 2.1 lists cabling specifications (speed, media and identification scheme.)

Table 2.1 Cabling Specifications Chart

Speed	Media	Identification Scheme
10 MB/s	50 ohm coaxial cable	10Base5 or ThickWire
10 MB/s	50 ohm coaxial cable (RG 58)	10Base2 or ThinWire
1 MB/s	twisted pair	1Base5 or StarLAN
10 MB/s	twisted pair	10Base2 single
10 MB/s	twisted pair	10BaseT or twisted pair/dual
10 MB/s broadband	75 ohm coaxial cable (CATV)	10Broad36 or broadband
10 MB/s	fiber	10BaseF or fiber

Addressing Ethernet

All Ethernet boards come with the node address factory set. You will have to set the board for the type of cable being used, that is thick or thin. You will also have to set the board for any DMA channels, and base I/O addresses used. See the documentation that comes with the board.

Most manufacturers of Ethernet boards have a file server board available. As an example, 3COM has a 16-bit Etherlink Plus board for the server. This comes configured with 256K of RAM expandable to 512. They provide on-board buffering and will reduce any bottlenecks at the file server NIC. Where these are available, use them except when using a 386 CPU. There is a 80186 CPU chip on the card and it does not transmit as fast as the 386 processes.

Thin Cable Parameters

These parameters can change slightly depending upon the NIC manufacturer. See the manufacturer's specifications for exact distances. The parameters are

- the maximum trunk segment is 607 feet (185 meters),
- using four repeaters, up to five trunk segments may be connected,
- the entire network trunk length is, 3035 feet (925 meters),
- the minimum distance between stations is 1.5 feet (.5 meters)
- including repeaters, there can be a maximum of 30 workstations per trunk.

NOTE: When using thin cable, you must set the NIC to use the internal transceiver if the card supports this feature. Then connect your T-Connector directly to the BNC connector on the back of the NIC. Make sure that both ends of the cable are terminated and one end is grounded. Do not use drop cables with thin cable; that is the internal transceiver was specified.

Thick Cable Parameters

The same as the thin cable parameters, these distances can vary slightly based on the manufacturer's specifications. The parameters are

- the maximum distance from workstation to external transceiver, is 164 feet (50 meters),
- using four repeaters, up to 5 trunk segments can be connected,
- the minimum distance between transceivers is 8 feet (2.5 meters),
- the maximum length of a single trunk is 1640 feet (500 meters),
- the entire network trunk length is 8200 feet (2500 meters),
- including repeaters, there can be up to a maximum of 100 workstations per trunk.

NOTE: When using thick cable, you must set the NIC to use the external transceiver. The same as thin cable, you must ensure that both ends of the cable are terminated and one end is grounded.

Parameters for a Combination of Thick and Thin Cable

- ensure the total trunk length is between 600 and 1640 feet,
- calculate the length of the thick and thin cable separately using this calculation:

$$\text{Thin Cable} \leq \frac{1{,}640 - \text{Total Trunk Length}}{3.28}$$

Thick Cable = Total Trunk Length minus Thin cable

Arcnet

Arcnet can be cabled as a distributed star or a linear bus network. Coax (RG62), fiber optic or unshielded twisted pair cabling can be used to connect Arcnet cards. Arcnet works better with unshielded twisted pair than other NIC on the market.

The main advantage of Arcnet is its flexibility. It is also the least expensive of the three systems discussed in this chapter, which makes it popular in the marketplace.

Arcnet's disadvantage is its low-performance rate. It transmits at 2.5 MB per second. Some vendors such as Thomas Conrad, have produced 16 MBps cards which helps performance.

Communication in Arcnet occurs using a token bus protocol. Lost packets or tokens are not as damaging to an Arcnet network as they are to other systems.

> **NOTE:** The network will transmit a re-configuration burst of 31 micro seconds whenever a node is physically turned on or off on the network.

Addressing Arcnet

Each node address must be unique, regardless of whether the node is operating as either a file server or workstation. Arcnet has a range of 1 to 255 available addresses. It is recommended that you record each microcomputer's address on the back of the machine, and on your installation record sheets.

> **NOTE:** Address zero is for system broadcasts and should not be used.

Cabling Arcnet

Arcnet uses 93 ohm, RG 62/U cable. As mentioned earlier in this cabling section, it can be cabled as a distributed star or linear bus network. To cable Arcnet as a distributed star, attach your cables to a central hub. This means that the file server and workstations are attached to a hub. The hub can be either active or passive.

Active hubs act as signal splitters and signal amplifiers. They can contain as many as 64 ports. Because they contain their own power supply, the signal is regenerated. This means that they can carry signals longer distances than passive hubs and can be daisy chained together.

Passive hubs only split the signal. They are an inexpensive way to cable a small number of workstations together. They only have four ports. This means that only four machines can be attached to this device. Any unused ports on these devices must be terminated. Because the passive hub does not contain a power supply, signal regeneration does not occur. Hence, these devices are used to cable short distances only. In addition they cannot be chained before any other passive or active hubs.

Unused ports on a passive hub that are not terminated will cause signal reflections which causes problems on your network and can bring it down.

Diagnosing problems on Arcnet is fairly easy because problem segments and nodes can be disconnected from the active or passive hub they are attached to.

Table 2.2 lists the maximum cable distances allowed.

Table 2.2 Maximum Cable Distances.

SOURCE	DESTINATION	MAXIMUM DISTANCE
node	node	2,000 feet
node	active hub	2,000 feet
active hub	active hub	2,000 feet
node	passive hub	100 feet
active hub	passive hub	100 feet
passive hub	passive hub	(should not work)

NOTE: The maximum distance between the farthest two nodes may not exceed 20,000 feet.

Token Ring

Token Ring is owned by IBM. It is similar to Arcnet in its flexibility and protocol. Its advantage over Arcnet is that it is faster. Its disadvantage over most network systems is that it is more expensive. It communicates using a token passing protocol. Token Ring is extremely popular with users operating larger networks.

IBM Token Ring transmits at 4 MBps or 16 MBps dependant on the cards and cable type you have purchased.

NOTE: If you are using Token Ring you are limited to a total of two NICs in the file server.

Addressing Token Ring

With Token Ring, you will need to select the base I/O address and the memory address. There are two selections to choose from

- primary, with an address selection of A20h which must be used if a remote reset PROM is used,
- alternate.

If you are addressing a bridge, make sure that the first card you choose is your primary and your second card is the alternate. You can not have two primary or two alternates in a file server or bridge.

All of these settings are established using IBM's setup program (microchannel only).

Cabling Token Ring

IBM's PC Token Ring network supports up to 96 nodes and up to 12 IBM 8228 MAUs (Multiple Access Units). The MAU acts the same as Arcnet's active hub. MAUs have a ring in (RI) port and a ring out (RO) port. These are used to create a physical ring link. In the same manner as most systems on the market today, there are two types of NICs available: standard bus and microchannel bus. These are also available in 4 and 16 megabytes per second speeds.

NOTE: If you use a 4 and 16MB card on the same ring, the 16MB card will be reduced to a 4MB card. Therefore don't do it.

The Token Ring system uses two types of cables: adapter and patch cables. Adapter cables are 8 foot lengths of IBM type 6 cable. These are used to connect the station boards with the 8228 MAUs or patch cables. Patch cables (type 6 cable) come in four lengths, 8, 30, 75 and 150 feet. A patch cable is used to extend the cable distance when it is required to extend past the 8 foot adapter. You also use this cable to connect MAUs together.

- maximum number of stations = 96,
- maximum number of MAUS (8228 units) = 12,
- maximum patch cable distance between MAU and station (excluding 8 foot adapter) = 150 ft.,
- maximum patch cable distance between two MAUs = 150 ft.,
- maximum patch cable distance connecting all MAUs = 400 ft..

NOTE: The MAU (8228 units) must create a ring. To accomplish this, the RO (ring out) port of the last MAU must connect to the RI (ring in) port of the first MAU.

Before connecting the cables, initialize the ports on the MAU with the Setup Aid provided. After a few seconds you will hear a click, signaling that the port has been initialized.

Broadband Cabling Scheme

Broadband LANs are used when many types of transmissions are required. They are used in large backbone installations. Large backbones of this type are typically installed by educational institutions, hospitals, and large industrial sites.

The same as cable television (CATV), broadband divides its bandwidth into multiple channels. To accomplish this, it uses a technique know as frequency division multiplexing (FDM). The FDM technique divides a voice channel into subchannels, each with a separate frequency. These subchannels can carry video, voice, or data on the same cable.

One broadband cable can carry a combination of video, data, and voice.

Broadband's advantages are

- it can carry many different transmissions on the same cable (telephone, data, fax, and video monitoring for security),
- it is durable cable,

- distance can be increased in broadband Ethernet from 2.5 kilometres to 3.5 kilometers,
- it is a proven product.

The disadvantage of broadband is its complexity. It requires many components to connect the network interface cards (NICs) to the cable system. These components require frequent tuning.

Broadband Topology

Broadband utilizes a tree topology. The main cable is referred to as a "trunk." This trunk is connected to a transmission facility known as the headend. The headend is a device that modulates data and changes the incoming signal's frequency to an outbound path, which is then sent to its destination (device).

Workstations, and other devices utilized by users are attached to the system with drop cables and frequency division multiplexers or specialized modems. These are then attached to feeder cables which connect into the trunk. All of these devices are required because broadband uses analog signals for transmission and all workstations use digital signals. The multiplexer and modems are used to convert the workstation's digital signals to analog that broadband transmits.

To connect this network to the headend, taps, splitters, directional couplers and other devices are required. The taps are used to connect the drop cables to the feeder cables. Splitters and directional couplers, are used in directing the transmission paths discussed in detail further on in this chapter. These devices are known as "active" because they have power, unlike cable which is "passive."

Hardware requirements

Modems: You have a choice of using fixed or agile frequencies.

In an environment where point to point communication is required, a fixed frequency modem would be used. These devices transmit signals at a factory specified frequency.

If a corporation's needs require the frequencies to be changed then the agile modem should be used. These devices can be either manual or automatic.

As mentioned earlier in this chapter, two paths are required for connection to the headend. One path carries transmissions to the headend (return channel), the other away from the headend (forward channel). These paths can either be virtual (single-cable system) or physical (dual-cable system).

The virtual system simulates a physical system by a division of forward and return transmission paths. This is a process of separating the sub-channels so that adjacent channels will not interfere with each other. This spacing is referred to as guard band, a principal also utilized in radio and television broadcasting.

Single-Cable System: Three methods can be used to divide the bandwidth of a single-cable system

- high split allowing 29 return and 30 to 40 forward channels,
- midsplit allowing 17 return and 38 to 46 forward channels,
- subsplit allowing 4 return and 40 to 55 forward channels.

Dual-Cable System: This system dedicates a specific transmission path to each cable. The forward and return paths use the same frequency with the headend moving the data from one cable to the other.

> **NOTE:** The advantage of a single-cable system is the initial financial savings. However, because single-cable systems divide their bandwidth, they support only half the channels that a dual-cable system does.

Design Considerations: Keep in mind that components such as cables, splitters, and taps reduce the signal strength through insertion loss. This loss of signal is measurable and should be compensated through the use of amplifiers. You will need to consider this when designing your broadband system.

Problems

Cross modulation: When two signals combine, distortion occurs. This is known as cross modulation.

Cross talk: When one signal duplicates another, signals frequency distortion occurs. This phenomenon also common on the telephone system is known as cross talk.

Compression: This results from improper amplifier settings, where the input and the output are no longer the same.

Ingress: When environmental interference (most likely radio waves) are picked up by the network, this phenomenon is known as ingress.

Jabbering modems: This occurs when a modem starts randomly transmitting. This will down the channel.

Broadband Ethernet

The IEEE organization has a standard for Ethernet on broadband cabling. This standard is known as 802.3 10Broad36. The primary differences between Ethernet on baseband versus broadband is cabling distance and the implementation of the CSMA/CD protocol.

Distance: With repeaters a maximum distance of 3.5 kilometers can be achieved. Compare this to baseband's 2.5 kilometer maximum and you can see the advantage.

Protocol: Ethernet on broadband still utilizes the CSMA/CD protocol. Because broadband communicates in analog, Ethernet cannot rely on the DC voltage level to indicate the occurrence of collisions. To accomplish this, it dedicates 4 MHz of its 18 MHz channel to detecting collisions while leaving the rest for transmission of data. When collisions are detected, notification occurs over this reserved channel.

Broadband has three ways to handle the detection of these collisions. They are

- an Unscramble Mode Delimiter (UMD) is added to the end of the preamble (See Part 1 CONCEPTS, Chap. 2 Hardware, Sec. 2.2.3 Cabling (Topologies, NIC Cards, and Bridging.) The first 1450 bits following the UMD are stored by the modem and compared to the bits on the received packet. If they match, the communication is successful. If they do not, a collision has occurred.

- after 34 bits, Ethernet looks for a UMD. If it cannot detect one, it assumes a collision has occurred. Hence this is known as UMD timeout.

- modems (used to transfer the computers digital signal to broadband's analog signal) can also identify collisions. This occurs when the modem receives a packet while the workstation is attempting to send a packet as well. The modem then does a 75 bit delay, in which time it strips away the preamble, then it sends a notification to the other modems. Sensing the signal, the modem's controller stops transmissions and reschedules.

Connecting a Backbone with Bridges

A bridge is comprised of multiple network interface cards in a machine and software. There are four reasons for bridging

- connect multiple file servers,
- split network traffic,
- connect unlike networks (network interface cards),
- extend your cabling parameters.

The function of the bridge software is to route packets to the appropriate destination on any connected networks. All of this occurs at the Data Link Level of the OSI module for those who really care. NetWare utilizes its IPX/SPX protocols to accomplish this communication.

There are two types of local bridges; internal and external. Internal bridges are for instances where you have multiple network interface cards within your server(s). This would be used if you wanted to connect multiple file servers and create a backbone. In addition you could use this to split network traffic to your file server in a process that is similar to adding lanes to a highway. You are providing for more traffic in and out of your file server. This is particularly useful if you have a large number of users. Also this could be used to connect unlike networks (network interface cards), although this is rarely used. External bridges are for instances where you have multiple network interface cards within a workstation. This could be utilized to connect multiple file servers if you had run out of slots in your server, or you may use this to extend your cabling parameters, although this is rarely used.

Internal bridging is established by the addition of the network interface cards to the server and the regeneration of NetWare through NETGEN. NetWare then handles all of the routing and protocol conversions automatically.

External bridging is established by the installation of the network interface cards in the workstation and running the BRGEN program. Once you run this software it generates BRIDGE.EXE which is loaded into this machine. You can have a bridge as dedicated (functioning only as a bridge) or nondedicated (as a workstation as well). Nondedicated bridges are not recommended because of memory constraints and user failures. If you do decide to go with a nondedicated bridge, you will need to specify the amount of memory for the bridge to function. For example, BRIDGE128 allocates 128KB of memory for the bridge.

> **NOTE:** You can bridge up to four network interface cards within one file server or workstation.

Addressing a Bridge

In an internetwork (multiple NICs in one server) you must specify a unique network (or internetwork) address for the LAN. The rule is that any NIC connected to a common cabling system must have the same network address in order to communicate. Any NIC connected to a different cabling system must have a different address. Just remember: same cabling-same address, different cabling-different address.

If after installing your network you need to change the address, you may do so with the utility DCONFIG.

NICs on the same cable system require the same network address. NICs connected on different cables require different network addresses. Figure 2.21 illustrates both internal and external bridging.

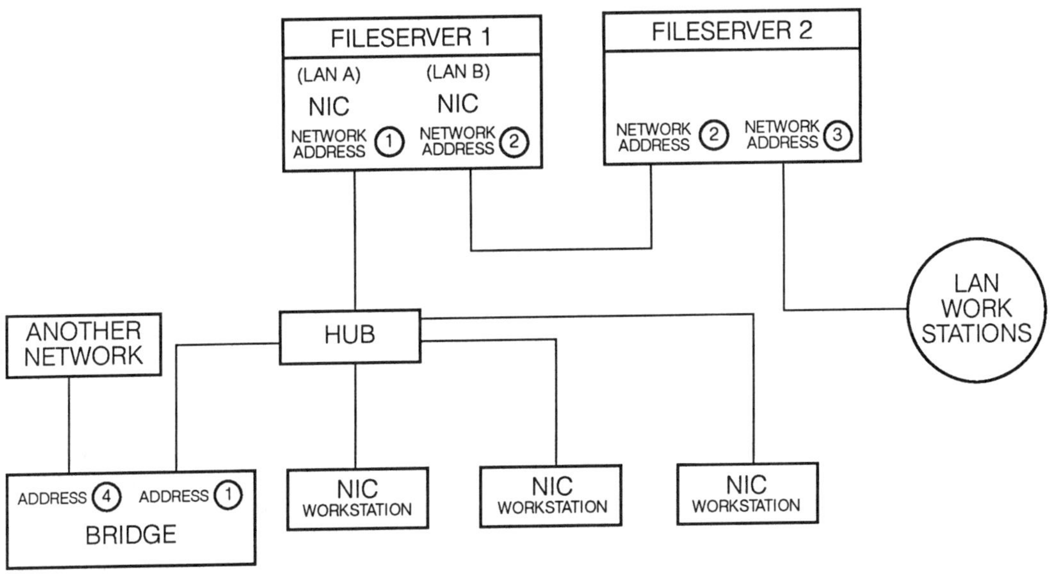

Figure 2.21 Both internal and external bridging have been shown in this illustration.

Connecting a Backbone

The most efficient method of connecting multiple file servers is through a "backbone" (See Fig. 2.22.) A backbone is a single network cabling system that connects only servers and bridges. Because the backbone sees the most traffic on an internetwork, no workstations should be attached to this leg of cabling. In addition, it is easier to troubleshoot and maintain if no workstations reside here. For best performance, a high-speed topology is recommended for your backbone.

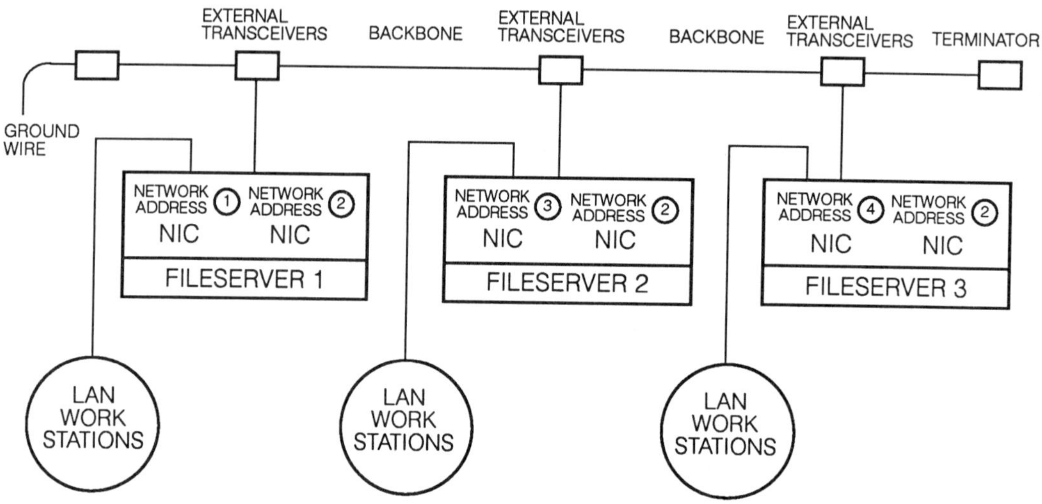

Figure 2.22 This "backbone" cabling schematic utilizes an Ethernet cabling system.

Cabling Design and Troubleshooting Enhancement Products

There are many add-on products available to enhance the cabling design of NetWare. Manufactures of these products include: Cabletron, 3Com, and others. We have included a sampling of these products available from one of these companies. Similar products are available from other manufacturers.

LanScanner

With 3Com's Multiconnect LanScanner, technicians and cable installers can quickly determine how well coaxial cabling and twisted pair wiring installations can handle data transmissions. The LanScanner device (See Fig. 2.23) analyzes the transmission of electronic signals giving users the advantage of identifying the location of wiring problems without the need to trace wires in ceilings, ducts, and cable trays.

Figure 2.23 3COM's LAN scanner, a valuable tool for technicians

Menus guide you in selecting either coax or twisted pair cabling and give you a choice of four test functions. These four tests are AutoScan, Manual Scan, Noise Detection, and DC Loop Resistance.

- AutoScan reports the length of cable, proper termination, and impedance variations.
- Manual Scan allows the user to manually examine cable impedance characteristics at any point along the cable.

- The Noise Detection Test indicates interference from an external noise source through the measurement of low-frequency noise. This test utilizes pulse detection to monitor voltage spikes or signal leakages.
- The DC Loop Test measures the total electrical resistance of a cable that is shorted at the far end, providing accurate loop resistance measurement without the need for a second test tool. Loop resistance is a critical parameter for installing twisted pair Ethernet.

NOTE: Cable types that are not compatible with a standard BNC connector, may be attached to the LanScanner using cable adapters.

CableTamer

The 3Com MultiConnect CableTamer is an impedance-matching device that makes it possible to implement Ethernet on a wide variety of currently installed cabling systems. The CableTamer is offered in two versions. The CableTamer/93 model allows connection between thin Ethernet cable and coaxial cable used in most IBM 3270 and Arcnet installations (See Fig. 2.24.) The CableTamer/75 model connects thin Ethernet cable to the type of wiring typically used in cable television (CATV) and Wang Wangnet installations.

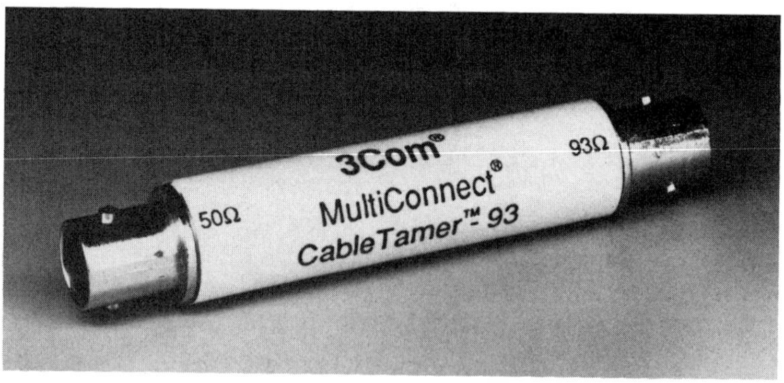

Figure 2.24 3COM's Multiconnect Cable Tamer allows you to run industry standard 10 MBs Ethernet over existing Arcnet (RG62) or 3270 cable.

PairTamer

3Com's MultiConnect PairTamer Ethernet allows network users to communicate over previously installed telephone wiring.

The PairTamer can replace an existing modular telephone outlet to connect microcomputers to the network (See Fig. 2.25.) Both the telephone and network plug into the PairTamer and operate in the same wiring bundle without interference. The PairTamer units are passive devices that do not contain internal power sources.

Figure 2.25 The PairTamer can replace an existing modular telephone outlet (jack) to connect microcomputers on the network.

Multiport Repeater

3Com's Multiconnect Modular Multiport Repeater is a concentrating device that makes it possible to attach multiple network segments consisting of one or more types of media together in a star configuration. Signals from each segment are "repeated" to all the other segments, enlarging and extending the reach of the network. These media types include thick and thin coaxial, fiber optic and single (10Base2) or dual (10BaseT) twisted pair wiring segments to form one enterprise-wide network.

> **NOTE:** Up to 100 repeaters may be installed on one Ethernet backbone segment.

This product offers several operational advantages such as easy workstation addition and removal without interrupting other modules or network segment connections, automatic or manual isolation of faulty segments and reconnection after the fault is corrected, connection of 50 ohm RG58, 75 ohm RG 59, 93 ohm RG62, 70 and 150 ohm single twisted pair or any IBM Type 1, 2, 3, 5, 6, 8, or 9 wire.

2.2.4 Network Printers

Printer types

When choosing printers for use with networks, there are some special considerations.

Network printers will be used much more than stand-alone units, therefore they must be high volume. On a stand-alone system you have one user, one printer, and on a LAN you have multiple users, one printer.

> **NOTE:** Hardware requirements are almost the same for stand-alone installations (See Part 1 CONCEPTS, Chap. 2 Hardware, Sec. 2.1.5 Printers.)

It is not necessary to purchase additional printer hardware to handle the extra workload imposed when it must deal with multiple jobs. NetWare places jobs in a "print queue" and sends them to the buffer in the printer, and the job is then processed by the printer. Depending on the volume of printing that you must process, you many wish to add additional memory capacity to the printer, thereby enlarging the buffer. For more information on print queues and their management (See Part 2 REFERENCE, Chap. 18 Printing with NetWare.)

Other Considerations

One of the main motivations for a network installation is its ability to share peripherals. Using NetWare to share printers has many advantages over the stand-alone mode

- security and management control is much easier, users can be limited to specified printers,
- print queues offer a variety of configurations and job priority functions useful for managing workload,
- fewer printers are required, therefore a higher quality of equipment can be purchased producing better printing for the same cash outlay.

NOTE: For more information on security, print queues, and printing, (See Part 2 REFERENCE, Chap. 18 Printing With NetWare.)

2.2.5 Backups (Tape, CD-Worm)

While it is possible to backup to floppies, this procedure is time consuming, much more prone to errors, and not recommended for networks. Backup to floppy is therefore not discussed in this text.

From a management perspective, most major concerns about network backup will be addressed by personnel designations and job descriptions, and in hardware and software choices. Questions to consider in any management decision on network backup are

- Does the tape backup unit have enough capacity?
- Is the backup reliable, and can it be restored easily in case of drive failure?
- Can portions of the backup be accessed, for example, one file?
- Is the backup easy to use, and is the software easily understood by anyone if the designated backup personnel is unavailable?
- Is the backup hardware an internal unit, or does it require the purchase of additional equipment?

Tape Backup Units

One of the most popular methods of backup for networks is the tape backup unit. This allows an entire network to be backed up easily (See Fig. 2.26.)

Tape backup units using the ¼" medium have been available for over 15 years. Relatively recent technological developments have increased their capacity from the original 5 megabytes to over 2 gigabytes with digital audio technology (DAT).

Figure 2.26 Tape cartridges have been specially designed for tape backup units.

CD Worm Backup Units

Compact Disk Write Once Read Many (WORM) backup units have one distinct advantage: a compact disk can store from 550 megabytes to over 1 gigabyte of data. These backup units have a reputation for reliability.

Other Backup Units

VCRs can also be used for a backup medium but are not that common.

3 SOFTWARE

In this chapter

Operating Systems, Applications, and Data Basics, Software Basics for Stand-Alone Workstations, Software Basics for LANs.

3.1 BASICS (OPERATING SYSTEMS, APPLICATIONS, AND DATA)

3.1.1 Software Interface Basics

Operating Systems

The Operating System (OS) is a collection of software programs that function in the same way in which a telephone switchboard operator directs calls. The OS is the interface between the application programs (i.e. WordPerfect) and your computer hardware. OS basics discussed in this chapter apply to both the NetWare, which runs on the file server and DOS which runs on the workstation.

We can communicate with both operating systems using commands such as **CHKDSK, VOLINFO**.

CHKDSK: This DOS command scans local workstation drives, checks the specified drive, and reports any errors found.

VOLINFO: This NetWare command scans a file server, and displays the information about total and free storage space, and directory entries for each volume on a file server.

3.1.2 Hardware Interface Basics

Communicating with the Hardware

The attached hardware is usually referred to as peripherals. Part of the operating system handles the input/output to these hardware peripherals. This is required because the hardware is controlled by very primitive commands.

Loading the Operating System

At start up, the operating system must be loaded into the computer's main memory. This is called the Boot-up process.

Boot-up process The boot-up process performs a number of hardware diagnostic tests, the Power On Self Test (POST) and then it loads the operating system and other optional commands. These specific programs are required for the computer to function.

When first switched on, a computer does a "cold boot", a name derived from the assumption that the machine is either new or cold. The "warm boot" is performed when the machine has already been turned on, and may have "lost its mind". The warm boot is usually the result of the three finger salute: <ctrl><alt><del>, or the reset button. This assumes that the POST sequence is not required. This initiates the boot process.

> **NOTE:** The warm boot, in most microcomputers, is not as comprehensive a restart as a cold boot.

The various boot-up steps for DOS are

- the computer goes to the Read Only Memory (ROM) and runs the POST to check the Random Access Memory (RAM), the keyboard, and the other hardware (peripherals),
- the computer looks first at the floppy drives for a system (bootable) disk, if it does not exist, it checks the hard drive(s) for this same information. If none of these drives contain a boot track, an error message will appear: for example, "Non system

disk, or disk error." If the disk is a boot disk, the computer looks for a boot track, usually located at track zero and if found, loads the operating system from that drive,

- next, two hidden files are loaded. These two files are part of the basic input/output system (BIOS). These files help establish the relationship between program input/output operations and peripheral devices. The Operating System contains routines for each peripheral device known as drivers or device handlers.

At this point, the computer is up with hardware functions running although the user interface does not exist. The computer checks the root directory of the boot disk for a CONFIG.SYS file. If this file is found, the commands are carried out. The CONFIG.SYS file is an ASCII text file that contains a series of commands. These commands allow you to tell DOS to perform particular functions and to load add-on device drivers, and so on. You can create this file with any ASCII text editor. It may contain commands such as BREAK, BUFFERS, FILES, COUNTRY, LASTDRIVE, SHELL, DEVICE, and so on. Here is a sample CONFIG.SYS file:

```
BUFFERS=26
FILES=32
DEVICE=MOUSE.SYS
DEVICE=ANSI.SYS
```

NOTE: For more information regarding the creation of a CONFIG.SYS file see your DOS manual.

- once the CONFIG.SYS has extended and modified the environment, the user interface is loaded. This is managed by the file COMMAND.COM. This file makes up the second part of the operating system, known as the command processor. The command processor translates user's requests and any application program calls and carries out the commands. COMMAND.COM provides the user with a prompt, and makes internal DOS commands available. The DOS Operating System is now fully loaded and operational.
- one last step is performed before control is turned over to the user. The operating system looks for the AUTOEXEC.BAT file. The same as the CONFIG.SYS, this is an ASCII text file, created by the user with a text editor. Users can customize their system using this file. If this file is not found, the user is prompted for the date and time, and control is passed to the user at a DOS prompt. Here is a sample AUTOEXEC.BAT file:

```
ECHO OFF
PATH = C:\;C:\DOS
PROMPT $P $G
CLS
```

Application Software

Once the computer is operational with the operating system loaded, you can run any application software available on your computer.

Basically, application software is the user interface for a specific task whether word processing, database management or a spreadsheet. Any one application package might encompass hundreds of man-years of programming, design, and testing time. We now have the ability to buy these programs as we would a book off the shelf. Re-inventing the wheel is not required to enable our computers to be a functional tool.

Application Programs

Microcomputers have changed the way we do business, in a short time frame. These small desk-top machines now have more computing power than their room-size ancestors. Costing less than most photocopiers, they enable us to do a wide range of business tasks such as word processing, spreadsheets, accounting, database management, and desktop publishing.

Tasks that once took days and even months can now be done in minutes. The increase in productivity this brings, is the main factor driving the computerization of business.

Electronic Spreadsheets

In 1979 a new software program was introduced for the Apple computer. Called VisiCalc, this "electronic spreadsheet" soon revolutionized the nations accounting departments. This spreadsheet brought the microcomputer from the hobbyist's or hacker's basement to the manager's desktop.

Users soon discovered that this new accounting tool was more than just another electronic calculator. Not only could an entire spreadsheet be recalculated in minutes, it was now possible to create complex models for forecasting profits, sales, costs, budgets, or just about anything else where a pencil, paper, and an calculator had been used previously.

Newer spreadsheet programs have enhanced capabilities to perform complex mathematical computations, create graphs, and enable the user to develop an attractive, graphics oriented and easy-to-read presentation.

Management now has more immediate access to spreadsheet information which can be presented in graph or chart form for easy reference. Using generated graphics, spreadsheets can automatically update graphs with the latest data. Graphs can be redrawn in a fraction of the time previously required. Business decisions can now be made based on more accurate and comprehensive information. Charts and graphs easily identify trends and conditions that can be missed in a mass of accounting data, making the spreadsheet with its graphic capabilities an essential management tool.

Word Processing

Word processing packages have dramatically reduced the time required to produce reports, letters, memos and even books. The difficult task of typing and editing has been made easier, faster, and vastly more efficient. It is possible to insert or delete individual characters, lines, or paragraphs and move, copy, or delete them as required. Centering, bolding, and underlining are now simple tasks. Today's software packages can check spelling (for multiple languages), create a table of contents, number every line, and even format the document with headers and footers. Form letters can be written once for regular use. Contracts or proposals can be pieced together from multiple source documents all stored on drives which serve as an electronic "filing cabinet" for documents. Access to these files is more efficient than was ever possible with paper based filing systems. Specific text can be located with features in some word processors, or with special utilities.

Database Management

A database management system (DBMS) is one of the most useful tools in the computer library. In its simplest form, the database manager is a filing cabinet where large amounts of electronic information can be stored and retrieved in a logical way.

Businesses can use a database management system to keep customer order information, address and mailing lists, inventories, or just about any other data that must be retained and updated. The database facilitates storage and retrieval by letting users organize the way information enters the system, saving the information electronically, and then reporting on the information in almost any fashion requested by the user.

For example, a database with customer address information can be told to generate a printout of mailing labels for all customers within one zip or postal code allowing "target" mailings. As another example, you may wish to send a special Christmas greeting to all customers that have dealt with the firm for over 10 years. The database can complete this task in less time than it used to take to decide where to start to gather the information.

Desktop Publishing

Desktop Publishing (DTP) is a software package that combines the word processing power of the microcomputer with the capability to typeset the written text. Graphics can be created or added, and text can be manipulated to create professional output at a fraction of the cost. This fairly recent software application enables a firm to create their own newsletters, or marketing literature in-house. Desktop publishing packages are similar to word processors but are more graphics oriented. They can be used as an electronic tool for paste-up and layout.

When completed, the publication can be printed on a Laser printer to produce near typeset quality. It is possible to take the electronic file to production houses that have sophisticated Laser printers to produce professional quality prints.

Compatibility Between Software Applications

With software applications, it is often necessary to have one package communicate with another. For example a word processor can be used for the text, and a desktop publishing package must be able to import that text. For more information see "Can You Import/Export Data?" later in this chapter.

Data

Data is a generic term that encompasses documents, accounting files, database files, and any other electronically stored information that can be processed by the computer with or without an application program. Data is the primary reason for having and using application programs to input, store, retrieve and manipulate this data.

3.2 SOFTWARE BASICS FOR STAND ALONE WORKSTATIONS

3.2.1 Copyright

The easiest way to operate your system is to have only legitimate software on your system. To be completely legal, every computer software package installed on the machine should be a registered copy. That means that you must own a copy of

- your Disk Operating System (DOS),
- any word processor on the System,

- any spreadsheet program on your computer,
- any utilities you may have.

If you do not have the DOS manuals, you probably do not have a legal copy of DOS. Owning a legitimate version is very assuring, however, the DOS manual included with legitimate copies is really only useful for reference.

Freeware

Freeware is just that-totally free, and is usually available from an electronic bulletin board accessible through the use of a modem. In some cases the author of the freeware will ask for a voluntary donation, but by definition there is no requirement to pay for the software in order to use it. Freeware usually identifies itself as such on the first screens that come up when the software is run.

Shareware

Shareware is the same as freeware in that it can be downloaded from an electronic bulletin board. It does have a difference however, there is a charge for its continued use. Software authors will agree to have their programs distributed by "electronic bulletin board systems" (usually called a BBS). In fact that is one of the best ways to get a program to market. They agree to allow various distributors to send their program to BBS operators who list their program and a brief description of what it does. If you want to try the program, download it and assess it. If you use one of these programs, copyright dictates that you must pay for it. By using it you are accepting the terms and conditions that are a part of continuing to use the program. The justification for this is simple. An author must spend time writing the "source code" that makes the program work. He or she has every right to expect to get paid when their program is used.

Commercial Software Application Packages

Some, but not all software has some form of agreement sealed in a package with a strategic floppy like the PROGRAM disk. It will say something like, "By opening this seal you are accepting the terms and conditions. . . . . ." That means you are subject to the copyright laws. You cannot give copies of your registered software to anyone, for most jurisdictions in the world you can be held personally liable if you knowingly distribute copies of software you own. The same as any other commodity, software you own can be sold, or donated, however you should first read your license for terms, and if necessary, contact the software manufacturer. WordPerfect for example allows users upgrading from 5.0 to 5.1 to donate the old software to a registered educational institution in their area. WordPerfect must be notified of this situation using a special form which comes with the 5.1 upgrade.

The Demo Copy

Some software developers will issue demo or assessment copies. These, however, are not intended for daily use. If you have a demo copy, and you like the package after assessing it, buy a real version. There are great benefits. Upgrading usually costs a fraction of the retail price, plus you will have the proper documentation, which makes understanding and using any program much quicker and easier.

Copyright infringement of computer software is a serious matter, and you should make every effort to ensure that your system contains only legitimate application software.

3.2.2 Single User Software Basics

The majority of microcomputer-based application software has been designed as single user. This means it has been written for use by only one user at a time.

Network Compatible Is Not the Same as Multiuser Software

You will notice when you buy software that many packages claim to be network compatible. This can be extremely misleading, as it implies that it is multiuser, this is not normally the case.

If a package is listed as "network compatible" this only implies that it can be successfully installed on the network file server hard drive. This does not mean that it is a multiuser program, or one that allows you to share datafiles.

Buying a network, and installing single user software on the file server hard drive will not make it multiuser. (See Part 1 CONCEPTS, Chap. 3 Software, Sec. 3.2.3 Multiuser Software Basics.)

When you install any software on the file server, you must consider the copyright implications. Many licensing agreements specifically spell out that the installation of their package on a network is considered a violation of that agreement.

System Managers Concerns

If you do not install any single user software on the network, you can avoid licensing and support concerns. If you make the software available on the network as a single user package, and it proves to be popular, it will only be a matter of time before the users make requests that you cannot legally fulfil. One possible exception to this would be if a demo or evaluation copy of a multiuser package is only available as a single user version.

> **NOTE:** For more information on upgrades, and dealing with users reluctance to accept change (See Part 1 CONCEPTS, Chap. 5 System Maintenance, Sec. 5.2 Upgrades.)

What Not to Do

There is one situation which can lead to endless problems and that is if you install a single user package on a network accessible by several users (multiuser). Single user software often has not been designed for networks, where programs and datafiles can be shared. For example, if there are two users (A and B) accessing a single user package, and user A loads a datafile, and is in the process of modifying the file, adding or changing information, and at the same time, user B loads and modifies the same datafile. User B saves his changes, and user A saves her changes, user B just lost all his work, which may have taken minutes or hours to create.

Situations such as this can have a major impact on productivity and user trust in a network. Even more important, the data loss in this example may not be discovered immediately, if ever.

3.2.3 Multiuser Software Basics

Your choice of application software has considerable long term network implications.

NetWare is designed to allow multiple users simultaneous access to the same data files. For this to function, the file attributes (called flags) must be changed. Setting file flags correctly is part of a successful multiuser application software installation. (See Part 2 REFERENCE, Chap. 17 Application Installations.)

Multiuser software has the ability to lock a file. In a word processing environment, this is an extremely valuable feature, since you seldom have the requirement for two users to edit the same document at the same time. Unfortunately this is not the case with a database management program, or an accounting package. An accounting system that will only let one user access a file at a time is not a realistic approach to the way in which most businesses operate. The same holds true for database management programs that take this approach of one user per file. This approach is referred to as "file locking."

Realistically to have true multiuser capabilities, application software must have "record locking." This means that if user A is in accounts receivable doing a customer inquiry, on COMPANY ONE, user B can be also doing an update or inquiry on DELTA COMPANY all in the same database. This data is read and saved to the same datafile. If user B requests the information on COMPANY ONE, he or she should receive a message such as

The record you have requested is in use.

Depending on the language used, and the programmer's utilization of the record locking functionality, user B might also be told that it is user A that is locking the record.

Therefore, a truly network compatible database or file system, must have a record locking capability built into it. This software must take into account different types of file and record locks. For example, if a user is printing out all accounts receivable customers, you would not want your software to lock the entire file. The software should recognize that the printing is a read-only operation, and with no requirements for changing or updating the datafile. The opposite also holds true. If user A tells the software to re-sort the customer file and user B is adding a new customer at the same time, then the software should inform user A that the operation cannot be started until all users have exited the required files.

Software that does not have the capability to understand the situations outlined, will allow user A to re-sort the customer file, while user B is still in the file. Ultimately this will corrupt the datafile. With most accounting systems, inaccuracies (corruption) only comes to light at month or year end.

3.3 SOFTWARE BASICS FOR LANs

3.3.1 Copyright

Network Copyright

If you install "legal" software copies on your network, you will never have to be concerned about copyright infringement. Network users should be advised not to install any software that is not legally acquired, to ensure that your network remains legal.

Using Programs

Often a network program can be used to create a document, a database or even another program which is then offered for sale. It is a wise precaution to contact the owner of the original program and clear the use of their software in this context, and confirm your conversation in writing.

Many single user software packages explicitly state that they cannot be installed on a network or a shared system under any circumstances. In some special conditions these companies will enter into an agreement to allow the installation, usually for use as a single user package. Conditions such as diskless or floppy only workstations would require a special arrangement of this nature. If you install one of these packages on the network, you should be aware that many of these packages have never been designed to run on a network.

Copyright and Backup

Many copyright provisions spelled out in license agreements stipulate that only one backup copy can be made, however, the legal concept of fair use is usually the overriding consideration. That means if backups are made for backup purposes only, and not for other use, multiple backups of software should not be a breach of the license agreement.

3.3.2 Network Compatibility

Network Compatibility

When choosing software that is to be installed on the file server and/or run on a workstation attached to the network, there are several compatibility considerations that should be part of your criteria

- Is the software network compatible, will it co-exist in the workstation RAM with the NetWare shell and/or the network interface card (NIC)?
- Can the software be installed on a drive letter greater than "E:"?
- Will the software recognize and therefore access data using logical drive letters greater than "E:"?
- Does the software use copy protection which attempts direct hardware writes to sectors on a local hard drive?
- Are the specified and/or actual minimum memory (RAM) requirements below the 640K DOS boundary compared to available workstation RAM after LOGIN?
- Are import/export files compatible with other software on the network.

If the software does not meet all one of these requirements, it will cause continual installation, support, and maintenance concerns.

3.3.3 Network Licensing

Network Licensing

Most application software packages have a license agreement included in the documentation, or with the disks.

True multiuser software is supplied with specific network licensing to legally install and use the software on a network. Failure to comply to any specified licensing terms is a violation of copyright.

For example, WordPerfect charges a flat fee for the initial single users installation of its package on a file server. There is a fee for each additional workstation that will be using WordPerfect on the network connected to the file server where WordPerfect has been installed. WordPerfect Corporation actually recommends that users contact their local dealer for the best pricing on licensing, whether it will be separate node packs or a site license.

Another example, Paradox (Borland's database program) charges a base price for their network version, and then a set price for every five users that require Paradox at the same time. Paradox tracks each user on a NetWare network by their user name and station ID as they start Paradox, and keeps a current count of "active" users in Paradox. You will be unable to exceed your legal license because Paradox counts the users as they start or exit Paradox. You only receive a partial set of documentation (not including the Paradox Application Language (PAL) manual or Network Guide) for each user with the node packs.

Other software packages have individual requirements. Their licenses may be based on a per file server fee, or on the number of users. Most license agreements describe the terms and conditions, for details, check your license agreement.

3.3.4 Can You Import/Export Data?

Compatibility between different types of application software packages on your network will quickly become an issue if it was not considered before the software was acquired. This refers to many different levels of compatibility of file formats. Here are some examples:

- A database is the most efficient way to maintain customer information, including names and addresses, however databases have very unsophisticated word processing capabilities. This becomes critical, for example, if you are planning to do a mail merge, sending a customized letter to all of your customers. This should be considered at purchase time. Buy only a database and a word processor that have compatible file formats, or some level of import/export capabilities, you will end up in a situation where you will have to enter the data twice, once in the database format, once in the word processor.
- A possible requirement of your accounting package might be its ability to export data in a spreadsheet format, and possibly to import other spreadsheet data.
- Desktop publishing packages are most often used for proposals, reports, and promotional materials. Wordprocessing documents, spreadsheets, and graphic files are often imported into desktop publishing documents. These factors should be considered in the initial planning stage when purchasing software, if there are any plans for desktop publishing.
- All software packages today should accommodate the demand by business users for a graphics-oriented user interface and output in hard copy. To accommodate this need for graphics, spreadsheets produce pie charts (See Fig. 3.1), and bar graphs to graphically represent data. Therefore you may also need to import/export graphics as well as data between packages.

One possible solution to meet these interchange requirements is an integrated software package. There are many in the marketplace which claim some level of data interchange. An integrated package might include the following functions

- spreadsheet,
- database,
- wordprocessing
- graphics,
- communications.

If you compare a specialized word processing package to the wordprocessing module of an integrated package you will usually find that the capabilities of the specialized package are much more enhanced.

Therefore depending on your requirements an integrated package might meet your minimum requirements, and guarantee a higher level of file format compatibility.

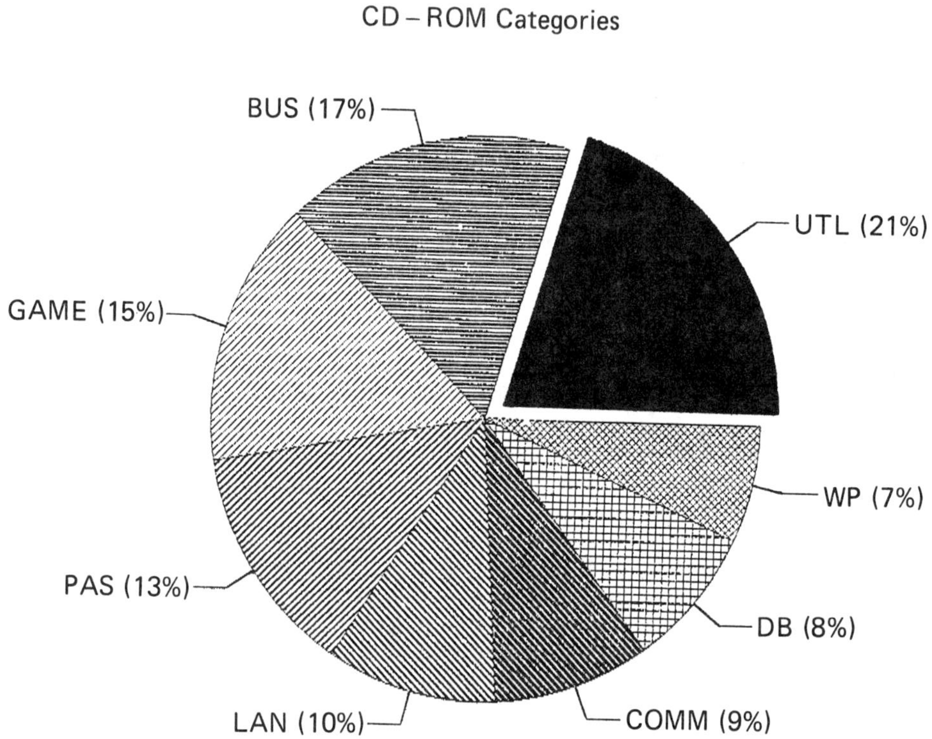

Figure 3.1 Some database applications offer excellent graphing capabilities of their data. This graph was generated by Borland's Paradox database.

4 USER SUPPORT

In this chapter

User Support: Stand-alone Workstations, Application Software Configurations, User Training, Hardware and Software Troubleshooting, Local Hard Drive Backup, Documentation, Security Issues, File Transfer, Enforcing Company Standards, User Support: Networks, Application Software and/or User Configurations, User Training, Hardware and Software Troubleshooting, Security Issues, File Transfer, Enforcing Company Standards.

4.1 STAND-ALONE WORKSTATIONS

A stand-alone workstation refers to a system that is not attached to the network. The reasons for this might include: application software that will not run with the network shell loaded; physical inability to attach to the network such as distance, user reluctance, and so on.

Part of the system managers responsibilities include user support. Depending on the network size, this support might be handled by a microcomputer support group, or hot line. Unfortunately, the majority of LANs are of a size where you have one person who is responsible for all support issues including:

- application software configurations,
- user training,
- hardware and software troubleshooting,
- local hard drive backup,
- documentation,
- security issues,
- file transfer,
- enforcing company standards (choice of programs, style sheets, macros, fonts etc).

User support on stand-alone computers provides unique management and personnel challenges. You might be dealing with a user that has no computer literacy, or on the other hand you may have a "super user," who feels that they know it all. Therefore every user must be handled individually both from a knowledge level and personality basis.

> **NOTE:** For more information on upgrades, and dealing with users reluctance to accept change (See Part 1 CONCEPTS, Chap. 5 System Maintenance.)

4.1.1 Application Software Configurations

The majority of application software requires some sort of setup or configuration at the initial installation. Once you have successfully installed the software you may be required to set up individual user and/or physical workstation configuration (See Fig. 4.1.) These "configuration files" might include:

- video card type and screen color,
- default printer drivers and/or ports,
- location of datafiles, and
- any user specified default options in effect at software startup.

4.1.2 User Training

User training issues can be addressed in a multitude of ways, depending on your company's policies and budget limitations. You must also consider each individual's ability to utilize any on-line help, tutorials, and Computer-Based Training (CBT) available for a particular program. The majority of popular application packages are shipped with extensive help and usually tutorial files. You will find that these tools will be used by your more experienced users, but not by new users.

New users will benefit by an introduction to both the computer environment and any software they will be using, by professional instructors. This approach to training in general will pay for itself many times over if your users come back from the course with less fear, and an open mind to learning.

4.1.3 Hardware and Software Troubleshooting

A major upper level management concern is system downtime. Users are unable to work if their tools (computers) are nonoperational. As either management, or a support person your troubleshooting abilities for both hardware and software will be tested usually on a daily basis. You should assemble a "tool kit" of hardware and software diagnostics/utilities before they are required. When a user is "down," they usually are unimpressed if you tell them you have no idea what the problem is. You will be in a much more confident position if you can state what the problem is, and be able to estimate the time required to fix it. (See Part 2 REFERENCE, Chap. 19 System Management.)

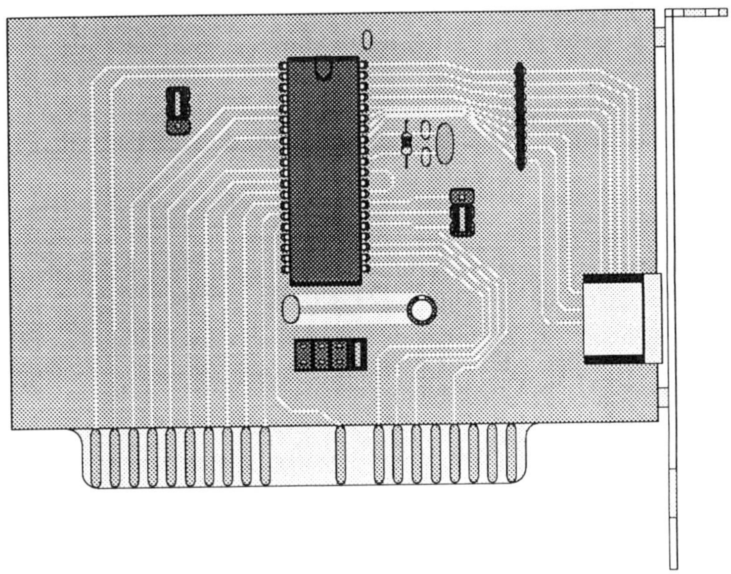

Figure 4.1 Individual video cards require special "video drivers" which must be custom configured for many software applications.

4.1.4 Local Hard Drive Backup

A major concern with local hard drives is the necessity of maintaining timely backups of the programs and/or data on these local hard drives. Unfortunately, in most situations you will be required to support a local hard drive when it crashes or has been accidentally formatted, but usually you have no authority to ensure that regular backups are being run.

> **NOTE:** It's a wise precaution to maintain at least one monthly backup physically accessible only by support personnel, and one backup off-premises.

4.1.5 Documentation

Local hard drives should be documented in the same manner, and for the same reasons as the network (See APPENDICES, Sec. A.3.1 Why Document a Network?)

4.1.6 Security Issues

Security for a stand-alone workstation must be considered for the following reasons:

- physical removal of the workstation (which would include all data and programs on the hard drive),
- DOS lacks the implicit ability to limit user access to the system and any specific datafiles,
- accessibility to confidential data,
- DOS lacks the ability to prevent illicit copying of Executable (EXE) or program files.

4.1.7 File Transfer

With stand-alone workstations, any floppy drive misalignment, sizes, or incompatibilities between systems, will be discovered the first time a file is transferred by floppy. It will then become a major problem. For ease of file transfer and support issues, it is desirable to have both 5 ¼" and 3 ½" media capability. This will enable the stand-alone workstation to have the capacity to transfer files to any other DOS based microcomputer.

> **NOTE:** This issue should be acknowledged and planned for when specifying hardware configurations.

4.1.8 Enforcing Company Standards

Depending on your company policy, covering choice of software application programs, style sheets, macros, fonts, and so on, this might not apply to your situation.

If applicable, then you must consider how to enforce these standards in your particular situation. In most instances trying to "wean" a user from their old favorite program is a losing proposition at best. Success can sometimes be accomplished by dazzling the user with a package that is newer, better, greater, flashier, and has more features.

4.2 NETWORKS

Part of the system managers responsibilities include network user support. Dependant on network size, this support might be handled by a microcomputer support group, or hot line. Unfortunately the majority of LANs are small, where there is only one person who is responsible for all support issues including:

- application software and/or user configurations,
- user training,

- hardware and software troubleshooting,
- documentation,
- security issues,
- file transfer.

NOTE: For more information on upgrades, and dealing with users reluctance to accept change (See Part 1 CONCEPTS, Chap. 5 System Maintenance, Sec. 5.2 Upgrades.)

4.2.1 Application Software and/or User Configurations

The majority of application software requires some sort of setup or configuration at the initial installation. This is more complex when you have to install the software on a network in a multiuser configuration. Depending on the programmers logic, every software package will have different very specific requirements to run properly in a multiuser environment. Unfortunately many software manufacturers do not specifically understand a network's environment requirements, so they are inclined to give you installation instructions such as "See your Network Administrator/Supervisor". Once you have successfully installed the software, you may be required to set up individual user and/or physical workstation configurations. These "configuration files" might include:

- video card type and screen color,
- default printer drivers and/or ports,
- location of data and/or users private files,
- any user specified default options in effect at software startup.

4.2.2 User Training

All of the same training approaches discussed in the previous section apply to networks (See Part 1 CONCEPTS, Chap 4 User Support, Sec. 4.1 Stand-alone Workstations.) You will find that user fear is magnified in a network situation, because the user is placed in a situation where they cannot see or hear hard drive storage, or the printers. Users also find it extremely confusing and difficult to conceptualize the process when they are saving or printing a datafile to a network.

4.2.3 Hardware and Software Troubleshooting

All of the same troubleshooting considerations discussed in the previous section apply to networks (See Part 1 CONCEPTS, Chap 4 User Support, Sec. 4.1 Stand-alone Workstations.)

These concerns are magnified in a network situation, since a network file server hard drive crash will affect more than one user.

You should add to your repertoire of stand-alone workstation diagnostics/utilities a selection of network specific tools. When acquiring these tools, consider the number of users supported, and reflect this in your cost justifications.

4.2.4 Security Issues

Security for network support must be considered for the following reasons:

- support personnel by virtue of their position have access to absolutely all company data,
- if you have a network support package installed, which for example lets you view and manipulate another NetWare user's screen, this package can enable support personnel to play "Big Brother,"
- users will request access to programs or data to which they should not have rights,
- user requests for absent employees datafiles.

4.2.5 File Transfer

All of the same file transfer concerns discussed in the previous section apply to networks (See Part 1 CONCEPTS, Chap. 4 User Support, Sec. 4.1 Stand-Alone Workstations.)

A good rule of thumb to use on a network is to supply the group "Everyone" with trustee rights to a directory called PUBDATA. This directory name implies that this is a public data directory. Users can use this directory to transfer files between users "private" directories. It is usually easier to explain the location of this directory to users if you assign (map) a permanent drive letter to it, such as P:.

4.2.6 Enforcing Company Standards

The considerations for the enforcement of company standards are discussed in the previous section (See Part 1 CONCEPTS, Chap. 4 User Support, Sec. 4.1 Stand-Alone Workstations.)

Enforcement of any standards is much simpler on a network.

5 SYSTEM MAINTENANCE

In this chapter

Preventative: Hardware Preventative Maintenance, Monitoring Resources, Upgrades: Annual NetWare Upgrades, Upgrading Application Software--As Required, Compatibility of New Software, User Support After Upgrades, Backups: Why Do a File Server Backup? Doing Regular Backups.

5.1 PREVENTATIVE

Network user surveys have shown that on an average, a network fails twice monthly for a total of about 10 hours downtime *every month.* A lack of preventative maintenance is often the culprit for this excessive downtime which is frustrating to both users and management and is usually costly.

After a network has been correctly installed and configured, system preventative maintenance is the key element to ensuring that your network continues to run efficiently and without crashes. A program of preventative maintenance should be included at the initial planning stage (See Part 1 CONCEPTS, Chap. 1 Local Area Network Concepts, Sec. 1.3 LAN Planning and Design.)

When planning preventative maintenance it is vital to formulate a plan that will actually be carried out, using the best tools and utilities available (See Part 2 REFERENCE, Chap. 19 System Management, Sec. 19.2 House Cleaning.) A workable preventative maintenance plan can and will prevent unnecessary problems and catastrophic file server crashes. Any preventative maintenance plan should consider all the elements of a network including all hardware and software components.

5.1.1 Hardware Preventative Maintenance

All network hardware components should be regularly maintained, including the file server, cable, hardware, and printers. These procedures should only be carried out by qualified personnel.

File Server-Annually The main file server components should be dismantled, cleaned and reinstalled insuring that all chips and cards are "seated" properly into their respective boards (See Fig. 5.1.)

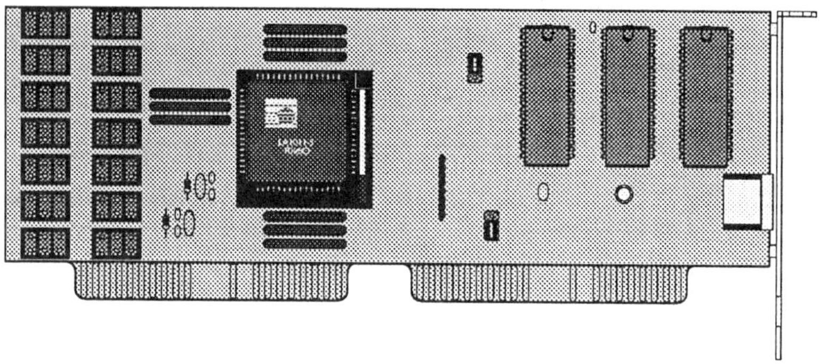

Figure 5.1 All cards and chips on the boards such as this one should be cleaned and reinstalled annually by qualified personnel.

Cable Connections-Annually Check all cables connecting to the power source, keyboard, monitor, printer(s), and to the network.

Cable Hardware-Annually, or Semiannually

Check all cable runs and connectors to and from closets, hubs, concentrators, or Multistation Access Units (MAUs). Examine these components for visible damage, or any signs of wear. If any of these are suspect, they should be replaced immediately by qualified personnel.

Compare the cabling blueprints, diagrams, or specifications to the system physically in place. If necessary revise and upgrade the documentation to a "currently installed" status.

Printer-Monthly Insure that local and network printers are being maintained or serviced by qualified personnel. The frequency of this maintenance will depend on the level of usage, however, in most cases monthly checking and cleaning will suffice.

5.1.2 Monitoring Resources

From time to time it will become necessary to modify or reassign resources on a dynamic basis. For example, you could have the situation where an application program's datafiles have grown faster and/or larger than originally planned. Whenever possible, you should accommodate this change before it becomes critical. A solution can be as simple as moving the data, or could be as complex as adding another file server.

The most important thing is to be aware of upcoming situations, and to try to stay ahead of the need.

5.2 UPGRADES

5.2.1 Annual NetWare Upgrades

One of the necessities of maintaining an efficient network is the requirement to keep up to date on current technology. If you cannot do this yourself, find a dealer that is reliable, and who stays on the "leading edge" and is aware of the latest releases.

Ideally you should upgrade only after a "new" version or release has been shipping for six months. This is to avoid being a beta test site for any software that has "Undocumented Features."

With NetWare, the network server operating system, you can estimate that you will have to upgrade or at least assess your system approximately every year. This is true because

- the older the version, the more difficult it becomes to get qualified personnel for NetWare support,
- qualified support personnel are "not enthusiastic" about supporting older versions,
- software is continually being upgraded, and this will produce compatibility problems with an older operating system, or older software,
- you may not be able to run new application software which may have many desirable new features, if your file server is running a much older version of NetWare.

5.2.2 Upgrading Application Software-As Required

The same reasons dictate software upgrades, as mentioned in the previous section.

Software upgrading, however, presents a new set of problems. Users can have a certain resistance to upgrades. "It works fine for me, and does everything I want, please don't change it" they often state. You are dealing with a personnel problem, and some explanation here may be of assistance.

Users soon establish a "comfort zone" when they grow accustomed to using any software. They know the keystrokes required to accomplish their tasks, and rarely venture outside the zone. Unfortunately most users learn the keystrokes not the concepts.

To solve this inertia, you must encourage your user to "take a small risk" to accept the software upgrade and venture into unfamiliar territory. Risk taking outside the comfort zone is the time tested way to deal with this problem, and a way to redefine, and therefore, expand a users comfort zone boundaries.

When you introduce a new software version, you must encourage the users to take the risk explaining the direct benefits to them such as improved features, perhaps easier printing, available fonts and so forth.

5.2.3 Compatibility of New Software

If possible, determine if a proposed new software package is compatible. This decision requires many considerations

- batch files (for printing and/or package startup), if any might have to be updated,
- user menus, if any might require changing,
- drive mappings in login scripts may have to be altered to reflect any new application software/data locations,
- printer setup files and drivers might require reconfiguration,
- special user configurations such as document macros, style sheets, SET or INI files might have to be upgraded.

5.2.4 User Support After Upgrades

Ideally users should be trained before an upgrade. A NetWare upgrade should be transparent to end users, however an application software program upgrade might require extra training and support. A training concept that has worked successfully for many companies is a short course at noon called "Lunch and Learn." This session can give the users a brief overview of what can be expected and helps lessen their fear of changes. This is also a good time to encourage communication with your users and hopefully will bring to light any users' considerations that you were unaware of.

5.3 BACKUPS

5.3.1 Why Do File Server Backup?

Network operating systems are usually reliable and are not normally vulnerable to mass corruption. On the other hand, with all of the technological advances of hardware over the past few years, we still find that the hardware in any computer system is prone to failure. Mean Time Before Failure (MTBF) measures the life expectancy of any hard drive, controller, or hardware component. This is usually in the range of 30,000 and 60,000 working hours. Unfortunately file server hard drives are the "Achilles heel" of the network hardware configuration. Networks are drive intensive, and therefore, decrease the MTBF of these components.

As a result, one of the prime responsibilities of the network administrator is to ensure that the system is always functioning. This means doing regular backups.

5.3.2 Doing Regular Backups

One of the first considerations in purchasing a backup system is compatibility. You must ensure that your chosen system backs up the hidden and system files. Most importantly "Does it back up NetWare's bindery files?"

The second consideration is, "Does it back up zero byte files and empty directories?" Some of the application software on the market create zero byte files for reference purposes and require their existence to function correctly.

One item to consider is that NetWare allows you to create directories with names longer than DOS's limitations of eight characters with a three character file extension. Ideally, you should not be creating directories outside the DOS limitation, however you should be aware of this possibility when purchasing a backup system, that is, will it backup and restore directories with names in excess of the DOS limitation. Further, will it allow you to restore a directory name in excess of the DOS limitation to a DOS drive, and prompt you to input a name within DOS limitations-one that will make sense to you after the restore has been completed.
Now that we have discussed some of the purchasing considerations lets talk about the ease of doing it

- Install the backup interface card, if one is used. Most system supervisors install this at their workstations.

- Next, you will need to set up any required device drivers on your boot drive. Make sure they do not conflict with any of your applications. If you find this a problem you will need to create a separate boot disk for backups.

- Create a directory below the root called "BACKUP" and copy the backup files into this directory, or follow the install instructions for your backup device. Insure that as supervisor you are the only one with rights.

- For unattended backups, you will need to set up a script or configuration file in this directory. This file will contain some sort of "WAITUNTIL" commands to back the system up at a specified off-hour time. Your backup software will have to support this feature for this to function.

- You will want to backup your system when no one is logged on. Backup software might not backup files that are open in nonshareable mode. However, the backup software creates a backup log which usually includes all the files backed up, any files skipped (including open files), and any corrupt files that the backup process has encountered.

Doing incremental backups (changed data) every day, and a full backup at the end of every week runs the risk of losing data. This can be caused by application software that does not update the "archive" bit. Because the file attribute "modified since last archive" is not always updated, there is no guarantee that your changes will be included in incremental backups. Also if you need to restore your complete system, you run a higher risk of media (tape) failure on any one of the sets.

A better plan of action is to match your tape backup system as closely as possible to your file server storage capacity. A complete system backup run daily, rotated, and a weekly set rotated gives you a much more comprehensive restore capabilities. For example, a user may come to you in a panic because a spreadsheet that is only accessed once a month is "missing." With weekly backups, you will be able you step backwards and find their latest spreadsheet. Audit policy might require that you also do an "Archive" tape monthly.

An off-site backup should be maintained with a minimum of one backup set off-site at a time. These should be updated on a regular basis in case your company has reason to need them.

6 HIGH-END SYSTEMS AND SPECIAL REQUIREMENTS

In this chapter

High-End Systems, Multiple-Bridged File Servers,, Network Accessible Data Communications and/or Gateways.

6.1 HIGH-END SYSTEMS

This term usually refers to a larger network with requirements that might include the following:

- multiple-bridged file servers,
- network accessible data communications and/or gateways,
- dedicated specialized servers, for example, print servers,
- network accessible CD ROM or WORM drives.

6.2 MULTIPLE-BRIDGED FILE SERVERS

In many business environments, the requirement for multiple file servers is common. This is usually caused by a combination of reasons such as: physical location of different departments, lack of a full time system manager or network administrator, or the requirement to have more users attached to a network than can be reasonably supported by one file server.

6.3 NETWORK ACCESSIBLE DATA COMMUNICATIONS and/or GATEWAYS

As the number of computer users and/or network workstations increases, data communication requirements will become an issue. If you have multiple network users who require data communications, it is usually more cost effective to have them share one resource that is attached to the network. These resources can be a combination of asynchronous communication servers, fax servers, e-mail servers, or gateways to host systems. There is a vast selection of both Novell and third party products to accomplish all of these services. The choice of products to fulfil your requirements must be considered using the same method that you use to choose an application software package.

6.4 DEDICATED SPECIALIZED SERVERS, for example, PRINT SERVERS

As the size and complexity of a network grows, the establishment of workstations dedicated to one particular task becomes more efficient and cost effective. These specialized servers meet the needs of multiple users and at the same time offload some or many of the processes that the file server previously handled. This of course decreases the workload on your NetWare file server allowing it to dedicate more time to serving users' requests.

Some specialized servers can include

- print servers,
- database servers,
- fax servers,
- communications servers,
- backup servers (tape or WORM),
- e-mail servers,
- CD ROM, WORM servers.

6.5 NETWORK ACCESSIBLE CD ROMs or WORMS

Optical Disk Cartridges are standardized as follows:

- 4.75" CD ROM disk, with a 552 megabyte capacity,
- 5.25" WORM disk, with an 800 megabyte capacity,
- 8" Optical disk with a 800 megabyte capacity per side,
- 12" Optical disk with a 1 gigabyte capacity per side.

This capacity has made both CD ROMs and WORMs a desirable medium for massive amounts of data. Currently, available titles include not only the expected such as encyclopedias, but also such diverse publications as an agriculture library, various newspapers and magazines, drug and poison indexes, medical databases, and various reference manuals. The number of titles and units is growing dramatically as new uses for the technology are identified.

These information resources can be made available to network users through a variety of third party hardware and/or software add-ons.

WORM was developed to fill the requirement of many large computer sites to store or archive massive amounts of data on a virtually indestructible media. There are products available to enable the user to backup or copy from any DOS device, and also do network backups or copies. A requirement might exist for the ability to archive sensitive or very valuable data for long periods of time. For example, an oil company's exploration seismographic data often must be archived for a long time before it is required again.

6.6 LARGE CAPACITY HARD DRIVES, TERABYTES ON LINE

The processing capability of computers has changed dramatically over the years. For example, the Univac computer in 1949 was capable of 320 calculations per second which was considered a remarkable achievement at the time. In contrast, by 1990 a Compaq SystemPro had increased this to 4 million instructions per second.

The cost of hard drive storage must also be put into historical perspective to fully appreciate the technological progress that has been made in the last few years.

For example in the October 1981 issue of "Interface Age," the advertised price for a North Star 18 megabyte hard drive was $3923. By 1985, the technology and the prices had changed dramatically. In the May 1985 issue of "PC World" the largest hard drive advertised was a 42 megabyte Rodime, at $1595. In the 1990s the price per megabyte has dropped dramatically. The future trend is toward larger faster hard drives, and the "dollars per megabyte" will decrease even further. This will be caused by both advances in technology, and economies of scale effected by mass production.

7 NETWARE 386

In this chapter

Introduction to NetWare 386, New Features of NetWare 386: Overview, File Server Memory (Allocation), Hard Drives and Volumes, System Reliability, Security: File and Directory Security, Trustee Rights, Bindery: Bindery Security-Privileges, Bindery Security-Encrypted Passwords, Summary of NetWare 386 Utilities, Modified Utilities: Modified Command Line Utilities (including changes in the user interface), Utilities No Longer Available, Console Commands: Console Command Description, Printing with NetWare 386: PCONSOLE, Backup Considerations.

7.1 INTRODUCTION TO NETWARE 386

This section on NetWare's new operating system, has been included for system managers who have 386 NetWare and are looking for easy to understand, reference material on this new operating system.

NetWare 386 may look and feel the same as previous NetWare versions to end users, however, it is a totally different operating system designed specifically for the 80386, and 80486 as the file server CPU.

Many of the basic NetWare concepts outlined in this text apply to this new operating system, however some commands, and the security structures have been modified, and other features have been added. NetWare 386 is a completely new operating system, written specifically to take advantage of the features of the 80386 CPUs (and above).

In a major redesign of the operating system, Value-Added Processes (VAPs) (see Glossary) has been eliminated, and has been replaced by Network Loadable Modules (NLMs). This significant change is, however, virtually transparent to the end user.
Installation of 386 has been made much simpler. You are given the ability to dynamically load and unload hard drives, network interface cards (NICs), protocols, and various diagnostic utilities

while the NetWare 386 file server is operational. Previously, everything in this list had to be generated using NETGEN, and operated on the file server only when the server was down.

This installation can be accomplished in 15 minutes, which makes the operating system seem deceptively simple, however it is not. The more knowledgeable the installer, the easier it looks, that can be deceptive. NetWare 386 is not a "take it to the office and plug it in" type of operating system. Like any network operating system, if it is not correctly installed and configured, you will be unable to take full advantage of the enhanced features and reliability that this new operating system offers.

One of the most impressive features of NetWare 386 is its ability to dynamically reallocate memory resources.

7.2 NEW FEATURES OF NETWARE 386

7.2.1 Overview

The 80386 CPU chip has specific features and capabilities that NetWare 386 utilizes

- protected Memory Mode,
- 32-bit program instructions,
- 32-bit data paths,
- no memory segmentation.

NetWare 386 was designed to support a variety of enhancements to take advantage of the 80386 environment, which includes:

- a maximum of 4 gigabytes of RAM on the file server (theoretical only-limited by current hardware availability),
- a maximum of 32 Terabytes of file server drive storage (theoretical only -- limited by current hardware availability),
- NetWare 3.0 version of the Shell has a limit of 250 concurrent connections to a file server. The design specifications for the NetWare 3.1 shell version will theoretically support 1000 concurrent connections,
- a maximum of 100,000 concurrently open files per NetWare 386 file server,
- dynamic memory allocation of file server RAM used by directory cache blocks, routing buffers, maximum number of open files, and so on,
- a maximum of 32 volumes with any one volume having the capability of logically spanning 32 physical hard drives.

Customized enhancements and/or services that can be simply added by the system manager as required by a situation or particular hardware environment include:

- communication and/or service protocols,
- file and directory systems,
- naming conventions,
- LAN drivers,
- other value added services.

NetWare 386 Loadable Modules (NLMs) are the tools you would use to dynamically configure a file server to your requirements. An NLM is a program code that has been written to perform a specific task (e.g. printing) and when you LOAD an NLM it becomes an integral part of your NetWare 386 file server operating system.

A set of specifications that the NLMs adhere to is called Open Data-Link Interface, which is a component to make NetWare 386 an "Open Server Platform." These communication specifications allow multiple protocols such as IPX/SPX, TCP/IP, and AppleTalk to share the same LAN driver and network interface card (NIC).

7.2.2 File Server Memory (Allocation)

Since NetWare 386 requires an 80386 CPU that can theoretically address up to 4 gigabytes of RAM, we need to consider minimum RAM requirements. A minimum of 2 megabytes of RAM are required to be divided between DOS, the NetWare 386 operating system, and cache buffers. DOS and the initial NetWare OS are relatively constant, however, the use of cache buffers requires some explanation.

A portion of the 386 file server RAM is required for the OS and a portion for cache buffers. Cache buffer default size is 4 KB, if required you can specify a larger cache buffer size of 8 or 16 KB.

NetWare 386 utilizes these cache buffers as follows:

- cache buffers are available for loan from the cache buffer memory pool to LOAD NetWare Loadable Modules (NLMs) and are returned to the pool when the NLMs are UNLOADed,
- required cache buffers are allocated to cache the File Allocation Table (FAT) of all volume(s),
- required cache buffers are allocated to cache parts of each volume(s) directory entry table (DET),

- cache buffers are utilized for file caching which ensures that the most frequently requested files are kept in RAM,
- cache buffers are utilized for a hash table containing all directory names,
- cache buffers are allocated to maintain turbo FAT indexing tables which contain a list of all open randomly accessed files that have 64 or more FAT entries.

Dynamic Configuration

In NetWare 386, the following operating system requirements are dynamically allocated file server RAM, based on a balance between need and available memory

- directory cache buffers,
- file service processes,
- turbo FAT index tables,
- FAT tables,
- routing buffers,
- disk elevator size,
- directory hash tables,
- router/server advertising memory,
- maximum number of open files,
- file locks,
- kernel processes,
- kernel semaphores,
- TTS transactions,
- memory for loadable modules.

When memory is dynamically allocated, the file server waits a few seconds to react to sudden or infrequent peaks of activity. This is to allow the file server dynamic memory allocations to remain relatively stable.

This process of dynamic memory allocation loans memory from the file cache buffer memory pool as required, however, not all loans are returned to this pool.

These allocations are returned to the file cache buffer memory pool:

- nonmovable memory, utilized by NLMs and returned when NLMs are UNLOADed,
- movable memory (cache block allocations that might require expansion), utilized by system tables that can increase in size as a result of dynamic configuration.

These memory allocations do not return to the file cache buffer pool but can be returned to the memory pool of origin:

- allocation pool (short time allocations),
- permanent memory allocation pool (never returns memory to this pool), and
- permanent returnable (long time allocations).

NOTE: The file server must be downed to return these allocations to the file cache buffer memory pool.

7.2.3 Hard Drives and Volumes

New features of NetWare 386 include the capability to perform hard drive and volume functions while the server is up and running, with the volume MOUNTed and being accessed including:

- partitioning the drive,
- creating (adding) a new volume segment, as part of an existing volume from unallocated drive space.

The volume name with NetWare 386 can consist of up to 16 bytes, with one byte indicating the name length and up to 15 for the name.

Disk Partitions With NetWare 386 you must boot up from an active DOS partition on the hard drive or from a floppy drive on the file server. The NetWare partition contains four copies of a volume definition table.

Drive Input Output (I/O) Elevator seeking is a disk ordering technique used by NetWare 386 to provide disk I/O efficiency. NetWare 386's elevator seeking implementation uses two queues, one to "enqueue" file system requests, and the other to "dequeue" disk driver requests.

Previously, NetWare would initiate an I/O process and wait until the drive controller device driver replied that it was ready for I/O. With NetWare 386, utilizing a controller such as an SCSI disconnect, the driver does not wait while the device prepares for I/O thus allowing concurrent I/O on multiple channels.

The capability of scattering a volume over multiple hard drives enables you to increase the number of I/Os to the volume per second. You must remember however, that if one of your hard drives fail, you could damage many files since portions of a file may be on multiple hard drives, because NetWare 386 scatters data being written to a multiple drive volume evenly over all the physical drives.

Disk Allocation Blocks NetWare 386 volumes store data in physical units called "Disk Allocation Blocks", whose sizes can be configured when the volume is added. This disk allocation block size of 4, 8, 16, 32, and 64 KB will be your minimum physical file allocation space to each and every file on that volume. For example, if you have a batch file that is 800 bytes, it would be allocated 64 KB, if the volume it is located on has had that 64 KB disk allocation block size specified. This specification must be carefully thought out with the types of application to be stored on the volume considered.

File Allocation Tables (FATs) Every volume contains a file allocation table which consists of an index listing the location(s) of each and every block in which a file resides. To enable quick access to any block of data in the volume, these FATs are cached in the file server memory.

Turbo File Allocation Table (Turbo-FAT) A Turbo-FAT is created and added to whenever you have a datafile that uses more than 64 FAT entries. The Turbo-FAT consists of a table which indexes the disk allocation blocks locations for any and all of these larger datafiles.

> **NOTE:** The disk allocation block size you have specified will govern the size of the datafiles locations included in the Turbo-FAT. For example, with a 4 KB disk allocation block, any file equal to or greater than 262,144 bytes (256 KB) will be listed in the Turbo-FAT. With a 64 KB disk allocation block the file size would have to be equal to or greater than 4,194,304 bytes (4 MB).

Total Storage Capacity With NetWare 386, the theoretical limit for file server drive storage has been increased to 32 terabytes. This limit is determined by three factors:

- 8 byte size of a FAT entry,
- 386 CPU's ability to address up to 4 GB of RAM,
- a disk allocation block specification of 64 KB.

In reality, NetWare 386 version 3.0 will support up to 1024 hard drives of 32 volumes by 32 drives per volume.

Files and Directories NetWare 386 has new file and directory features, altering the method of file and directory organization

- directory tables,

- multiple name spaces,
- sparse files,
- salvage files.

Directory Tables

A directory table is created for each volume. This file has one or more directory blocks, which contain information about files, directories, file or directory trustees, and so on. This information can be in various formats, depending on the workstation operating system.

At installation, the volume SYS: has six directory blocks in its directory table, all other volumes start with two blocks. Blocks are added as required to a maximum of 65,536 directory blocks per volume. The maximum number of directory entries per volume is 2,097,152 since each directory block contains 32 entries. Directory caching is only applied to directory blocks in use.

Multiple Name Spaces

Multiple name spaces refers to NetWare 386's ability to support multiple directory entries for different workstation operating systems. These operating systems (DOS, OS/2, Unix, Macintosh) have different file naming convention requirements, including length, legal characters, case sensitivity, data and resource forks, and so on. NetWare assigns a DOS name to every file stored with a workstation operating system other than DOS. Multiple name spaces also applies to directory names.

Workstation operating systems that require 2 bytes to represent one character are now supported by NetWare 386 with multiple byte characters for file, directory, and bindery names.

Sparse Files

This feature has been introduced to maximize the available drive space. Sparse files refers to files that are created "empty" by some application programs. NetWare 386 will not allocate disk space to an empty file, but only writes the actual data ignoring zero filled disk allocation blocks. When the application program tries to access the empty (zero filled) portion of the file, NetWare returns zeros, usually fooling the application program into believing that the file is intact.

Salvage Files

NetWare 386 has the ability to SALVAGE deleted files, a feature with limited use in previous NetWare versions. Previous versions allowed the SALVAGE of only the most recently deleted file, or files. On busy networks, your chances of a successful file SALVAGE were slim.

NetWare 386 also deals with deleted files from deleted subdirectories, a situation which previous versions did not address. By default, all deleted files are saved in their default directory until the server runs out of disk allocation blocks, or the user deliberately "PURGEs" the deleted files. If a files default directory has also been deleted, the file is saved in a DELETED.SAV directory located at the root of the volume.

Using the SALVAGE utility, a users can view the list of any deleted files in a directory and recover them. The length of time that your volumes will retain these deleted files is dependant on available disk allocation blocks. When the volume requires these disk allocation blocks, NetWare 386 then purges deleted files on a FIFO basis (oldest deletions purged first).

Both files and directories can be forced to PURGE immediately on deletion, defeating the enhanced SALVAGE capabilities of NetWare 386. This can be accomplished by disabling the salvageable file feature with the SET command, or setting the file and directory attribute to purge.

Accounting Services

NetWare 386 has enhanced the accounting features found in previous versions. It is now possible for a server to charge for the use of its services such as

- blocks read,
- blocks written,
- connect time,
- disk storage,
- service requests.

The system manager must determine the charge rate for each of these. An authorized accounting server can perform the following:

- submit charges against a users "account,"
- place a hold on a users account,
- query a users account status,
- create and maintain an audit trail file of charges.

Properties

Accounting Services uses three "properties" in the file server's bindery to perform accounting tasks.

ACCOUNT_SERVERS Property An ACCOUNT_SERVERS property has security access levels equal to a supervisor and is authorized to submit accounting records to that server.

ACCOUNT_BALANCE Property This property stores an object's account balance and minimum balance. If this property does not exist, servers will deny services to this object. The account balance limits the object's network resource use.

If the object has been flagged as having no minimum balance, services will never be refused.

ACCOUNT_HOLDS Property The ACCOUNT_HOLDS property is dynamic, and stores holds on a user's account. These holds are placed on the account by the affected server (holding server) before servicing a request, insuring sufficient funds are available in the account to pay for the service. After servicing a request, the server submits its charge, then releases the hold.

Holds are cleared by a holding server disconnection and can be explicitly cleared by a holding server request.

Audit File

NetWare 386 monitors network resources and keeps an audit trail of all charges in a file located in the SYS:SYSTEM directory.

Activity Log

NetWare 386 version 3.1 features an Activity Log that records all activity on the file server by supervisors and workgroup managers.

Audit Trail System

NetWare 386, version 3.1 features the NetWare Audit Trail System which allows auditing of all read and write requests to the file server. These audit files contain file access information of who has accessed the file, and when they accessed it. The NetWare Audit Trail System is only supported on file servers that have the Transaction Tracking System (TTS) enabled.

> **NOTE:** The files created by the NetWare Audit Trail System will grow until they have run out of volume space. You should regularly archive or delete these files. A warning message will appear and the audit trailing turned off if the volume fills up.

Audit trails will only be maintained for files that have a read and/or write audit file attribute.

7.2.4 System Reliability

Transaction Tracking System (TTS)

In NetWare 386, Transaction Tracking System (TTS) is used to protect the NetWare bindery and other operating system dynamic files from corruption and is integral to the design on NetWare 386.

TTS is utilized to guaranty that all changes (transactions) to a file are either completed in full or not initiated. To apply TTS to user data, the file must be FLAGged as transactional.

Enabling and Disabling TTS

TTS is not an option with NetWare 386 as was the case with previous NetWare versions. TTS is automatically enabled dependant on drive space and memory when the volume SYS: is first mounted. TTS can only be disabled by DISMOUNTing the TTS backout volume (usually SYS:) or using the console command DISABLE TTS after the file server has been booted and TTS enabled automatically. TTS is automatically disabled if the volume SYS: becomes full or the file server runs out of available free memory.

System Fault Tolerance (SFT)

NetWare 386 version 3.0 supports both System Fault Tolerance (SFT) Levels I and II. Added to SFT Level II is a feature called Hot Fix 2 which re-issues read requests to a mirrored drive and writes the good data to the Hot Fix redirection area. NetWare 386 version 3.0 has a limitation of 25,000 concurrent transactions, which is part of SFT Level II.

Write File Audit (WFA) and Transaction Roll Forward (TRF)

Write File Audit (WFA) and Transaction Roll Forward (TRF) are new features added to NetWare 386 version 3.1. These features insure data integrity for applications (database) datafiles by recording all datafile writes to a TTS file which is utilized by TRF to rebuild any corrupted datafiles.

NetWare Loadable Modules (NLMs)

NetWare 386 Loadable Modules are the tools you would use to dynamically configure a file server to your requirements. An NLM is a program code that has been written to perform a specific task (e.g. printing) and when you LOAD an NLM it becomes an integral part of your NetWare 386 file server operating system. When an NLM is UNLOADed all resources are returned to the file server for reallocation.

Although NLMs are similar to the replaced Value-Added Processes (VAPs) which resided and operated in the file server memory, NLMs have much greater capabilities. These include a more direct access to the operating system through a number of application program interface (API) system calls, called the Loadable Module Interface.

This loadable module interface includes:

- ANSI.C runtime library,
- POSIX API,
- existing Microsoft, Borland, and Watcom C runtime libraries,
- OS/2 execution thread API,
- netWare C Interface library,
- NetWare 386 C RunTime Library.

Types of NLMs

NetWare 386 includes NLMs from four basic groups. They are: utilities, LAN drivers, disk drivers, and name space modules.

Utilities / application modules (.NLM)

DISKSET
INSTALL
MONITOR
PSERVER
UPS
VREPAIR
BTRIEVE

LAN (network interface card) drivers (.LAN)

NE2
NE1000
NE2000
RXNET
TOKEN

Disk drivers (.DSK extension)

DCB
DCB2
EDCB
ESDI
IBMSCSI
ISADISK

Name space modules for multiple file systems (.NAM)

MAC

NOTE: NetWare 386 version 3.0 supports multiple file naming conventions, by including an NLM for Macintosh since support for DOS and OS/2 are built into the NetWare operating system.

NetWare Care Protocol (NCP) Service Protocol

A workstation shell or requester and a file server communicate using a language referred to as the NetWare Core Protocol (NCP), a service protocol. These functions comprising the NetWare Core Protocol are also called the NCPs.

7.3 SECURITY

7.3.1 File and Directory Security

Only the changed or modified capabilities of NetWare 386 in the file and security area have been included in this chapter.

File/Directory Attributes

File or Directory Attributes assign special properties that can override effective trustee rights. You can use the attributes to restrict or inhibit copying, deleting, renaming, viewing, writing, and sharing.

File Attributes	Letter
Copy Inhibit	C
Delete Inhibit	D
Execute Only (previously E)	X
Indexed	I
Purge	P
Read Audit	Ra
Read Only	Ro
Rename Inhibit	R
Write Audit	Wa

Directory Attributes	Letter
Delete Inhibit	D
Purge	P
Rename Inhibit	R

Copy Inhibit

Applicable to files only, this attribute restricts the copy rights of users logged in from a Macintosh workstation. Users can remove the copy inhibit attribute if they have been granted the Modify right.

Delete Inhibit

Applicable to files and directories, this attribute prevents users from erasing even if they have the Erase trustee right. Users can remove the delete inhibit attribute if they have been granted the Modify right.

Execute Only

Applicable to files only, this attribute assignable only by a Supervisor, prevents users from copying executable programs (.EXE or .COM). Most programs that are flagged execute only will execute, but are not able to be copied or backed up. Use this flag with caution, since it cannot be removed! Insure that you have another copy of the program file before assigning this attribute.

Purge

Applicable to files and directories, this attribute "purges" the file or all files in a flagged directory when they are deleted. These files cannot be recovered with SALVAGE.

Read Audit

Applicable only to files, available with NetWare 386 version 3.1. This attribute causes an audit trail to be created and maintained, listing users and time of file reads.

Read Only

Applicable only to files, this attribute prohibits users from writing to, deleting, or renaming a file. When the Ro attribute is assigned, NetWare automatically assigns the Delete and Rename inhibit attributes. This will prevent users from writing to, deleting or renaming a file even if they have been granted the Write and Erase rights at the directory or file level. Users can remove the read only attribute if they have been granted the Modify right.

Rename Inhibit

Applicable to both files and directories, this attribute prohibits users from directly renaming either files or directories even if they have the Modify right. Users can remove the rename inhibit attribute if they have been granted the Modify right.

Write Audit

Applicable only to files, this NetWare 386 version 3.1 attribute causes an audit trail to be created and maintained, listing users and time of file writes.

7.4 TRUSTEE RIGHTS

NetWare 386 has some changes in the security structure and its application. The maximum rights mask (directory rights) has been replaced by the inherited rights mask. The inherited rights mask is more extensive than the former directory rights. It can be applied to both directories and files. The individual trustee rights have been enhanced, including an implied open with read, write and create, and a new supervisor trustee right has been added.

The following is a description of each trustee right.

Right	Directory/File Trustee Assignment
Read	Allows you to read files. This right now has an implied open.
Write	Allows you to write to files. This right now has an implied open.
Create	Allows you to create both files and subdirectories and has an implied open. It will also allow you to salvage a file if it has been deleted.
Erase	This right is the same as the delete right of previous versions. It now applies to directories. Be aware that a user can not delete a directory unless they have the ability to delete files within it.
Access Control	This right is similar to previous parental access. Unlike parental you can not assign rights to yourself but can assign more rights to other trustees than you possess.

File Scan	This right replaces the former search right.
Modify	This right allows you to change file attributes and rename a directory where this right has been assigned.
Supervisor	This is a new trustee right. Similar to the former parental right, it allows you to create users below where it has been assigned. Be aware that once this right is granted it can not be revoked below. In addition this right grants a user the ability to assign or limit space in directories.

NOTE: Trustee rights assigned to directories can be blocked by the inherited rights mask or trustee file rights assignment.

7.5 BINDERY

The bindery is NetWare's internal database used to track resources such as file, print, and database servers and users usage of resources. NetWare uses the bindery to control its security not its file system. It consists of three files (formerly two), stored in the SYS:SYSTEM directory. These three files are: NET$OBJ.SYS used to track objects, NET$PROP.SYS used to track an object's properties, and NET$VAL.SYS used to track the property's value. An object is any user, group, file server, print server, or any other logical or physical entity on the network that has been assigned a name. Objects have a maximum of 16,777,216. Associated with each object is a set of characteristics, which are called properties, and each of these properties has a specific property value. A property can be a users password, account balance, and a list of groups they are a member of. Properties have a maximum of 16,777,216.

NetWare controls its file system's directory trustee information through directory entries which are part of the physical directory structure.

7.5.1 Bindery Security-Privileges

Various degrees of privileges are enforced by the bindery of each server: Supervisors, Workgroup Managers, Users.

The SUPERVISOR object of each server is granted special bindery security privileges. This "object" may grant special administrative privileges to other objects with the security equivalence feature in SYSCON. This security equivalence feature allows an "object" to be granted equal access rights as another object.

Two new properties called the WG_MANAGER and OBJ_SUPERVISOR are features of NetWare 386. Associated with the object SUPERVISOR is a set property called WG_MANAGER. Created with SYSCON by Supervisors giving limited supervisory privileges to other "objects" that require workgroup manager rights.

7.5.2 Bindery Security-Encrypted Passwords

Part of login security is provided by the bindery with the password property. With NetWare 386, Encrypted passwords at the workstation and on the wire are supported by the bindery. Password protection can be disabled.

7.6 SUMMARY OF NETWARE 386 UTILITIES

In this section, we describe only the new and modified utilities.

The new Command Line Utilities are: ALLOW, CHKDIR, PSC, and RPRINTER.

ALLOW	This command allows a user to set and modify the Inherited Rights Mask of a directory/file.
CHKDIR	This command allows a user to view user disk space restrictions, both volume and directory level.
PSC	This command stands for Print Server Command. It allows users to control printer servers and network printers faster than through the use of a menu utility.
RPRINTER	This command stands for Remote Printer. It allows users to connect/disconnect any remote printer from a print server.

The new Menu Utilities are: DSPACE, FILER, INSTALL (NLM), MONITOR (NLM), NBACKUP, PCONSOLE, and UPGRADE.

DSPACE	This menu allows supervisors to view and set user's disk space restrictions. This can be done from both a volume and directory level.

FILER	This menu now handles the new file/directory and security information. These include: up to 32 TB volumes sizes, increased file sizes of up to 4 GB, case sensitive directory/file names of up to 32 characters, the new trustee rights for directory/files, new directory/file attributes, and the new directory/file Inherited Rights Masks (IRM).
INSTALL	This menu is a NetWare Loadable Module (NLM). It is used by installers for creation and maintenance of NetWare's file server hard drives, partitions, and volumes. This menu can only be run from the console.
MONITOR	This menu is similar to the v2.1x MONITOR and FCONSOLE utilities, and is an NLM. It is used to display the following information: percentage utilization, file server activity, memory (cache) statistics, user activity, disk drives, volumes, LAN drivers, and NLMs. This command can only be run from the console.
NBACKUP	This menu utility replaces NetWare v2.1x MACBACK, LARCHIVE, LRESTORE, NARCHIVE, and NRESTORE menu utilities. Users may back up data to local drives, optical drives, and other network drives. In NetWare 386 v3.0, various DOS devices and tape drives are supported. Other third party device drivers will be supported by Netware 386 v3.1 with Device Independent Backup Interface (DIBI).
PCONSOLE	This menu utility allows users to communicate with the printer, this includes, viewing printer information, setting up the print server, and controlling network printing. The user interface has been modified to include printer condition information. As an example, the print server will notify users when their print jobs are finished and will notify a list of users when a printer needs attention, such as requiring new forms to be mounted or paper refilled.
UPGRADE	This menu utility is used by installers that are upgrading from V2.1 to NetWare 386 v3.0.

7.7 MODIFIED UTILITIES

In NetWare 386 the following utilities have been modified. In some cases the change has been the user interface, in others the actual function of the utility has been modified.

7.7.1 Modified Command Line Utilities (including changes in the user interface)

ATOTAL: (not changed) This command now supports OS/2.

ATTACH: (not changed) The only change with this command is that encrypted passwords are now supported.

BINDFIX: (changed) This command has been changed to include the support of the three new bindery files: NET$OBJ.SYS, NET$PROP.SYS, and NET$VAL.SYS.

BINDREST: (changed) This command has been changed to include the support of the three new bindery files located in SYS:SYSTEM.

CAPTURE: (changed) This command now recognizes the Print Server (PSERVER) NLM.

CHKVOL: (changed) This command allows you to view information regarding the server, volume, volume space, and number of files. Support is included for the new volume space of 32 TB (can only see 4 GB maximum), file size of 4 GB, and information about deleted files.

FLAG: (changed) This command can access and change the new file attributes including: Read Audit, Write Audit, System, Hidden, and Purge.

FLAGDIR: (changed) This command now supports purge on deletion.

GRANT: (changed) This command allows you to assign trustee rights (new rights) to directories/files.

LISTDIR: (changed) This command now supports OS/2, and new trustee rights.

LOGIN: (changed) This command now supports the new login features including encrypted passwords.

MAP: (changed) This command now supports both the MAPROOT utility, and encrypted passwords.

NCOPY: (changed) This command can accomplish recursive file copies, maintains file attributes including TTS, and handles any Macintosh file.

NDIR: (changed) This command supports the new features for varied block sizes, 4 GB files, Macintosh files, directory/file trustee rights and NLMs. Also there is no mention of the indexed file attribute as all files are automatically indexed when they reach a 64 FAT entry size.

NVER: (changed) This command will now display both the version and serial number of the operating system.

PAUDIT: (not changed) This command now supports OS/2.

PURGE: (changed) This command will purge any salvageable files in specified directories. Also, it will recognize all of the 386 paths and patterns.

REMOVE: (changed) This command will remove trustees of both files and directories.

RENDIR: (not changed) This command now supports OS/2.

REVOKE: (changed) This command will take away any of the directory/file rights (including the new ones), from a user.

RIGHTS: (changed) This command now supports the new directory/file accesses.

SECURITY: (changed) This command now supports the new trustee directory/file accesses.

SEND: (not changed) This command has been enhanced to provide both supervisors and workgroup managers with broadcasts and alters. In addition it now supports OS/2.

SETPASS: (changed) This command has been enhanced to support the encrypted passwords feature.

SLIST: (not changed) This command now supports OS/2.

SMODE: (not changed) This command now supports OS/2.

TLIST: (changed) This command now supports the new directory/file trustee accesses.

VERSION: (not changed) This command now supports OS/2.

VOLINFO: (changed) This command has been enhanced to provide support for the new 32 TB maximum volume sizes.

7.7.2 Modified Menu Utilities (including changes in the user interface)

DISKSET: (changed) This menu utility is an NLM that allows you to set, view, or change the settings of your disk coprocessor boards (DCB) or hard drive. It can only be run from the file server console.

FCONSOLE: (changed) Much less functionality than NetWare v2.1x FCONSOLE. The menu choices: File/Lock Activity, LAN Driver Information, Purge All Salvageable Files, and Statistics are NOT SUPPORTED by NetWare 386 v3.0.

MAKEUSER: (changed) This menu utility has the same primary functions of v2.1x for creating users, groups and assigning restrictions but now it includes the support of the new directory/file trustee rights. This can be used by workgroup managers.

PRINTCON: (not changed) This menu utility has not changed except for the support of workgroup managers.

PRINTDEF: (not changed) This menu utility has not changed except for the support of workgroup managers.

PSERVER: (changed) This menu utility is new and is an NLM. It is used to provide 386 printing services including: down the print server, stop printer, pause printer, rewind printer, view printer status, notify users of finished jobs, controlling remote printers, and notify queue operators of printer service requirements. Formerly, many of these features were done at the file server through commands or where not available.

SALVAGE: (changed) This command has been enhanced to allow users to specify directories to view, salvage, or purge specified salvageable files.

SHCONFIG: (changed) This menu utility has an altered user interface.

SHGEN: (changed) This menu utility has an altered user interface.

SYSCON: (changed) This menu utility has been enhanced to provide support for the new directory/file trustee access rights, user volume disk space restrictions, and includes workgroup managers.

USERDEF: (changed) This menu utility allows you to restrict disk space by volume or directory.

VREPAIR: (changed) Written to access the new NetWare 386 file system. Run form the console as a NetWare Loadable Module (NLM).

7.7.3 Utilities No Longer Available

The following Command Line Utilities are no longer available with NetWare 386:
HIDEFILE, and SHOWFILE.

The following Menu Utilities are no longer available with NetWare 386:
LARCHIVE, NARCHIVE, LRESTORE, NRESTORE, MACBACK, MAIL, and NETGEN.

7.8 CONSOLE COMMANDS

Console commands can only be entered at the server console command line. Most console commands can be used in the AUTOEXEC.NCF file but not in the STARTUP.NCF file.

The AUTOEXEC.NCF file is a batch file for the file server. It is located in the SYS:SYSTEM directory. This file contains commands that name the file server, specify the IPX address, load your LAN drivers, bind the IPX to your LAN drivers, and mount your volumes. This file is run after the STARTUP.NCF file.

The STARTUP.NCF file is located on the network startup disk (either floppy or hard disk partition) and is used to load your disk driver.

Server console commands can also be saved in NetWare Command Files (NCF) other than the AUTOEXEC.NCF file. These files have a default file extension of .NCF and are placed in the SYS:SYSTEM directory. These NCF files can then be executed by typing the file name (without the .NCF extension) at the console.

Console Command	Description
ADD NAME SPACE	Used to allow non-DOS files to be stored on a NetWare 386 volume. The MAC.NAM NLM must be active.
BIND	Binds the IPX to a specific NIC (Network Interface Card) or to a specified protocol stack.
BROADCAST	Used to send a message to all, or specified users logged in/attached to the file server.
CLEAR STATION	Logs out the user from the specified station and removes that user's connection to the server.
CLS	This command is used to clear the file server console screen.
CONFIG	This command is used to displays all hardware settings used by your file server.
DISABLE LOGIN	Prevents any additional or new users from logging into the file server. DOWNing the server automatically disables login. This command is used to prevent additional or new users from logging in to the file server.
DISABLE TTS	This command is used to turn the TTS feature off. Users can still work in a database FLAGged as TTS, the database is not protected.
DISMOUNT VOLUME	This command dismounts a specified volume. If any files on that volume are open (in use), the server warns you, and you will be prompted for confirmation prior to the dismount.
DISPLAY NETWORKS	This command will list the router's known networks. Included in this list is the IPX number, the number of hops (# of NICs that the packet must be cross

to reach its final destination), and approximate ticks for the packet to complete all the hops (a tick is a measurement of 1/18 of a second).

DISPLAY SERVERS — This command will list the router's known servers. Included in this list is the server's name, the number of hops (# of NICs that the packet must be cross to reach its final destination).

DOWN — Downs the server and insures data integrity by writing cache buffers to the hard drives, closing all open files, and updates the Directory Entry Tables (DETs) and the File Allocation Tables (FATs). If there are open files in use by a workstation, the server warns you, and will prompt for confirmation before DOWNing.

ECHO OFF — **The default**-commands in any .NCF files will not appear on the server console as they are executed.

ECHO ON — This command will display anything in the NCF file to the file server screen.

ENABLE LOGIN — This command allows users to log into the file server (usually used after the DISABLE LOGIN command).

ENABLE TTS — The default is that TTS is enabled when the volume SYS: is mounted. Normally only required after the DISABLE TTS command or the file server has automatically disabled TTS. Insure that any problem that has occurred is rectified before you ENABLE TTS again.

EXIT — Returns to DOS from the server program after the server has been DOWNed. This cannot be used if the REMOVE DOS or SECURE CONSOLE command has been used.

IPX INTERNAL NET — This command can only be used in the AUTOEXEC.NCF file. A new feature of NetWare 386, this command sets the logical network number that the router uses to identify all services/clients that reside in the same machine as the router.

LOAD	This command precedes the name of an NLM to load. You may specify a DOS or NetWare path to load NLMs. Optionally you can use the SEARCH command to set up additional paths for searching automatically.
MODULES	This command lists the name and description of all currently loaded NetWare Loadable Modules (NLMs).
MOUNT	All or specified volumes can be MOUNTed.
NAME	This command displays the server's name.
OFF	This command clears the screen.
PROTOCOL	This command lists the protocol identification numbers (communication protocol and media type is the basis for these numbers) registered with your file server.
REMOVE DOS	This command releases memory being used by DOS, and adds it to the server cache. Because DOS is no longer resident in the file server, files (e.g. NLM's) located on DOS drives are not accessible. The EXIT command will NOT be supported after DOWNing the server.
RESET ROUTER	This command is used to clear the router of all known servers and networks from its tables. It then rebuilds these tables with new server and routing advertising packets.
SEARCH	This command displays and lets you change the servers search path for NLMs and NCFs. Default is the SYS:SYSTEM directory (hard drive boot), and A: if the server was booted with a floppy.
SECURE CONSOLE	This command places the following security measures on the server: Restricts the loading of NLMs to SYS:SYSTEM, prevents the use of the built-in operating system debugger, restricts the changing of the DATE or TIME to console operators, and removes DOS from the file server memory.
SEND	This command sends a message to all or only specified users logged in/attached to the file server.

SERVER NAME	This command can only be used in the AUTOEXEC.NCF file to set the file server name and it must be unique and at the beginning of the file.
SET	This command lists and enables changes of the file server's configuration information. The list includes the configuration parameter name and current setting, the limits of those settings, and a brief description of what this parameter controls.
SET TIME	This command sets the file server's date and time.
SPEED	This command lists the speed of the file server's CPU.
SPOOL	This command is used to create, change, or list current spooler mappings. MUST be used since there are no default print queues for NPRINT and CAPTURE.
TIME	This command lists the current file server date and time.
TRACK OFF	This command tells the router to quit listing the server and network advertising packets on the router tracking screen.
TRACK ON	This command will activate an existing router, or if none exists, it will create a new one, utilizing the network advertising packets received or sent.
UNBIND	This command is used to remove NICs from a specified protocol stack.
UNLOAD	This command removes NLMs which have been previously LOADed.
VERSION	This command lists the file server's operating system version information and a copyright notice.
VOLUMES	Lists all currently mounted volumes on the file server.

7.9 PRINTING WITH NETWARE 386

NetWare 386 printing has been drastically enhanced over previous NetWare versions. It uses print servers loaded either at the server or in a dedicated workstation, to handle all of its printing services. The print server running in a dedicated workstation can handle queues on up to eight file servers. If you use the NLM print server, only queues on the current file server can be accessed. A print server supports up to 16 printers, five of which can be located off the print server, with the remainder spread throughout the network workstations.

The printing services of NetWare 386 are made up of a print server module known as PSERVER.NLM, and executable file known as PSERVER.EXE, software for remote printers known as RPRINTER.EXE, and printing utilities.

The PSERVER.NLM, like all NLMs is utilized through the file server. It is used to take print jobs from the file server's queues and send them to the appropriate printer.

The PSERVER.EXE is the command that you would load if using a dedicated workstation as your print server. It is responsible for sending jobs from the queue(s) to the appropriate printer located either on the print server, or on any remote printers. Remote printers refers to printers attached to user's workstations.

The RPRINTER.EXE is a command that is loaded after PSERVER is up and configured. It is a Terminate and Stay Resident program (TSR), that enables the print server to use your workstation's printer for the network. You can return your printer to stand-alone mode with the PSC command. This command can also be used to remove the TSR from memory.

The following is a list of printing utilities available to you: PCONSOLE, PRINTDEF, and PRINTCON. These commands are also available: SPOOL, NPRINT, CAPTURE, and ENDCAP.

7.9.1 Pconsole

Users can communicate with the print server with the PCONSOLE menu utility. The uses of PCONSOLE include: setting up the print server, controlling network printing, and viewing printer information.

The NetWare 386 server utilizes two types of bindery objects for print server support. These are created and modified through the PCONSOLE utility.

> PRINT_SERVER: Allows a print server to access and scan a server and/or user that has requested print services to determine the applicable access rights to the print server.
>
> ADVERTISING_PRINT_SERVER: Allows the print server to use NetWare's Service Advertising Protocol to advertise on the internet to enable users to locate the print server from the internet.

There are two types of print server clients (and their different level of privileges) in interacting with the print server and controlled using the PCONSOLE utility:

> Users: Can request print server status information, submit print jobs to the queue, and modify or delete these (their own jobs).
>
> Operators: Can request print server status information, can control print job handling by the print server, and can down the print server. Can manage (including delete) all print jobs while they are in the queue.

Printdef/Printcon

There have been no changes to the user interface in these two utilities. The only difference is that they support the new print servers, but this is all transparent.

Spool

If you want to create, change, or list spooler mappings, use this command.

Nprint/Capture/Endcap

These commands have the same user interface but now support the new print servers. This is all transparent.

7.10 BACKUP CONSIDERATIONS

Backup is accomplished with NetWare 386 by use of the NBACKUP, a menu utility which backs up files to a DOS addressable device. NBACKUP can be used when the network is running. Users with the appropriate rights can backup data to their directories using the NBACKUP utility.

> **NOTE:** DOS addressable devices include: network drives, floppy drive(s) at a workstation, hard drive(s) at a workstation, and ROM and WORM drives.

PART 2 REFERENCE

8 INSTALLATION OVERVIEW

In this chapter

Step-by-Step (Suggested Procedure for Installing NetWare), Using Netgen to Generate the NetWare Operating System, SHGEN: Generating the Workstation Shells

8.1 STEP-BY-STEP

8.1.1 Using Netgen to Generate the NetWare Operating System

The installation of NetWare is a two part process. First you install NetWare on the file server with the utility NETGEN, then you install the workstation shells with the utility SHGEN. Only NETGEN and SHGEN are discussed in this chapter, however, it is important to realize that all cabling and hardware will need to be correctly installed and configured (not discussed in this chapter).

The NetWare utility NETGEN is used to generate and maintain the NetWare Operating System. NETGEN will ask you to identify the type of network interface card(s) (NIC), and the hard drive installed in your file server. You must also specify the appropriate drivers to enable NetWare to communicate with the network interface board(s) you have chosen. Everything you choose will then be linked to the operating system generated by NETGEN. The file created by NETGEN including the chosen drivers is

NET$OS.EXE

When the NetWare file server is first booted up, NET$OS.EXE loads into the file server's memory.

After the NET$OS.EXE has been generated by NETGEN, NetWare must be installed on all network file server hard drives. By default, the first hard drive is setup as a system disk with a volume label of "SYS:". Also by default, it will contain the NetWare system, login, and public files. Any additional hard drives must be initialized in preparation for NetWare's directories and datafiles.

After the operating system file has been generated and all network hard drives have been initialized for NetWare, the file server is ready to be booted and begin serving the network.

NetWare 2.15 Netgen: Installation Overview

The NetWare installation manual has some perforated sheets in the back. These should be used for documenting your installation. It is far easier to record all settings made during NETGEN, at the same time. We recommend that all installations and system configurations be documented for future changes and support.

Step 1. Boot up the machine intended to be your file server with a DOS disk (3.X).

Step 2. Make working copies of your original NetWare diskettes. You will then use your working copies and put your originals away in a safe place.

You must have copies of the following diskettes (although it is recommended to make working copies for all):

5.25" diskettes	3.5" diskettes
NETGEN	NETGEN
AUXGEN	AUXGEN
SUPPORT	OSEXE-1
OSEXE-1	UTILEXE
OSEXE-2	SHGEN-1
UTILEXE-1	
UTILEXE-2	
SYSTEM (only when using G-Net due to GINSTALL)	
SHGEN-1	
SHGEN-2	

These diskettes will be modified or written to later (NetWare will prompt you).

Step 3. Insert the diskette labeled NETGEN in the floppy drive. Then type NETGEN <enter>.

Step 4. NETGEN will prompt you for some diskettes. Follow the prompts. Then a menu will appear. Select the **Custom Configuration** (See Fig. 8.1.) option by moving to that selection and pressing the enter key.

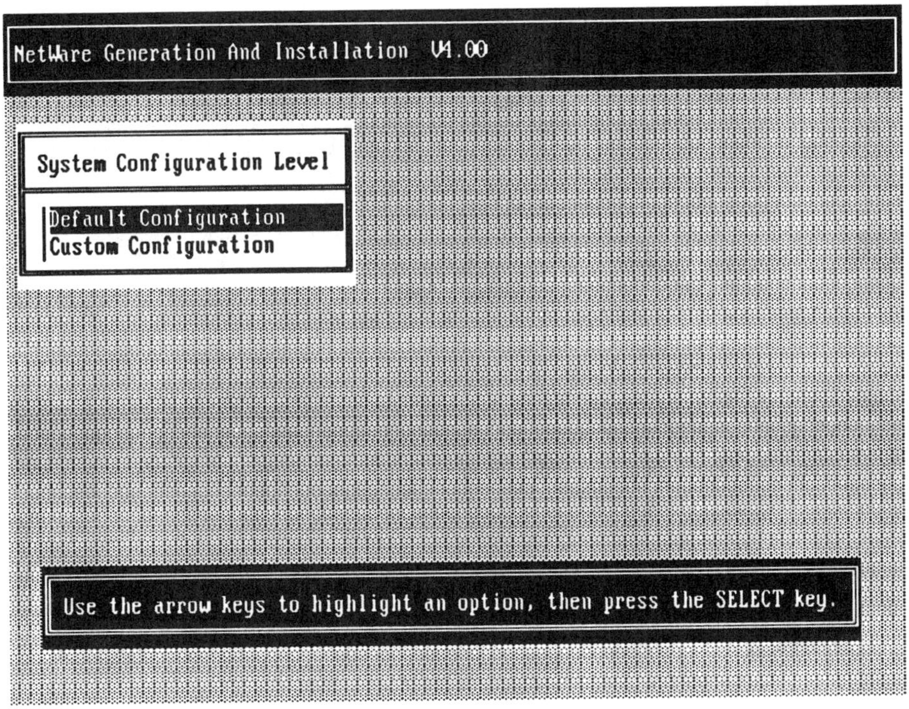

Figure 8.1 NETGEN Menu Utility, System Configuration Level.

We will only be discussing the "Custom" installation. This option allows more flexibility in configuring hardware and software. The default installation assumes default settings and configurations.

Figure 8.2 illustrates the screen that will be displayed.

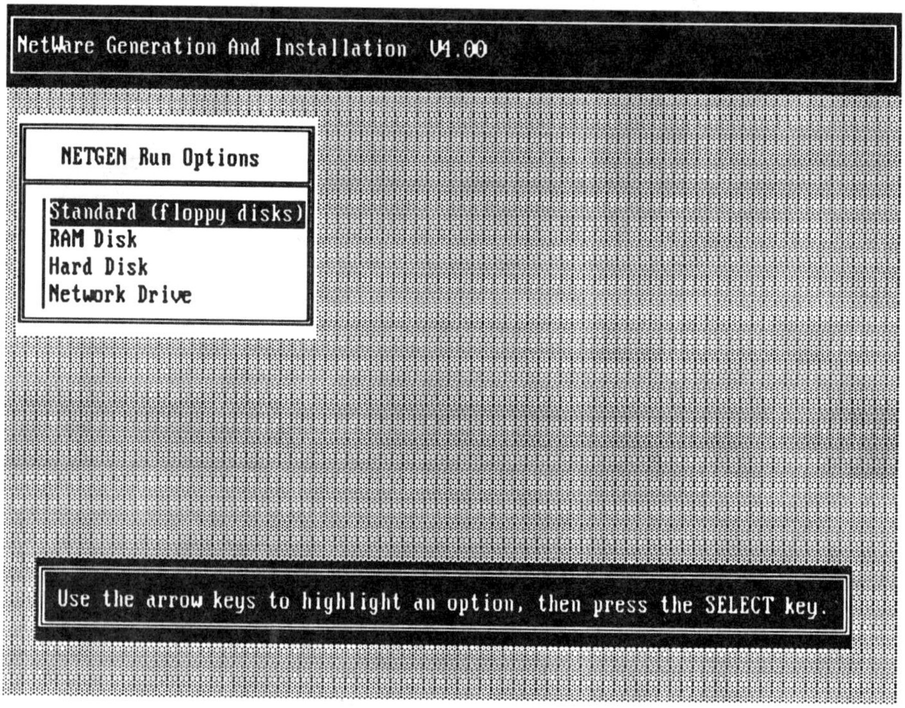

Figure 8.2 NETGEN Menu Utility, NETGEN Run Options.

You now have a choice of how you wish to install NetWare.

FLOPPY: The floppy method will prompt you for floppies all through the installation. This is the most time consuming of the methods.

HARD DRIVE: The hard drive method will prompt you for your working copy diskettes. It will then make a directory on the hard drive in your machine called NETWARE and copy all of the diskettes into their appropriate directories below this. The examples below are dependant on whether you are using 5.25" or 3.5" floppies:

(Main Directory)	(Sub Directories)
NETWARE ---	
	--NETGEN
	--SUPPORT
	--AUXGEN
	--GENDATA
	--LAN_DRV_.001
	--LAN_DRV_.002
	--DSK_DRV_.001
	--SFTOBJ.1
	--SFTOBJ.2
	--TTSOBJ-1
	--TTSOBJ-2
	--OSEXE-1
	--OSEXE-2
	--UTILOBJ.1
	--UTILOBJ.2
	--UTILEXE.1
	--UTILEXE.2
	--SHGEN-1
	--SHGEN-2

NETGEN will also copy the following files into the NetWare directory:

File	Disk
NETGEN.EXE	NETGEN
SHGEN.EXE	SHGEN-1
DISKSET.HLP	DSK_DRV_001

The advantage of this method is its speed. At one point towards the end of the installation you will be prompted to return to floppies. You will need to do this because you will be formatting this hard drive, if it is to function as a file server.

RAM DRIVE: The ram disk method, also a fast procedure is an alternative way to do the installation.

NETWORK: You must have an existing network to select this method. You will be using the computer that is intended as your file server, as a workstation on the existing LAN. You will create the same directories as discussed in the hard drive method in this chapter. The difference is these are created on the existing file server and downloaded to your workstation (future file server) when needed. The advantage of this method is that it is very fast and you will not have to return to floppies when you format your file server hard drive. This method is very useful for re-sellers or environments where you are adding a server to an existing network.

Make your desired selection by moving to that option and press the <enter> key. Now follow the prompt on the screen for the appropriate diskettes.

Step 5. Choose the **Select Network Configuration** option (See Fig. 8.3.)

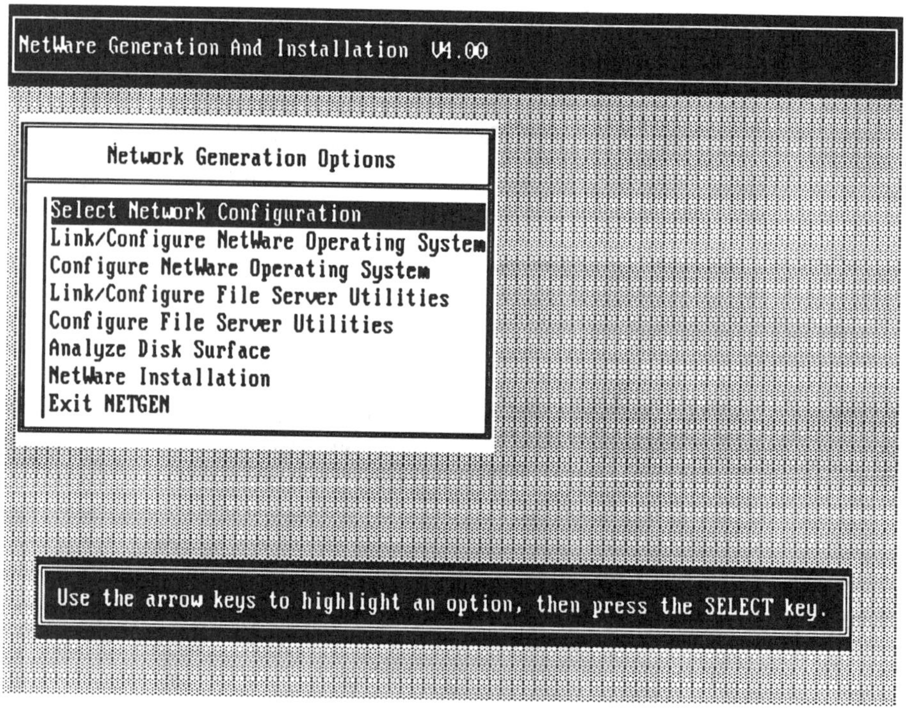

Figure 8.3 NETGEN Menu Utility, Network Generation Options

NOTE: You will be returning to this screen after you have made several selections. At that point, this screen will have changed and many new options will be available to you. You will have noticed that the option screens have been surrounded with double bars. The double bar in ALL NetWare menus means that you can perform an additional function. That might be adding/deleting an item or utilizing an additional window. A single bar means view only or you have gone as far as you can in this series of windows. One more thing to keep in mind is that you start at the top of all the windows and work your way down through the options. Selecting an option might bring new menus to the screen but you will eventually return to your original location. At this point you will move to the next item and carry on. Again the windows will have options added to them as you go through the screens based on the selections that you make.

Step 6. Now you will be in the Available Options window. You will now select the Set Operating System Options (See Fig. 8.4.)

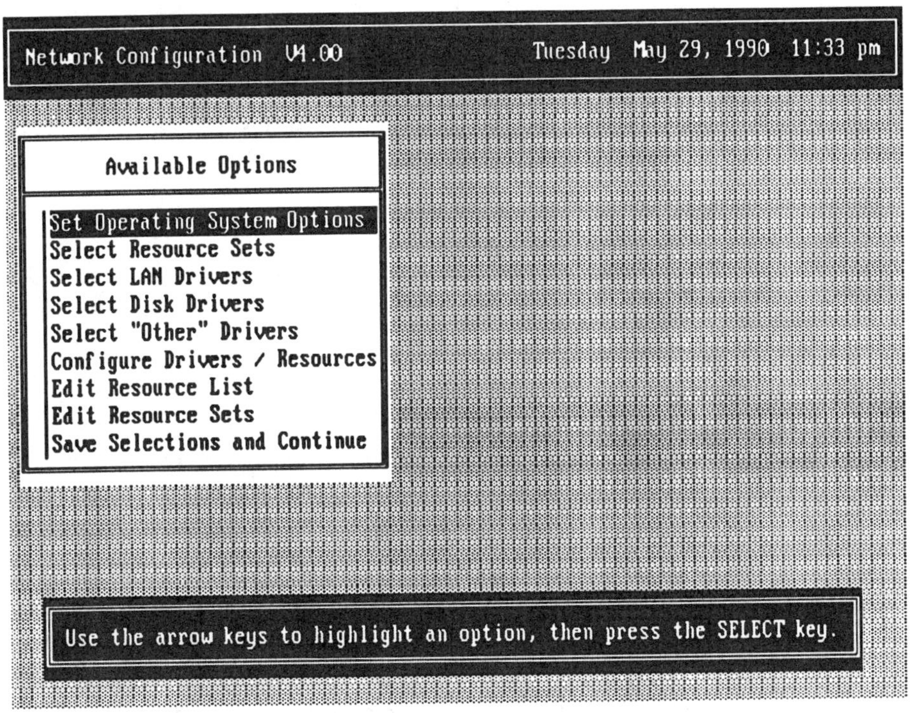

Figure 8.4 NETGEN Menu Utility, Available Options

If you are installing SFT NetWare, you will need to make the decision to install with TTS or without. If you are installing either Advanced or ELS NetWare, you will have to indicate either a dedicated file server or nondedicated. We recommend that you always select dedicated (See Fig. 8.5.)

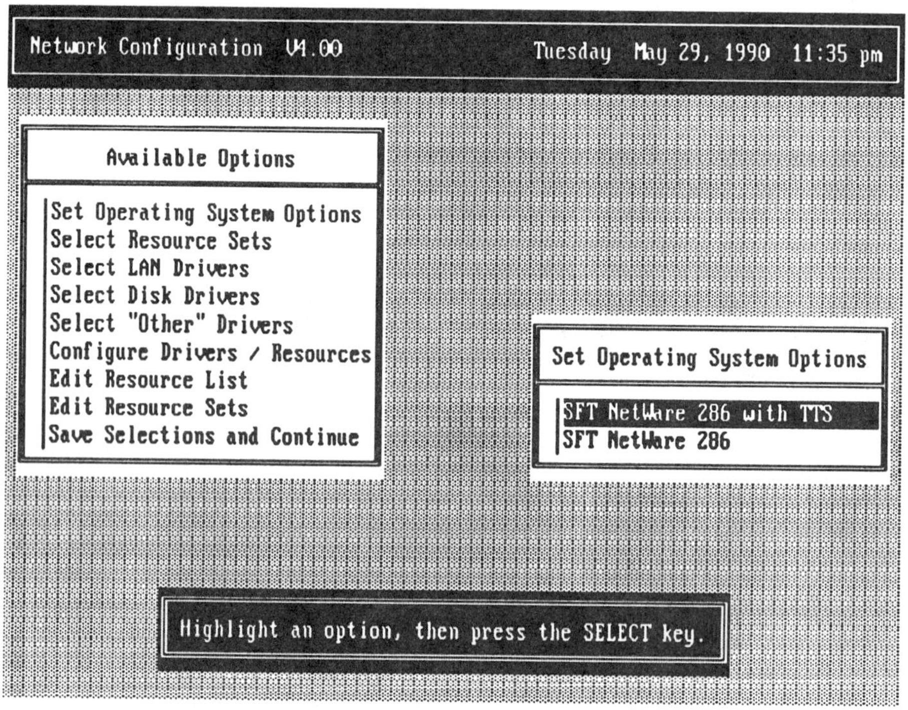

Figure 8.5 NETGEN Menu Utility, Set Operating System Options

Step 7. Next you "can" select the Select Resource Sets Option. A window will appear showing the available resource sets. A resource set is a list of hardware parameters which might be contained within your file server. For example, the type of machine you are using, LPT and COM ports, clock cards, and so on. NETGEN will take your selections into consideration when displaying available hardware settings. For example, you might select a IBM model 80 file server, then later on when NETGEN displays only the available LAN (NIC) drivers, that function in a micro channel machine will be displayed. (Also see step 11 if the item you want does not appear in this screen.)

Selection of a resource set is not required. We usually do not use this option. If you are installing hardware and NetWare, then you should already be aware of potential conflicts and therefore do not need this option. If you are unsure however, you can go ahead and select this option. To select a resource set, highlight the item you want and pressing ◄┘ (See Fig. 8.6.) Press Esc to return to the previous window.

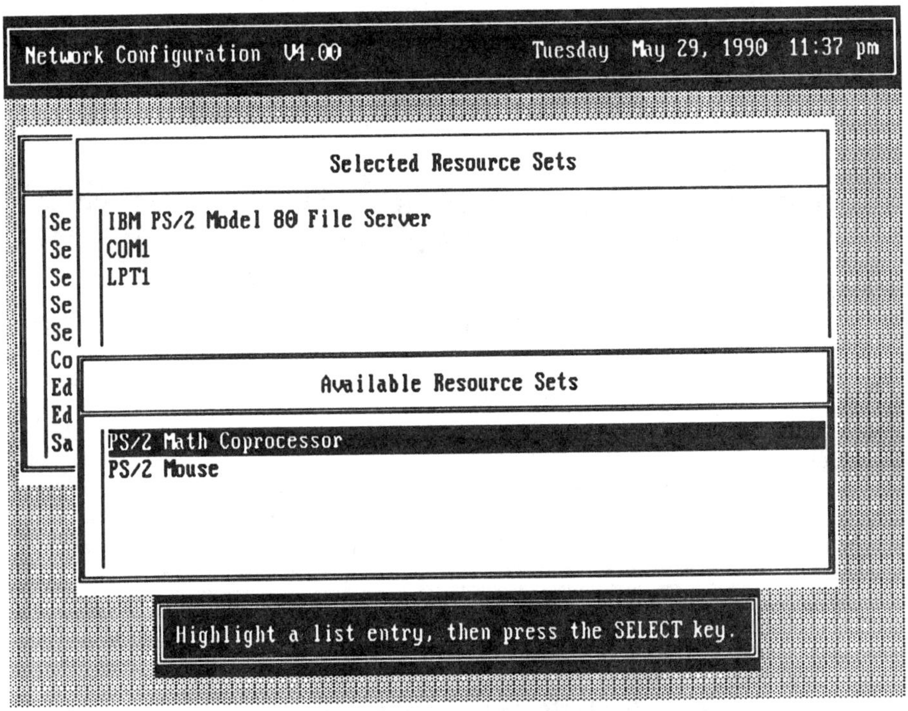

Figure 8.6 NETGEN Menu Utility, Selected Resource Sets.

Step 8. Now you are returned to the Available Options Window. You will now be selecting the LAN Drivers. This is where you are telling NETGEN what kind of NICs will be in your file server.

NOTE: Selection of multiple NICs in this screen tells NETGEN that you are doing an internal bridge.

Choose the **Select Lan Drivers** option from the Available Options menu.

Choose **Select Loaded Item**. A new window will open with available Lan drivers (Fig. 8.7.) Select the appropriate driver then press the Esc key to return to the Available Options menu.

NOTE: If the NIC that you are using in your LAN does not appear on this list you will need to add the drivers included on a diskette with the NIC you purchased. To do this exit the installation process, and

- if using a diskette, add the NIC driver to the diskette, or
- if using the hard drive, add the NIC driver as a subdirectory of LAN_DRV_.001, or LAN_DRV_.002.

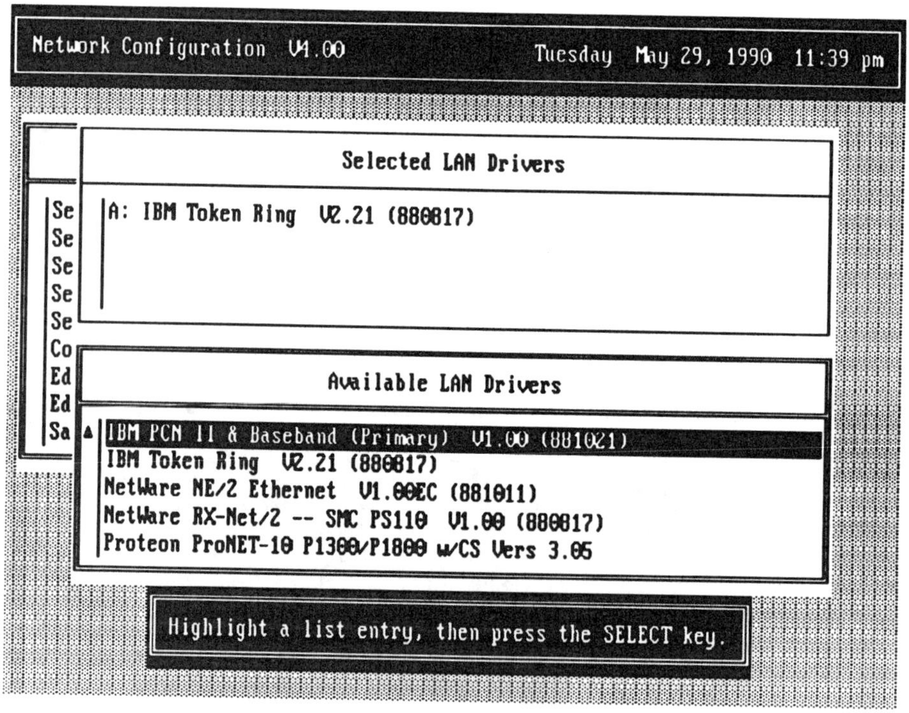

Figure 8.7 NETGEN Menu Utility, Available LAN Drivers.

Step 9. Again you are back at the Available Options window. Choose the **Select Disk Drivers** option from the menu.

This is where you are indicating to NETGEN what hard drive controllers you will be using in your file server. You will choose ESDI, MFM, or SCSI depending on your hardware.

NOTE: If using third party SCSI drives besides that are supported by Novell, you must select the "generic SCSI" driver.

Choose the **Select Loaded Item** option. A window will then appear prompting for the disk channel.

NetWare 286 supports up to five hard drive channels (0, 1, 2, 3, & 4), each controlled by a hard drive controller. Channel zero is always your internal controller. All drives physically located within the file server case are attached to this drive controller. All external drives must be attached with Novell's Disk Coprocessor Board (DCB) or a third party equivalent.

The channel number you select will refer to the number of DCB or third party board you have purchased. Board 1 is channel 1, board 2 is channel 2, and so on.

Enter the appropriate channel number. If you select multiple DCBs you will have to select the appropriate disk per channel. You must have a matching drive for each channel if you are duplexing. A new window will open with available disk drivers. Select the appropriate driver by highlighting the option and pressing enter. Press the Esc key to return to the available options menu.

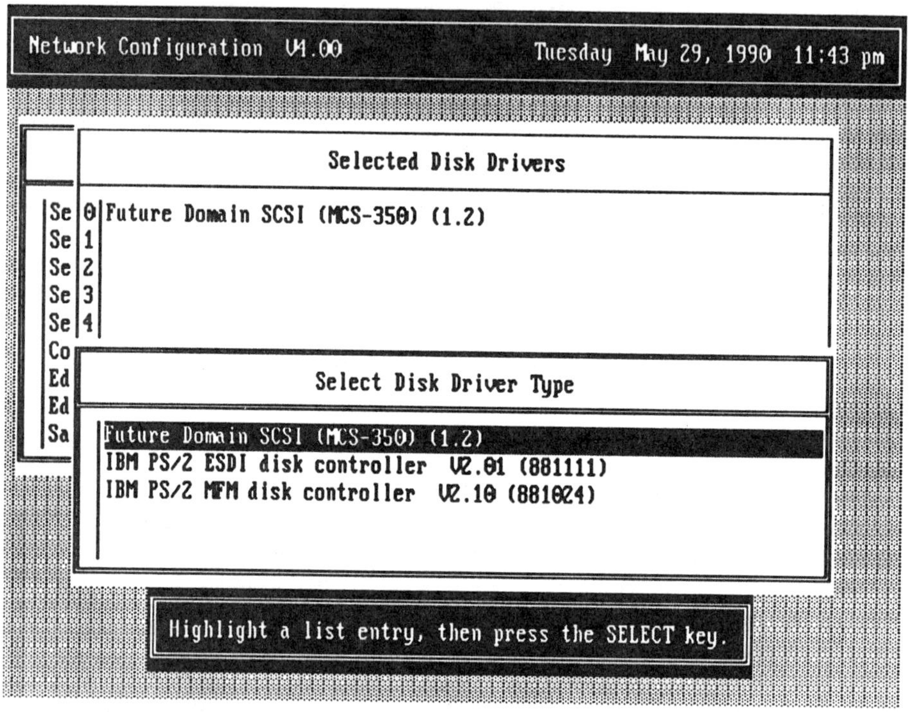

Figure 8.8 NETGEN Menu Utility, Selected Disk Driver Type

Step 10. Your next choice of the Available Options window will be to Configure Drivers / Resources. It is at this point that you are telling NETGEN: what address settings your NICs are set to, what network addresses you want, and how many communication buffers you will need. The network address is a number that you specify to represent a NIC. For example, 1 can represent the LAN (NIC) in your server. This is most important when installing a Bridge (See Part 1 CONCEPTS, Chap. 2 Hardware, Sec. 2.2.3 Cabling (Topologies, NIC Cards, and Bridging).) The rule is: NICs on the same cable system must have the same network address, NICs on a different cable system must have a different network address. NetWare requires these addresses to identify NICs in servers and bridges. You will also see the option to change these network address and also required communication buffers in a menu option later on.

Select **Configure Drivers/Resources** from the menu (See Fig. 8.9.)

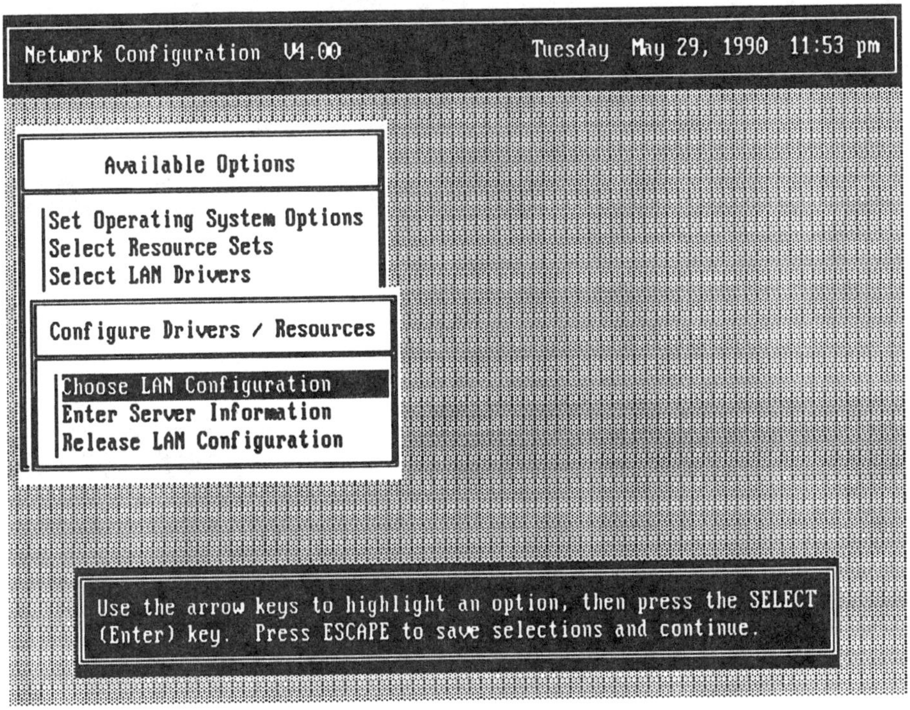

Figure 8.9 NETGEN Menu Utility, Configure Drivers / Resources.

NOTE: All drivers and resource sets that have been selected must now be configured in order to link the operating system in subsequent steps.

Select **Choose Lan Configuration**. NETGEN now asks for a configuration for each lan driver selected. Select a configuration (See Fig. 8.10) for each driver that does not conflict with other devices in the file server. Press the Esc key to return to the available Options menu.

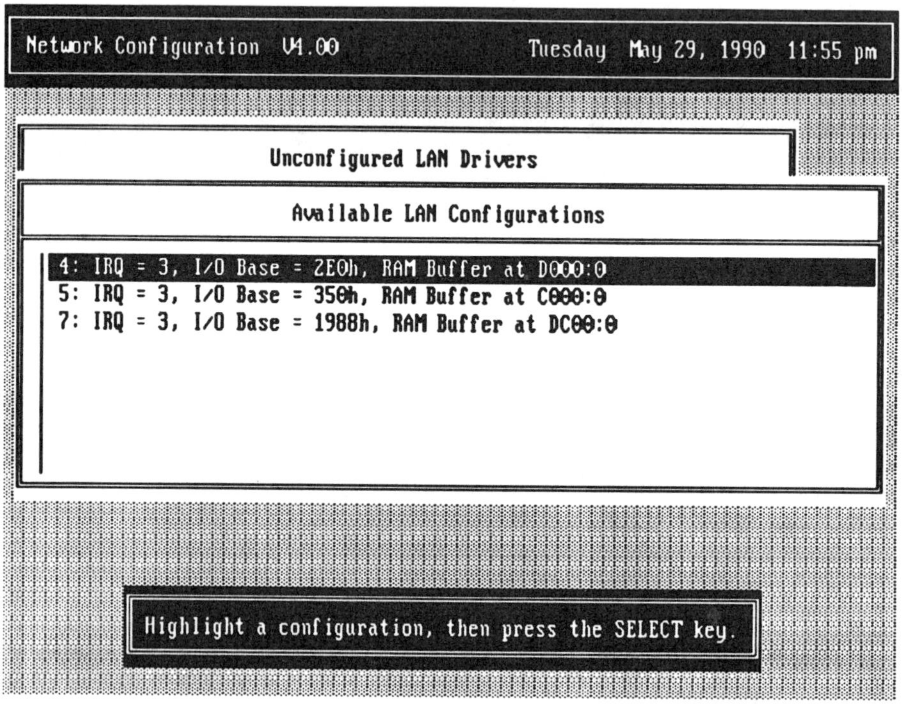

Figure 8.10 NETGEN Menu Utility, Available LAN Configurations.

Step 11. The Edit Resource Lists and Sets options can be ignored. These options allow you to change the lists you selected from in step 7. If the item you wished to include in step 7 did not appear, you could create it with these two options.

We are now ready to Save Selections and Continue. Select this option, and answer "yes" to the confirmation question. The Network Generation Options menu will now appear on the screen (Fig. 8.11.)

It will now look like this

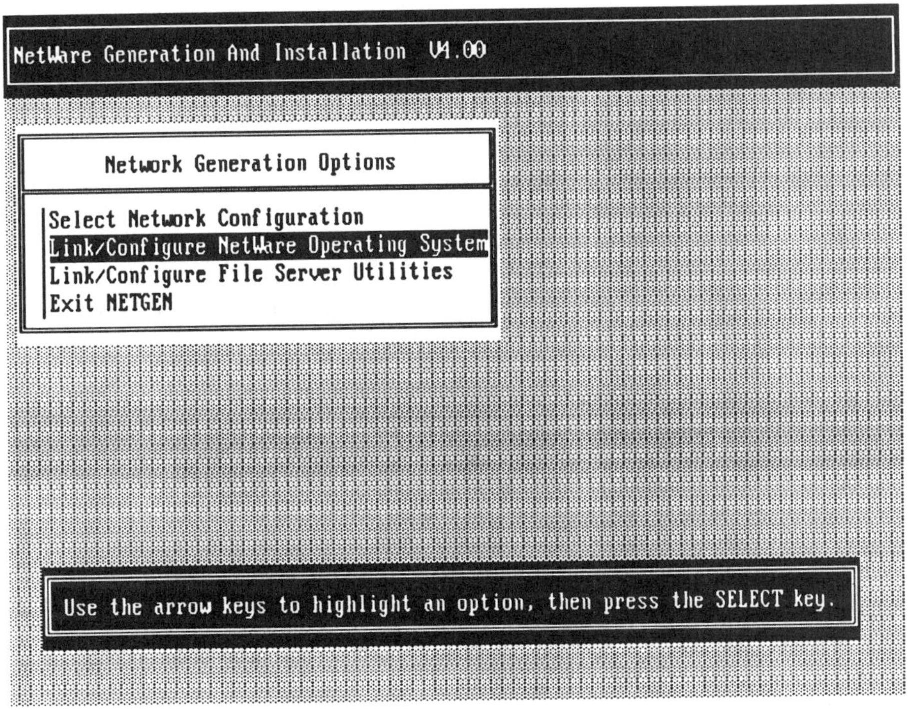

Figure 8.11 NETGEN Menu Utility, Network Generation Options.

Step 12. The next step is to link the operating system and other network utilities. Choose **Link NetWare Operating System**.

Step 13. Select **Link/Configure file server Utilities** from the Network Generation Options menu.

Step 14. What you are about to do now is to format the file server hard drive. You will need to exit NETGEN at this point, if you have been doing a hard drive installation or if you want to use a third party program to format your file server hard drive. The next step will be to format the hard drive. NETGEN will ask you if you want to download

to floppies. Yes, you want to. This will take all of the information you have selected so far and save it to your floppies so that you can recall it after your format is complete. NETGEN will prompt you for the required floppies and copy modified or new files to them.
Boot the server with a DOS disk, insert the NETGEN disk (working copy), and type **NETGEN**. Select the **Custom Configuration** again, and continue.

If you are not doing a hard drive installation just move on to the option to analyze the disk surface.

Step 15. Now format the hard drive to prepare it for NetWare. Select **Analyze Disk Surface** (Comprehensive Surface Analysis-CompSurf) option. A warning stating that all data will be destroyed will appear on the screen. Answer "yes" to the question to continue.

NOTE: This process can take up to 24 hours depending on the size, number of hard drives, and the speed of your drive controllers.

Step 16. The system will now ask for the UTILEXE-1 disk (if running from floppies now). Insert that disk and press Esc. Another warning will appear (press Esc to pass it by).

Step 17. Select the drive to be formatted and tested.

Step 18. Answer "yes" to the question to format the disk.

Step 19. Select the appropriate interleave for the disk drive. The normal interleave for AT type drives and controllers is 1, 2, or 3.

Step 20. Answer "no" to the question for maintaining the current media defect list, and "yes" to the next question about entering media defects. Enter this list manually.

Step 21. Select the number of passes for the surface analysis. This test is very time consuming. At least 3 passes should be chosen.

Step 22. Enter the number of I/O operations to be performed on the disk during the random test. The recommended minimum is 32000.

Step 23. Answer "yes" if all the parameters have been entered correctly, and "no" if any needs to be changed.

Step 24. Obtain the printed bad sector map attached to the drive or inside the system box and enter the bad sectors by head and cylinder. Press the **Ins** key for each addition, and Esc to stop entering bad sectors.

After all bad sectors have been entered, the surface analysis, known as CompSurf, will begin. When CompSurf is finished, the Network Generation Options menu will again appear on the screen.

Step 25. The next step is to install NetWare on the disk. Select **NetWare Installation** from the Network Generation Options menu. The system will ask for the NETGEN disk, then display the following:

Analyzing the system to determine the number and types of disk drives that are connected. This will enable NINSTALL to correctly install new drives, remove bad drives and/or change system configuration.

Please Be Patient!

The system will ask for the Support disk, the NETGEN disk and the Support disk again (if running from floppies). When the system prompts you to download to floppies answer yes and insert the floppies it will request.

Step 26. Check to be sure all drives are listed correctly, then press Esc. Select **Drive List is Correct** to continue.

Step 27. Select **install with either the Default or Custom Option**.

Both NetWare's Installation and Maintenance Manuals have a lot of details on this section. It is recommended that you read the appropriate sections of the NetWare manuals before completing this section of the installation.

The "Custom" option will have the following items in its main window: Miscellaneous Maintenance, Modify Hot Fix Redirection Table, Modify Partition Table, Re-initialize a Disk, Remove a Disk, and Return to Previous menu. The Miscellaneous Maintenance Menu can have the following options: Load Operating System, Load System & Public Files, System Configuration, Volume Information, Printer Maintenance, and Return to Previous Menu.

NOTE: Your Custom option menu can vary depending on several factors, including the type of OS you have selected, and other parameters you may have selected during NETGEN.

Selecting the Default option sets up the entire disk for NetWare and, assigns a default-2 percent of hard drive for the hot fix redirection table.

We have chosen the Default Option for this section.

Step 28. Press the Esc key. The system will now ask for a file server name. Enter a name as instructed on the screen.

Press the Esc key to continue.

Step 29. The system will now ask whether to spool for each of the printer ports in the server. Answer "yes" to the question for those ports that will be network printers, then Esc to continue. For any COM ports you select,you will have to set up the baŭd rate and protocol, and so on, that the printer will be using.

Step 30. Enter a network (LAN) address for LAN board A, then for any other boards installed. The system will then ask for the number of communications buffers.

Communication buffers are areas in the file server's memory set aside to temporarily hold network data "packets" arriving from the various stations. The packets remain in the buffers until the file server is ready to process them and send them to their destination on the network.

The default and minimum number recommended is 40, however, you can specify between 10 and 150.

If you want to change the default number, use the following formula:
Start with 40 then add 1 buffer for each workstation that will be connected (meaning having the shell loaded). For example, if you have 25 workstation connected at any one time, you should specify 65 buffers (40 plus 1 for each of the 25 stations).

NOTE: Each communication buffer uses approximately one half kilobyte of memory.

Step 31. Enter a number for communication buffers.

The system will ask for the AUXGEN disk, then the SUPPORT disk (if running from floppies), then will display the following messages:

Setting LAN and Disk driver configurations, Network Addresses and Communication Buffers in the operating system executable file (NET$OS.EXE).

Please be Patient!

NOTE: This can take from two to five minutes or longer depending on what has been previously selected.

The system will ask for the AUXGEN disk, the OSEXE-1 disk, then the SUPPORT disk (again if running from floppies), then display the Installation Options menu.

Step 32. Select the **Installation Complete** option. This option will begin actual installation of the software. Answer "yes" to the question to exit and install. The installation utility will now ask for floppy disks to be inserted. You will want to download to floppies. NETGEN will then perform the following:

- install the cold boot loader on the file server hard drive,
- copy the NET$OS.EXE file,
- copy the SYSTEM and PUBLIC disks.

After the files are copied, the Network Generation Options menu will be displayed.

Step 33. Select **Exit NETGEN** and answer "yes" to the confirmation prompt. The installation is now complete. Re-boot the server with no floppy disk in the drive and NetWare will come up. Next you will need to generate the workstation shell.

8.1.2 SHGEN: Generating the Workstation Shells

SHGEN is the installation program used to generate the workstation shell. The DOS workstation shell performs two functions:

- it directs workstation requests to the appropriate operating system (DOS or NetWare),
- it directs messages from the file server or another workstation to the appropriate destination on the network using a program called IPX.COM (**I**nternet **P**acket **EX**change protocol).

NOTE: NetWare workstations can run with a wide variety of network interface boards. However, each of these interface boards has its own communication language. Therefore, IPX requires a customized piece of software called a "shell driver" to direct communications between the various network interface cards in the network workstations.

As you generate the shell for each workstation using SHGEN, you must specify the network shell driver that corresponds to the specific type of network interface board being used in that workstation. SHGEN then links this communication driver with the NetWare IPX program to generate a fully operational IPX.COM file for each workstation.

When using the Custom level of SHGEN, select the network driver necessary for the work station. The Custom level also allows you to select configurations for "resources" that are not NetWare related such as

- hardware within a workstation defined according to the type of bus that can be used with a standard PC or Micro Channel,
- interrupt or DMA channels, I/O addresses, and memory addresses. The SHGEN program reserves these channels and addresses, or allows resources to be "configured" along with the network driver to ensure that no hardware conflicts occur at the workstation.

Procedure for Using SHGEN:

Step 1. Boot a PC with a DOS disk (3.x). The PC must have at least 640 KB of memory. If you run it from a hard drive there must be at least 1 MB free disk space.

NOTE: Before proceeding further, make copies of the following diskettes using DOS DISKCOPY: SHGEN-1 SHGEN-2 (Only SHGEN-1 for 3.5" disks). These disks need to be written to, so they must not be write protected. Make sure you use your working copies.

Step 2. Insert the disk labelled SHGEN-1 and type

SHGEN
The following screen will appear (See Fig. 8.12)

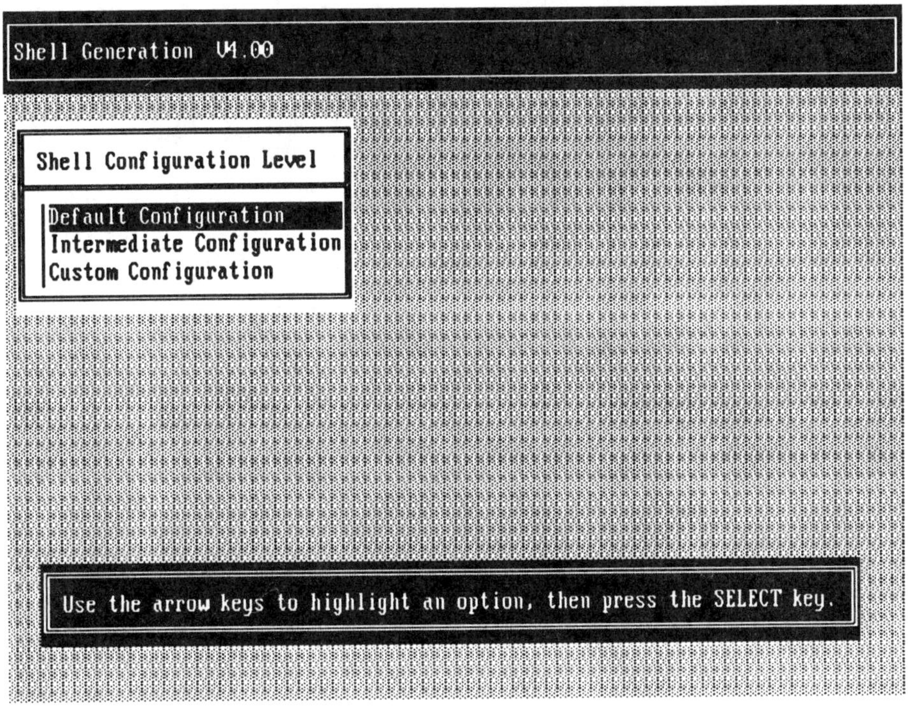

Figure 8.12 SHGEN Menu Utility, Shell Configuration Level.

Step 3. Select the **Custom Configuration** option, and then SHGEN run options: Standard, Hard disk, or Network Drive.

Step 4. Choose the **Select Shell Configuration** option. A new window will be displayed (See Fig. 8.13.)

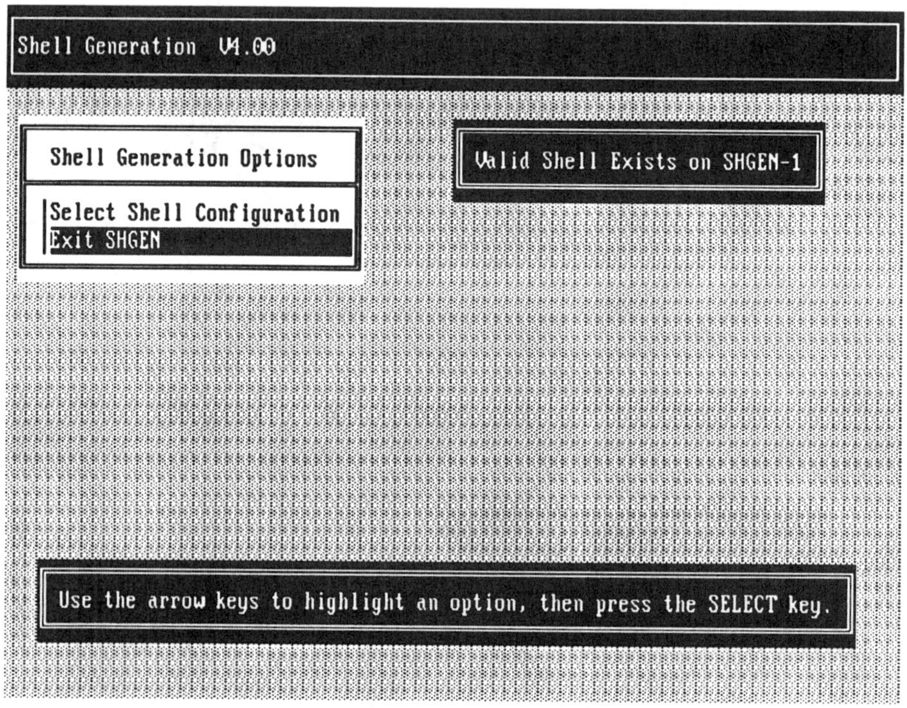

Figure 8.13 SHGEN Menu Utility, Shell Generation Options.

Step 5. Choose the **Select LAN Driver** option from the Available Options menu (See Fig. 8.14.)

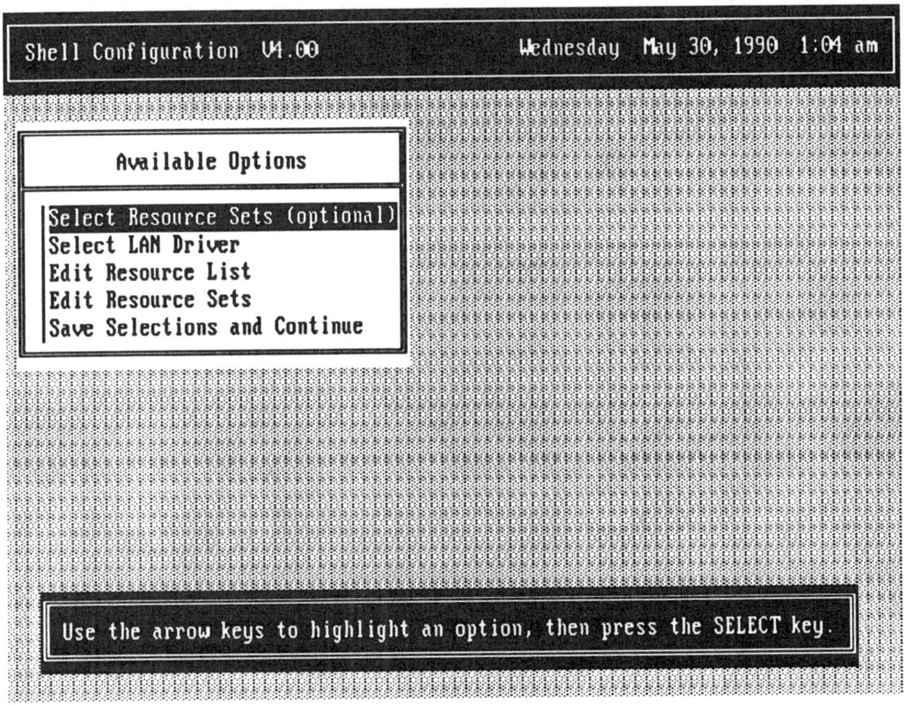

Figure 8.14 SHGEN Menu Utility, Available Options

Step 6. Choose the **Select Available Item** option. A window will open displaying the available LAN drivers.

Step 7. Choose a driver from the list by highlighting the entry and pressing Enter. The entry will be placed in the Selected LAN Driver window (See Fig. 8.15.)

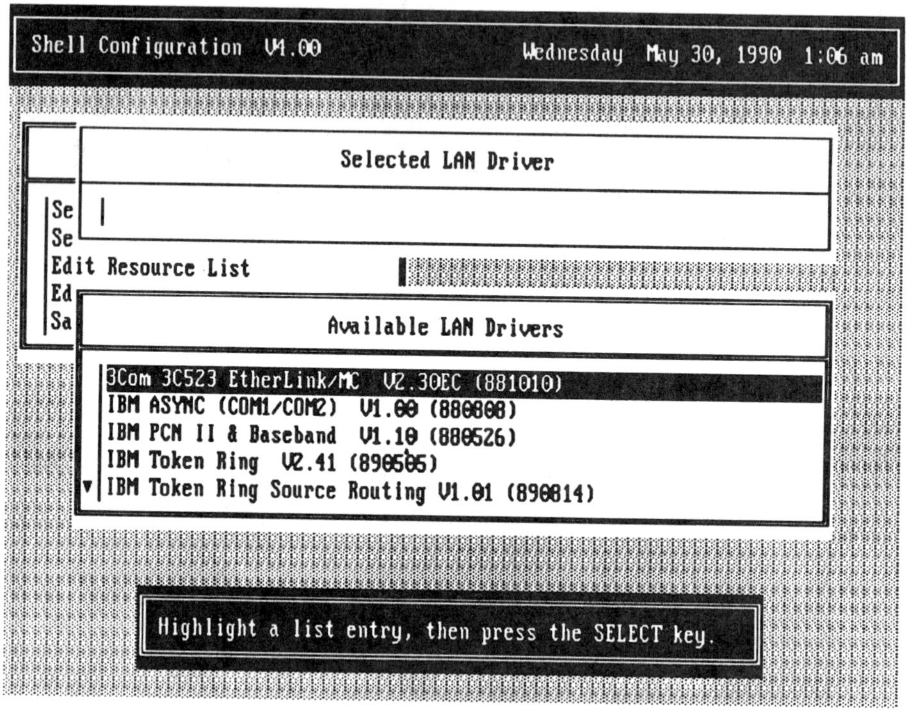

Figure 8.15 SHGEN Menu Utility, Selected LAN Driver.

Step 8. Now that your LAN driver appears in the window, press <esc> and you will be returned to the Shell Configuration "Available Options" menu.

Step 9. You will need to Configure Driver/Resources if the screen prompts you with "unconfigured driver/resources." This enables you to choose the hardware configuration settings for the drivers and resources you have selected.

Step 10. Now you will need to **Save Selections and Continue**. The following screen will appear (See Fig. 8.16.)

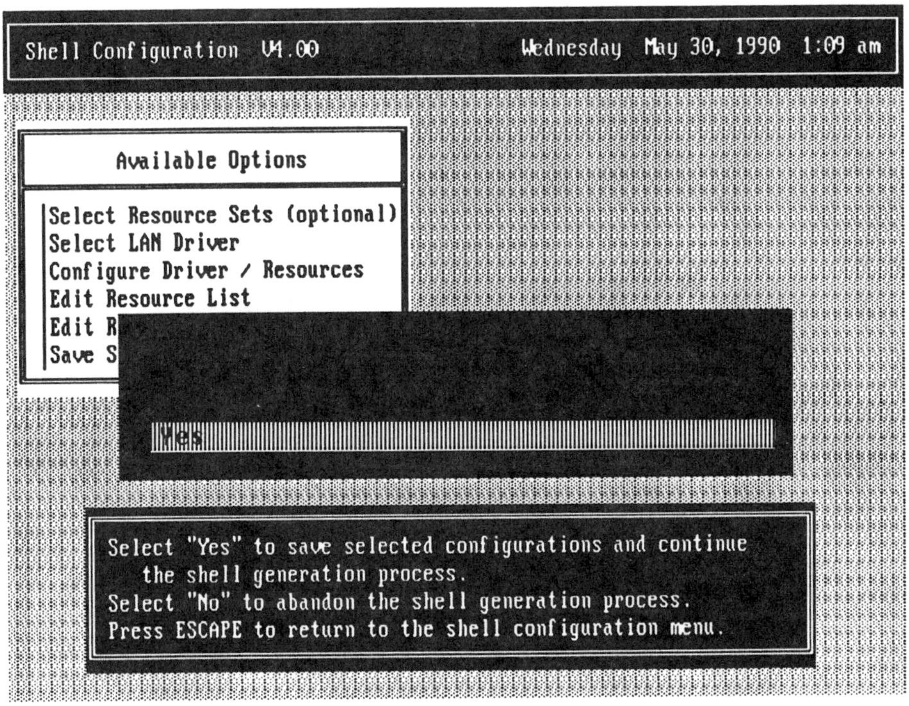

Figure 8.16 SHGEN Menu Utility, Yes to save and continue.

Step 11. Create a DOS boot diskette for each workstation and copy your shell to each disk. You may want to setup a config.sys and autoexec.bat file for your users as well.

9 DIRECTORY STRUCTURES

In this chapter

Directory Structures, Directories Given by NetWare, Moving Around the Directory Structure, PATHs, Example of DOS's PATH Command, NetWare's Map Command, Example of NetWare's Drive Pointers, Search Drives

9.1 DIRECTORY STRUCTURES

Novell utilizes a tree directory structure the same as DOS. The only difference is that you have a file server(s) name as the first level of your path.

All file servers are given a name during installation, this name thus appears as the first level of your directory structure. This is particularly important if you have a multiserver environment.

A volume in NetWare can be either an entire hard drive or a partition of the hard drive. Most people are familiar with C:\ (the root directory), or D:\ in DOS. In NetWare these will be called SYS: or DATA: and so on. When you install NetWare with (NETGEN) you must specify the volume names or accept the defaults. NetWare always creates SYS: as your first volume. The volume name appears as the second level of your directory structure.

Think of your directory structure as your filing cabinet system. The file server name is the entire cabinet. The volume names are the drawers. Inside the drawers are file folders or directories. These also can be further broken down to subfolders or subdirectories. Both folders and subfolders contain files (possibly letters, invoices, legal documents and so on.), in the same way your directories and subdirectories contain files. It is important to spend some time designing your directory structure as it can affect your security.

9.1.1 Directories Given by NetWare

NetWare gives you some basic directories during installation (See Fig. 9.1). Do not delete these!

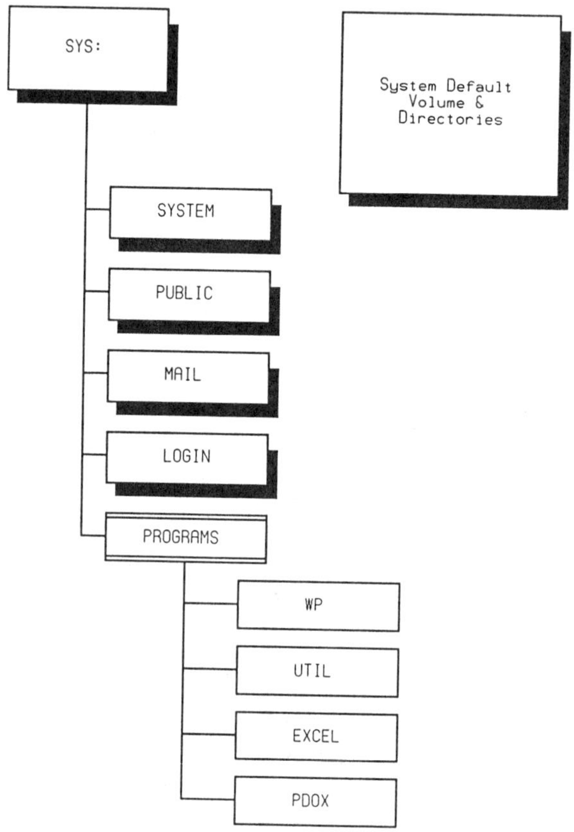

Figure 9.1 The Volume SYS:, and the four directories System, Public, Mail and Login are created by NetWare during installation.

NOTE: Notice the colon after SYS, this states that it is a volume. All volumes must be followed by a colon. A volume, as mentioned previously identifies a hard drive or a partition. It also acts as the root directory. NetWare 2.1x allows 32 volumes.

PUBLIC This directory is perhaps the most important in NetWare. This is where all of the user commands and menus are stored. Think of this directory as being the same as public transit, shared and accessible by all users (discussed in Security section).

SYSTEM This directory is the most important to the supervisor of the LAN. It contains all of the Supervisor/Console commands. It also contains the system files such as NET$OS.EXE. As a result, no user should have access to this directory with exception of supervisor equivalent (discussed in Security section).

LOGIN Think of this directory as the reception area of a building. This is where NetWare puts users after they have attached (run the shell) and are about to LOGIN. NetWare at this point has no information on the user logging in because the security profile has yet to be loaded. Therefore, this directory is a safe place on the system for the user to reside prior to their logging in. Once a user logs into the system, their security profile is then loaded and NetWare now knows where and what the user can access. This directory contains the command line utilities LOGIN.EXE and SLIST.EXE. These are used to allow users to login to the system while SLIST (stands for server list) allows users to see what servers are out there to login into. NetWare gives users the ability to read and execute these files for that purpose, therefore, you should not change this access.

NOTE: If you have a network that uses floppyless workstations, your boot files required for those workstations are also located in this directory.

MAIL Contains all of the mail boxes (directories) for the users. Even if you are not using NetWare's mail package (it no longer ships as part of the standard NetWare package but is available) but have purchased a more extensive third party package, you may want to keep these directories. The users login scripts are stored here. A login script is a file that is executed when a user logs into the system. It can contain everything from path statements to friendly messages such as "GOOD MORNING BOB," and so forth. This feature will be discussed more in-depth later. The mail boxes directories are identified by numbers, that is, 1, B0002 and so on. These hexadecimal numbers match the "USER_ID" number which identifies a particular user. NetWare assigns the rights to this area automatically.

To best appreciate directory structures, and to ensure proper management of directory structure, a diagram of the directories and volumes is most useful (See Figs. 9.2 and 9.3.). The directories illustrated may also have sub directories, however these have not been shown in the illustration.

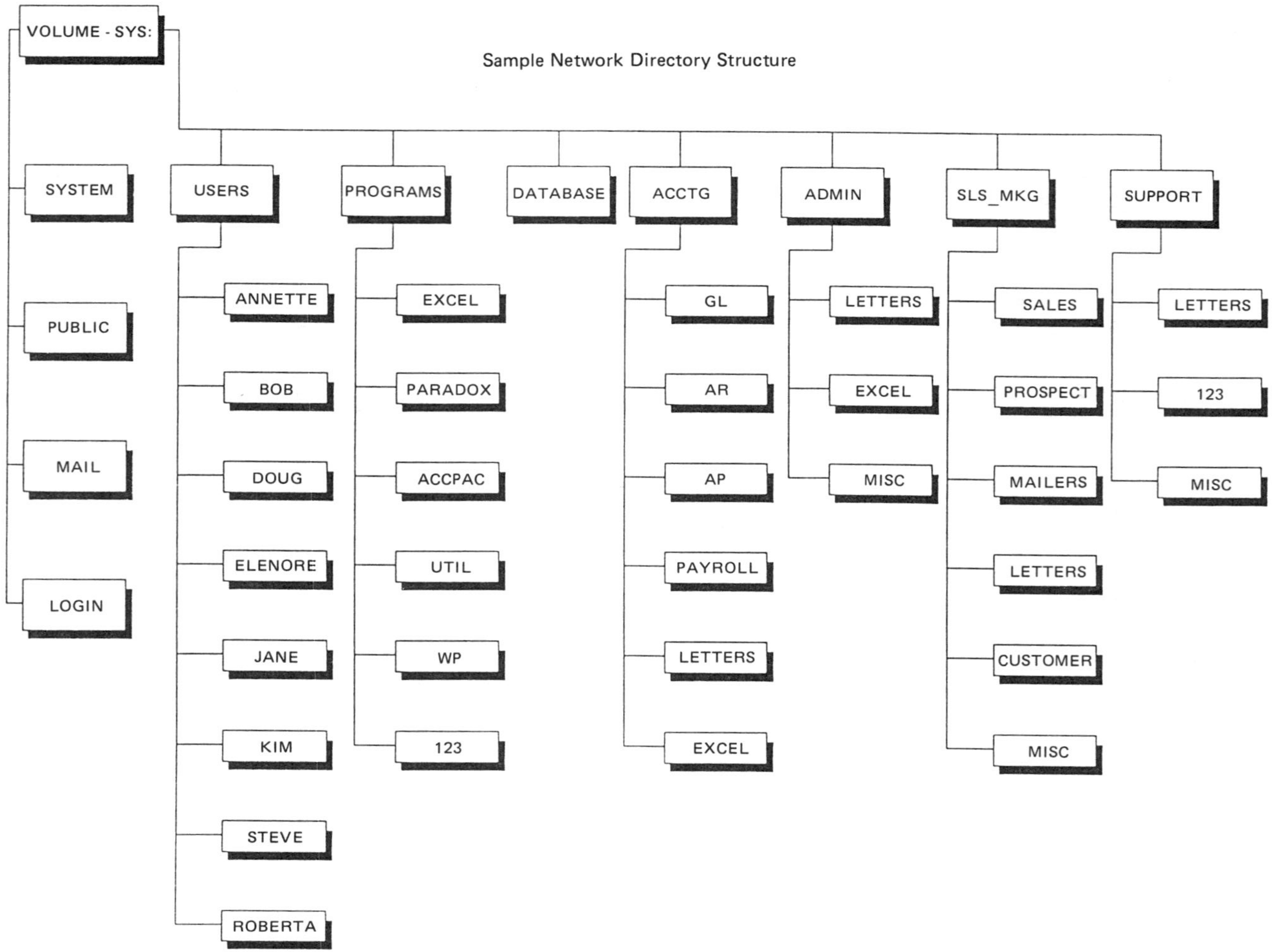

Figure 9.2 This sample network directory structure has NetWare created directories, as well as private directories and department directories, all in one volume.

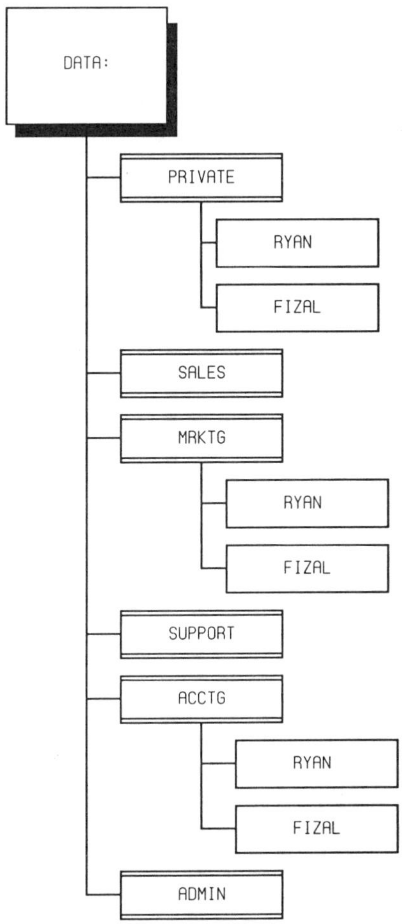

Figure 9.3 Users word processing files, datafiles, or accounting data can be placed in a separate volume called "DATA:."

9.2 MOVING AROUND THE DIRECTORY STRUCTURE

There are a couple of ways to move around in the directory structure. They are

- CD (DOS's change directory command),
- PATH (DOS command),
- MAP (NetWare's command).

No matter which method you use to move with, you must identify the location of the directory. This is the same as giving a person directions to find a building on a street. In this example, you would identify the area of the city, the main intersection, the directions to the desired street and the exact location of the building on that street. In computers you must tell the operating system (DOS or NetWare) exactly where to go to find any desired files or directories.

> **NOTE:** It is extremely important that you understand DOS (or operating systems) prior to managing your LAN.

Example of the DOS CD Command

```
C:\> CD\SALES\CUSTOMER\FORECAST
```

In this example you are moving to the forecast directory. The CD stands for change directory. See a DOS manual for further details

9.2.1 Paths

DOS also has a PATH command. First of all the term "paths" refers to the route that the computer will follow from the root directory to the desired subdirectory in your "tree structure." The command PATH has a slightly expanded meaning. It is used as a search path, for .exe, .com, and .bat files. In other words searching for your application software programs. DOS first looks in the directory you are currently in for the desired application program but if not found, starts searching through the known paths for these files. The known routes are those that you have specified with the PATH command. If you did not have a PATH command, the error message "file not found" would be returned, unless you are located in the directory of the application program.

9.2.2 Example of Dos Path Command

```
H:\> PATH H:\PROGRAMS\WP51
H:\> PATH H:\PROGRAMS\WP51,\PROGRAMS\123
```

In the first example, you are telling DOS to search below the root directory for a directory called programs and below that for a directory WP51. This way you could be in your private data directory and type WP51 and DOS would automatically search this route for necessary files to run the word processing package.

In the second part of this example we are demonstrating that multiple paths can be established with one path statement. The same process is occurring as previously however we are also telling DOS to search for a directory 123 for the spreadsheet program files. The semicolon (;) separates multiple path statements.

9.2.3 NetWare's Map Command

NetWare has a command that allows you to move around in the system VERY EASILY. Instead of typing CD followed by a path every time you wish to move to a directory, it is far easier to logically assign a letter of the alphabet to equal a directory path. Then when you wish to move to that directory you just type a letter followed by a colon and the enter key. You are familiar with doing this when moving between the floppy drive (A) and your hard drive (C). If you wish to move to the floppy you type A: <enter>. Well take that process one step further. In this case you are moving to a **PHYSICAL DRIVE.** When you assign a letter equal to a directory it is known as a **LOGICAL DRIVE.** This term is also associated with hard drive partitions.

PHYSICAL	LOGICAL
A: 1ST FLOPPY	D: HARD DRIVE PARTITION
B: 2ND FLOPPY	E: HARD DRIVE PARTITION
C: HARD DRIVE	

NetWare allows you a total of 26 logical drives **PER USER**. Why 26? Because there are 26 letters in the alphabet. In order to maintain compatibility with DOS, NetWare reserves the letters A through E as pointers to your local machine, although you can override these defaults if you wish. Therefore F: is almost always your first network drive. You will notice when you boot your workstation that you will need to change to F: after you ran the shell (IPX and NET3, or NET4). This places you in the network's reception area (LOGIN directory) from which you would login to the network. In this case F: is your first network drive.

The only reason you create drive mappings is for ease of moving around the directory structure. It is similar to assigning variables in algebra. The letter equals whatever value you assign it. When wishing to use that value again you just specify the letter.

9.2.4 Example of NetWare's Drive Pointers

LOCAL DRIVES	**A:**	**1**
	B:	**2**
(number depends	**C:**	**3**
on DOS version)	**D:**	**4**
	E:	**5**
NETWORK DRIVES	**F:**	**6**
	G:	**7**
	H:	**8**
	I:	**9**
	J:	**10**
	K:	**11**
	L:	**12**
	M:	**13**
	N:	**14**
	O:	**15**
	P:	**16**
	Q:	**17**
	R:	**18**
	S:	**19**
	T:	**20**
	U:	**21**
	V:	**22**
	W:	**23**
	X:	**24**
	Y:	**25**
	Z:	**26**

Example #1 Map Command

MAP F:=SYS:USERS/KIM
MAP G:=SYS:DATA/SALES

NOTE: Notice the equal sign. This tells the system that the drive letter F is now equal to Kim's home directory. Therefore if Kim wanted to move to her home directory to store a document she just has to type

F: <◂—┘>

To move to the sales data directory she types

G: <◂—┘>

Example #2 Map Command

```
MAP J:=SYS:DATA/LETTERS
```

NOTE: Unlike DOS it does not matter in whether you use a forward slash (/) or a backslash (\). Also notice that you do not need a slash after the volume name. As we had mentioned previously, the colon acts as a delimiter.

Example #3 Map Command

```
MAP J:=SYS:
MAP K:=J:DATA/LETTERS
MAP L:=J:PRIVATE/JANE
```

In this example we have mapped the letter J: to the SYS: volume. Then, in the second line, we are mapping the letter K: to the letters directory which is located below SYS:DATA. We can use the letter J: to equal SYS: because it was already assigned to that value. If you don't like typing, then you will use this.

Example #4 Map Command

```
MAP J:=DATA:
MAP K:=J:PRIVATE/JANE,L:=PREC;M:=LETTERS
```

In this example we are creating multiple MAP statements all on one line. If you don't like to type, you'll be happy with this. Otherwise they can be specified on multiple lines.

Example #5 Map Command

In the illustration that follows, the login script has map commands which use the logical drive letters F:, J:, and K:, to point to a volume, and these first definitions are used for subsequent mappings (See Fig. 9.4.)

```
NetWare System Configuration  V2.20d          Tuesday  May 29, 1990  8:15 pm
                  User EAMONS On File Server TAITO_DB

                           System Login Script

MAP F:=TAITO/SYS:
MAP J:=TAITO/DATA:
MAP K:=TAITO/DATB:
MAP G:=J:\USERS\%LOGIN_NAME
MAP H:=J:\SHARED
MAP P:=J:\PUBDATA

MAP S1:=F:\PUBLIC
MAP S2:=S1:%OS\%OS_VERSION
MAP S3:=F:\WINDOWS
MAP S4:=F:\
MAP S5:=F:\WORD
MAP S6:=F:\MHS\EXE
MAP S7:=F:\EMAIL\MAILUSER
MAP S8:=F:\PROC
```

Figure 9.4 A Login script can have simple or complex mappings, as required to establish management control of user access to data and application software. The system Login script can be created in SYSCON, System Login Script.

9.2.5 Search Drives

In the previous examples we were using the MAP command to create pointers to DATA directories. You can also use the MAP command to create search paths to APPLICATION PROGRAM directories. These are called SEARCH DRIVES. **A search drive is similar to DOS's path statements** and provides additional functions. Therefore, if you have a clear understanding of PATH, this is the same concept. A search drive allows a user located in one directory to access application program files that are located in another directory. Here you are creating a route that NetWare will search when you request .exe, .com or .bat files. The syntax is almost the same as the previous map statements.

> **NOTE:** If you establish path statements on your workstation using DOS, NetWare will automatically add them to your network search drives. If you use the PATH command after logging in, you will likely lose your network search drives. Therefore it is recommended that you only use NetWare's mapping.

Example #1 Mapped Search Drives

```
MAP S1:=SYS:PUBLIC
MAP S2:=SYS:PUBLIC/MSDOS/V3.31
MAP S3:=SYS:PROGRAMS/WP
MAP S4:=SYS:PROGRAMS/123
MAP S5:=SYS:PROGRAMS/UTILITY
```

In this example we have created search drives or search paths for the public directory, DOS version, word processing, lotus 123 spreadsheet, and a utilities directory.

> **NOTE:** You must have a search drive to public. Remember this is where all of your network user commands are located. This includes LOGOUT. Therefore, you can be in any directory and type LOGOUT, NetWare will locate this command for you and execute it.

Let's assume we have a user Kim and she wants to run the Wordperfect application to create a document. She would like to store this document in her private directory. NetWare facilitates this through the use of SEARCH DRIVES.

Example #2 Searching for WordPerfect

```
MAP F:=SYS:PRIVATE/KIM
MAP S1:=SYS:PUBLIC
MAP S2:=SYS:PUBLIC/MSDOS/V3.31
MAP S3:=SYS:PROGRAMS/123
MAP S4:=SYS:PROGRAMS/WP
```

This means that Kim is in her home directory thus seeing the following prompt on her screen

F:\USERS\KIM>

She then just has to type WP to execute her application

F:\USERS\KIM> WP <↵>

NetWare will then

1. Search Kim's private directory for a wp.bat, wp.exe, or wp.com file needed to run the application. Since these files are stored in the sys:programs\wp directory, NetWare will

2. Search the location designated in the first search drive. NetWare will not find the wp files here because we have stated with the MAP command that the first search drive (S1:) is equal to the public directory. NetWare will then

3. Sequentially search through the other search drives until the files for the application were located. In this example the fourth search drive.
NetWare will then

4. Execute this file loading wp.exe, leaving Kim in her private directory and any datafiles she creates in here.

NOTE: You only use search drives for applications. You are allowed a total of 16 search drives PER USER. Let's take a look at the break down of our drives available for assignment now.

Example #3 Break Down of Available Drive Assignments

LOCAL DRIVES	A:	1		
	B:	2		
	C:	3		
	D:	4		
	E:	5		
NETWORK DRIVES	F:	6		
	G:	7		
	H:	8		
	I:	9		
	J:	10		
	K:	**11**	**16**	
	L:	**12**	**15**	
	M:	**13**	|	
	N:	**14**	|	
	O:	**15**	|	
	P:	**16**	|	
	Q:	**17**	|	**SEARCH**
	R:	**18**	|	**DRIVES**
	S:	**19**	|	
	T:	**20**	|	
	U:	**21**	|	**(You may**
	V:	**22**	|	**assign up**
	W:	**23**	**4**	**to 16)**
	X:	**24**	**3**	
	Y:	**25**	**2**	
	Z:	**26**	**1**	

You can assign up to 16 search drives per user. This would assume that your user needed to search 16 application program directories. Most systems have approximately 6 or 7 search drives per user.

> **NOTE:** When you assign a search drive, it automatically takes up a letter of the alphabet. It starts taking these letters from the end of the alphabet. This means that S1: = Z:, S2: = Y: and so on. If you have already defined Y: you will notice that it moves up to the next available letter, in this case S2: = X:.

10 NETWORK SECURITY (SYSCON & FILER)

In this chapter

Users, Types of Users, Network Assigned Users, NetWare's Security System, Effective Rights, Security Flows Down.

10.1 USERS

10.1.1 Types of Users

NetWare provides the following statuses that can be applied to users:

1. Supervisor

   - Supervisor, a user name with an associated status of special rights.
   - The Supervisor sets up the security system.
   - The supervisor is responsible for creating users and groups.
   - If queue and console operators are required on the system it is the supervisors responsibility to assign these to specific users or groups.
   - The Supervisor has ALL rights on the system.

2. Security Equivalent

   - The security equivalence status is assigned to a specified user(s). It makes one user equivalent to another user. For example, creating a user equivalent to supervisor, effectively provides a "back door" into the system with a user having all the rights of a supervisor.

3. Console Operator

    - Any user assigned the console operator status can monitor and control file server activities through the FCONSOLE menu utility.

4. Queue Operator

    - Users with this status, designated queue operators, can edit print queue entry information.
    - A queue operator can delete any entry, from the print queue.
    - A queue operator can modify the queue's status.
    - A queue operator can change the order of the print jobs in the print queue.

5. Network User

    - This is any individual user who has access rights assigned to them by the network supervisor (or equivalent). Their security access is determined by the supervisor, as well.

10.1.2 Network Assigned Users

As part of the installation, NetWare automatically creates

- the user supervisor,
- the group everyone,
- the user guest.

A new user is automatically assigned as a member of the group everyone. This is a useful tool, for example you may want all of your users to have access to the word processing package. You can simplify this in one step by assigning the appropriate security rights to the group everyone. The user guest is there for occasional use only and can be deleted or restricted as you wish. When dealing with groups, a word of caution

NEVER DELETE THE GROUP EVERYONE

10.2 NETWARE'S SECURITY SYSTEM

The four levels of NetWare's security are:

1. Login / Password

- Access to the file server

    File server access can be restricted in any of the following ways, you may use any or all of these login and password restrictions through the SYSCON to customize your system security, and assume full management control of the use of your resources:

- User name

- These optional login restrictions can be added to restrict users access in a number of ways:

    time restrictions,
    station restrictions,
    account disable,
    account expiration date,
    limit concurrent connections,
    intruder lockout status.

- A password, is either required, or not required for system access.

- If a password is required, its use can be restricted in a number of ways:

    minimum length of password,
    force periodic (a date restriction) password changes,
    require unique passwords, NetWare will track up to eight previous ones for each user comparing each new password requested, and rejecting it if it matches one already used. Users should not be aware that there is a historical limit of eight.

2. Trustee Rights (user/group)

Trustee rights govern what a user can do in and below a specified directory.

Trustee rights can be assigned to individual users, or to groups. These can be used to restrict access to files, or restrict the allowable file operations. This ability to assign rights provides another excellent management tool.

Rights: . . . . Security Function:

- Read . . . . read from open files
- Write . . . . write to open files
- Delete . . . . delete existing files
- Open . . . . open a file
- Create . . . . create a new file (simultaneously opens)
- Search . . . . search a directory i.e., DIR, UDIR, NDIR
- Modify . . . . modify file attributes
- Parental . . . . create, rename, and erase directories and subdirectories beneath
  set trustee and directory rights in a directory and subdirectories below it

NOTE: Some software packages may create temporary files as part of their operation, and users must be able to create, write, and delete these temporary files, or the software will not run.

3. Directory Rights

Directory rights govern what a directory will allow any user to do while in its area.

The rights explained fully as trustee rights above can also be applied in the same way to directories. Directory rights can only be applied to directories.

> **NOTE:** Directory rights are just an extra security measure for a particular directory. Usually you leave them set to ALL (the default).

There is available a set of directory attributes which that can be assigned at a directory level with the FLAGDIR command line utility. You can specify any of the following attributes:

Normal — default with no attributes assigned, can also be used to cancel any attributes previously assigned.

System — acts the same as a hidden directory, and is used for directories that the system requires to function

Hidden — hides a directory so that it can not be seen when doing a directory search

Private	allows directories with this attribute to be seen without the files contained in the directory being revealed (now added to the directory)

4. File Attributes

File attributes govern what you can do with files.

Netware file attributes operate in much the same way as DOS file attributes. They can be assigned to files using the FILER menu utility, or use the FLAG command line utility. HIDEFILE and SHOWFILE command line utilities can be used to hide and unhide files for users with the appropriate rights.

Description . . . . Short Form

- Read / Write . . . . (RW)
- Read Only . . . . (RO)
- Shareable . . . . (S)
- Non-Shareable . . . . (NS)
- Transaction Tracking System . . . . . (TTS)
- Index / Non-Indexed . . . . (I/NI)
- Execute only . . . . (Filer only)
- System . . . . (Filer only)
- Hidden . . . . (Filer and HIDEFILE)
- Normal (non shareable
  and read/write) . . . . (FLAG only)
- Modified . . . . (M)

Read/Write	allows files to read from and written to
Read Only	allows files to read from but not written to
Shareable	allows multiple users to access the file
Non-Shareable	allows only one user at a time to access the file
Transaction Tracking System	enables NetWare's TTS to start tracking any files flagged with this attribute
Index/Non-Indexed	is used for files in excess of 2 MB, to keep an index of the file in RAM in the server thus providing faster access to large files

Execute only	allows the file to be executed or deleted, to protect the file from being copied
System	only NetWare can execute files with this attribute
Hidden	files with this attribute can not be seen in a directory search, nor can they be deleted, but they can be seen with the NDIR command or through filer if the user has the modify and search rights
Modified	this attribute indicates if the file has been changed or modified since the last backup

10.3 EFFECTIVE RIGHTS

If you start assigning rights to groups, users, and directories you will need to determine effective rights. Effective rights means "what can this user really do in a specific directory. The easiest way to understand this is to look at some examples.

EXAMPLE

Directory	→	**SYS:DATA/SALES**
User	→	**KIM**
Group	→	**SALES**

Let's assume that we have assigned rights to the user Kim, and she belongs to a group sales as well that also has certain rights. We have decided in this example that we will leave the directory rights to all for simplicity. Now we want to determine what "effective rights" Kim really has.

user rights	**ROS**
group rights	**RWOCDS (OR)**
TRUSTEE RIGHTS =	**RWOCDS**
trustee rights	**RWOCDS**
directory rights	**RWOCDPMS (AND)**
EFFECTIVE RIGHTS =	**RWOCDS**

Therefore Kim has RWOCDS in the SYS:DATA/SALES directory.

NOTE: You can see how this can get complicated. To keep everything simple it is therefore recommended that you

- first, determine if you are going to restrict directory rights,
- second, assign the trustee rights to groups,
- third, take care of any users special needs that do not fall into a group category like their private or home directories.

10.4 SECURITY FLOWS DOWN

There is one more aspect of security that you must keep in mind when designing your system, and that is, that trustee rights flow down through the directory structure until you change them. To best understand this concept, follow the examples given.

Security Example 1

Directory	→	**SYS:DATA/SALES**
User	→	**KIM**

If we assign ROS to Kim in the data directory, she will by default have ROS in sales (or any other directory located below DATA). However, we can restrict Kim to have no rights in sales by removing all rights to that area. Once you specify a rights restriction it will be activated.

Security Example 2

```
                                 SYS:
                                   ↓
 ┌──────────────────────────────────────────────────────────────────┐
   ↓         ↓           ↓          ↓             ↓        ↓
 LOGIN    SYSTEM     PUBLIC   APPLIC(ros)       MAIL    USERS
 (ros)                (ros)         |                      |
                                    ↓                      ↓
                     ┌─────────────────────┐      ┌───────────────┐
                         ↓       ↓      ↓          ↓          ↓
                        WP      SS     DB         JIM       KIM
                               (no)                         (all)
```

In this example, KIM's rights in the various directories are

at SYS:	NO RIGHTS
at SYS:LOGIN	READ OPEN SEARCH (ROS)
at SYS:SYSTEM	NO RIGHTS
at SYS:MAIL	NO RIGHTS
at SYS:USERS	NO RIGHTS
at SYS:APPLIC	READ OPEN SEARCH (ROS)
at SYS:APPLIC/WP	READ OPEN SEARCH (ROS)
at SYS:APPLIC/DB	READ OPEN SEARCH (ROS)
at SYS:APPLIC/SS	NO RIGHTS
at SYS:USERS/JIM	NO RIGHTS
at SYS:USERS/KIM	ALL RIGHTS (RWOCDPSM)

11 USING NETWARE'S MENU UTILITIES

In this chapter

Using the SYSCON Menu Utility, Options, Using the FILER Menu Utility, Directories/Subdirectories, Working with Files, View Volume Information.

All of NetWare's menu utilities are windowed. There are eight keys you need to remember to manipulate the windows

RETURN	Move to the next level of window (forward)
ESCAPE	Return to the previous window (backwards)
INSERT	Add an entry, that is, user, group, directory, etc.
DELETE	Remove an entry (same as above)
F1	Help (F1 twice gives you a listing of function keys)
F3	Modify, that is, rename a user, group, directory
F5	Mark (Toggle), that is, mark list of users for deletion
ALT F10	Quick exit from the menus from any location, changes are not saved.

11.1 USING THE SYSCON MENU UTILITY

Now that we have discussed directory structures, security, and users, our next step is to put this into effect. There are two utilities that accomplish this in NetWare. They are SYSCON and FILER. First, we will discuss SYSCON.

SYSCON stands for "SYStem CONfiguration." This menu utility is used to create, modify, or delete users and groups, assign rights, and so forth. A more in-depth look at its features is shown by the illustration (See Fig. 11.1).

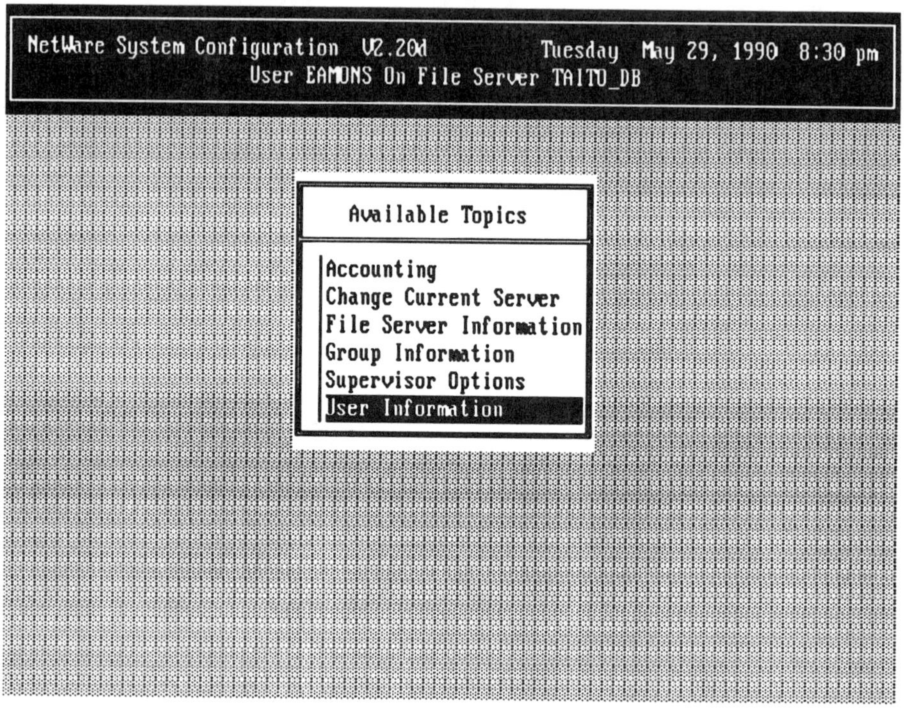

Figure 11.1 SYSCON Menu Utility, Main Menu.

11.1.1 Options

1. NetWare's internal accounting

    - These are the internal accounting billing choices available
      reading and writing from/to disk,
      connection to the file server,
      disk storage occupancy,
      service requests to the file server.

- View or modify (name the server) for which the above billing choices are to apply.

2. Change current server.

3. Display file server information.

4. **List and change group information.**
    - Full name
    - Group ID
    - **Member list**
    - Other information
    - **Trustee directory assignments**

5. View and Specify Supervisor options

    - Default account balance restrictions
    - Default time restrictions
    - Edit system AUTOEXEC file
    - File server console operators
    - Intruder detection/lockout
    - System login script
    - View file server error log

6. List and change user information.

    - Account balance
    - Account restrictions
    - Change password
    - Full name
    - **Groups belonged to**
    - **Login script**
    - Other information
    - **Security equivalences**
    - **Station restrictions**
    - **Time restrictions**
    - **Trustee directory assignments**

NOTE: The highlighted items are those used most frequently.

How to Create Users and Groups

STEP 1. To enter SYSCON type SYSCON press ↵. You are now going to create a user. Using the down arrow keys, move to the USER INFORMATION option, press ↵ to select it. Now press <insert> and it will prompt you for a user name. Type the name of your new user. You have just created a new user (See Fig. 11.2.)

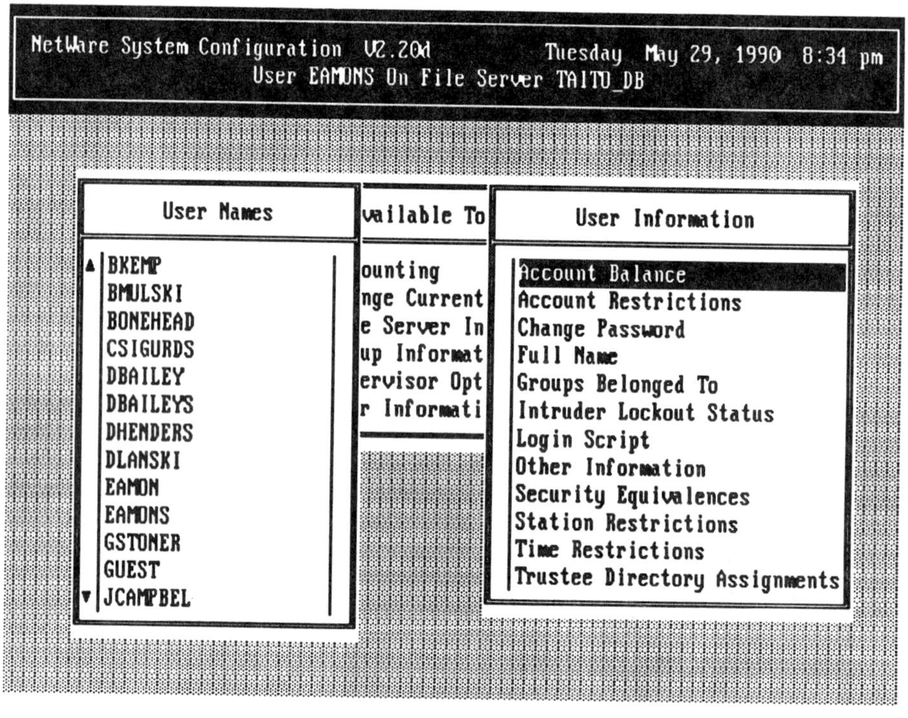

Figure 11.2 SYSCON Menu Utility, User Information.

STEP 2. Next you will create a group and add your user to the group. Also, you will view the member list of the group everyone. Press <esc> to go back to the main window in SYSCON (AVAILABLE TOPICS). Move to the GROUP INFORMATION option and press ↵. Now press <insert> and it will prompt you for a group name. Type in a unique name for your group. Now press ↵ on your group name. Go to the member list and press ↵ . Press <insert> and find the user you created, from the list, press ↵ , this adds the user to your group. Now press <esc> and go to the group EVERYONE and press ↵ . Go to the member list and view it. Notice that the user you created in Step 1. was automatically added to this group (See Fig. 11.3.)

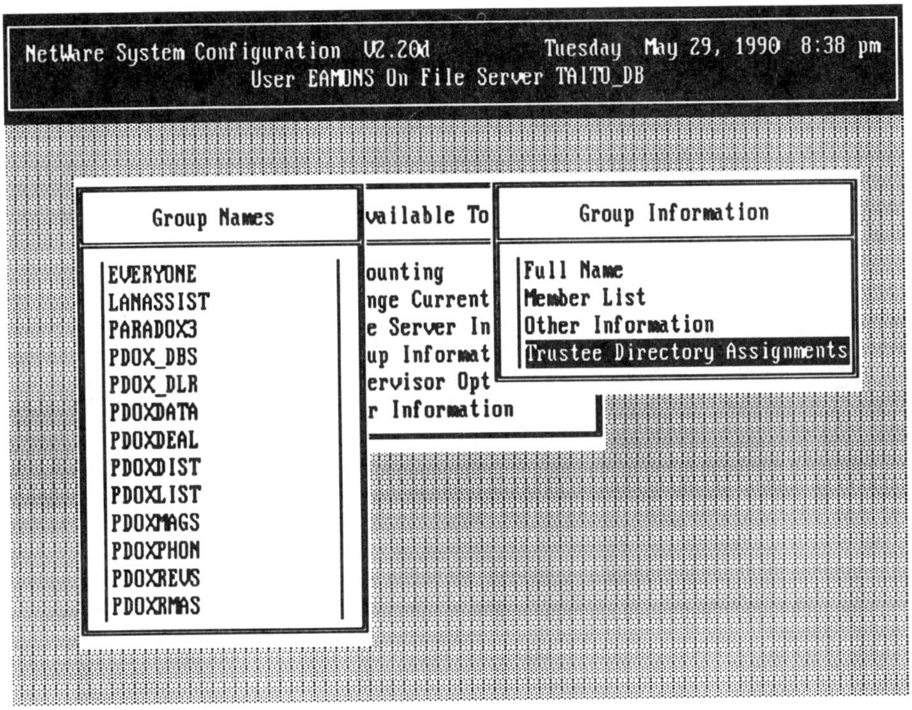

Figure 11.3 SYSCON Menu Utility, Group Information.

How to Delete Users and Groups

STEP 1. You are now going to delete users and groups. Staying in the GROUP NAMES window, move the highlighted bar to one of the groups you created. Press <delete>. You have just deleted a group.

NEVER DELETE THE GROUP EVERYONE

STEP 2. You are now going to delete the user you just created. Go back to the USER INFORMATION option on the main window and press ↵ . Now move the highlighted bar to the user you created and press <delete>. You have just deleted a user.

How to Delete Lists of Users and Groups

If you want to practice deleting a list of users or groups follow the same procedures used in the section prior, to make a list of users. Then using your mark key (remember F5) mark all of the users you just created then press the delete key. The same process can be used to delete multiple groups.

How to Rename a User or Group

If you want to rename an existing user, move to the User Information option on the main window and press ◄—┘. Move to the user you wish to rename and press the modify and rename key (remember F3). This same process can be used to rename a group (See Fig. 11.4.)

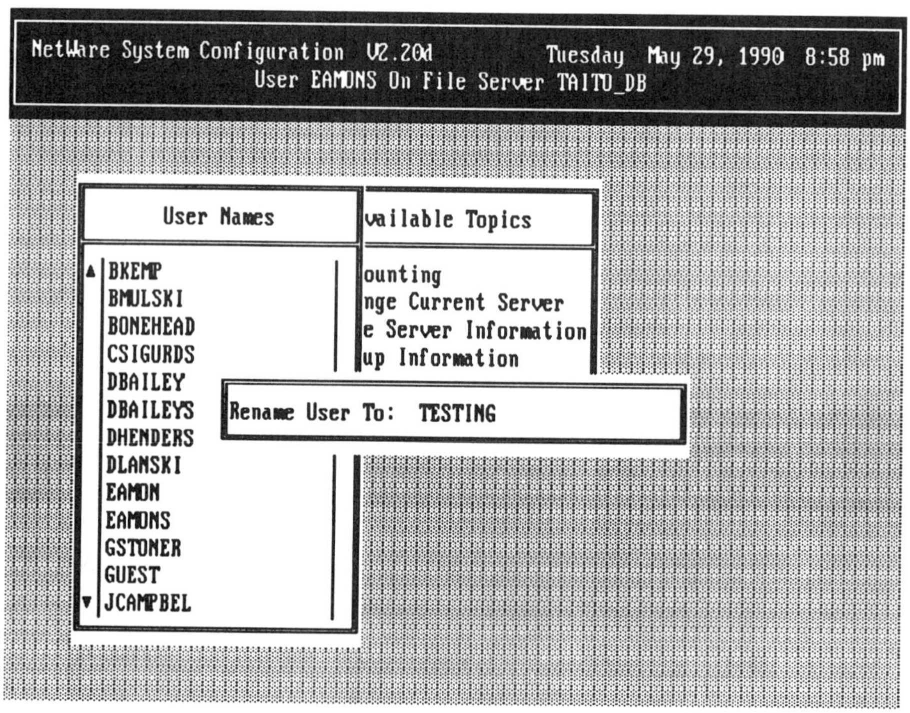

Figure 11.4 SYSCON Menu Utility, Rename User To, this menu can be accessed with the F3 function key.

CAUTION! There are ramifications to renaming a group. If a login script calls for a specific group, or user name that has been modified since the Login script was created, the Login will not execute properly.

How to Assign Trustee Rights to Groups and Users

Go to the USER INFORMATION option on the main window and press ↵. Find the user you wish to assign rights to and press ↵. Move your down arrow key to TRUSTEE ASSIGNMENTS and press ↵. Press <insert> and specify the directory path to which you want the rights assigned and press ↵. Notice the default rights it assigns you. Now assign the user the rights that they will require. To do this press ↵. Now select the rights by pressing (F5). Press ↵ to save it. You can create a directory and assign rights in the TRUSTEE ASSIGNMENTS window (See Fig. 11.5.) This is very useful for creating home (private) directories.

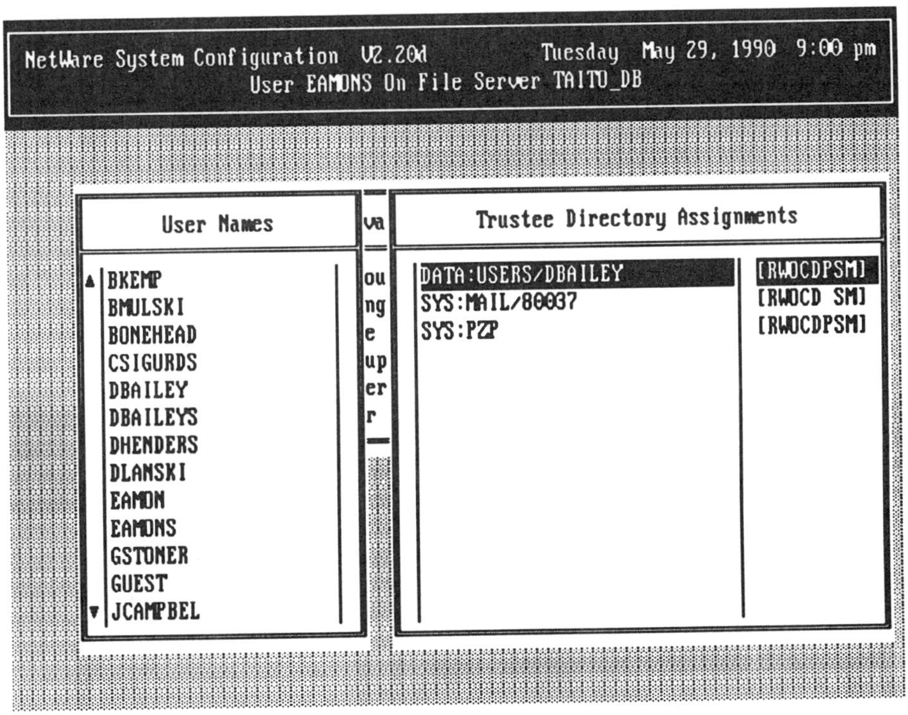

Figure 11.5 SYSCON Menu Utility, Trustee Directory Assignments.

How to Assign Account Restrictions

In this chapter you will be examining ACCOUNT RESTRICTIONS in detail. Position the movable lightbar on the ACCOUNT RESTRICTIONS option in the user information window and press ←┘. Move to the "Require a password" and type Y for yes. Now using your arrow (also called cursor) keys you can move to the minimum length option and specify the length that you require. You may also force the user to change the password every so many days. For example 30 days. Now every month they will be forced to change their password. The unique password option, if evoked, will track the last eight passwords. Therefore, a user can not reuse an old password until eight password changes have been made.

> **NOTE:** If you have not created any of your users (a new system), then you can create a "template" incorporating all of these options. This is created in the Supervisor Options Window selected from the main window of SYSCON (See Figs. 11.6A, and 11.6B.) The option to select is DEFAULT ACCOUNT BALANCE/RESTRICTIONS. Whatever you specify in this template will be assigned to any "new" users created after this template. This will then be automatic. For example you may wish to have all users forced to have a password, which must be composed of a minimum number of characters. At least five is recommended to maintain security.

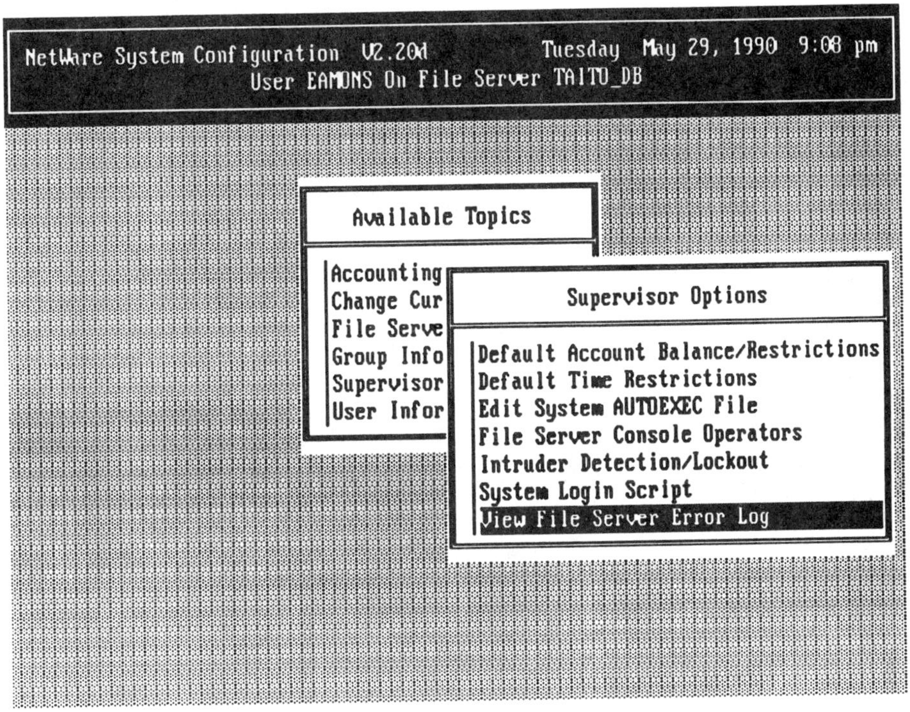

Figure 11.6A SYSCON Menu Utility, Supervisor Options.

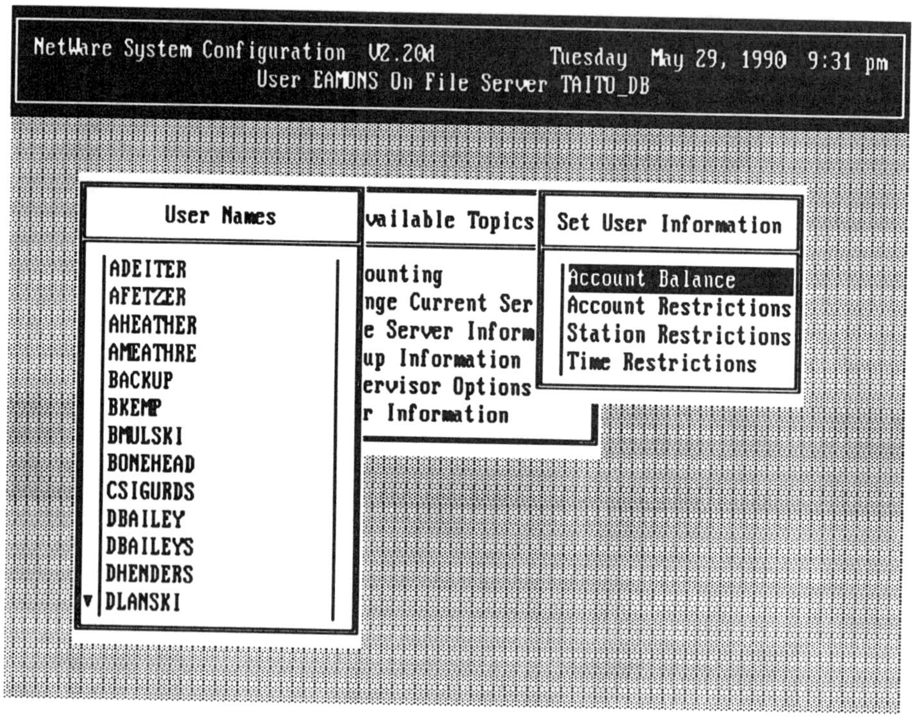

Figure 11.6B SYSCON Menu Utility, Set User Information.

If you have forgotten to do this template or you are working on an existing system, you can still set these options for multiple users. Move to the User Names window and mark the users you want to affect with the F5 key, an option allowing you to do all users at once. Now when you press ←┘, one of the options you can modify is account/password restrictions (See Fig. 11.7.)

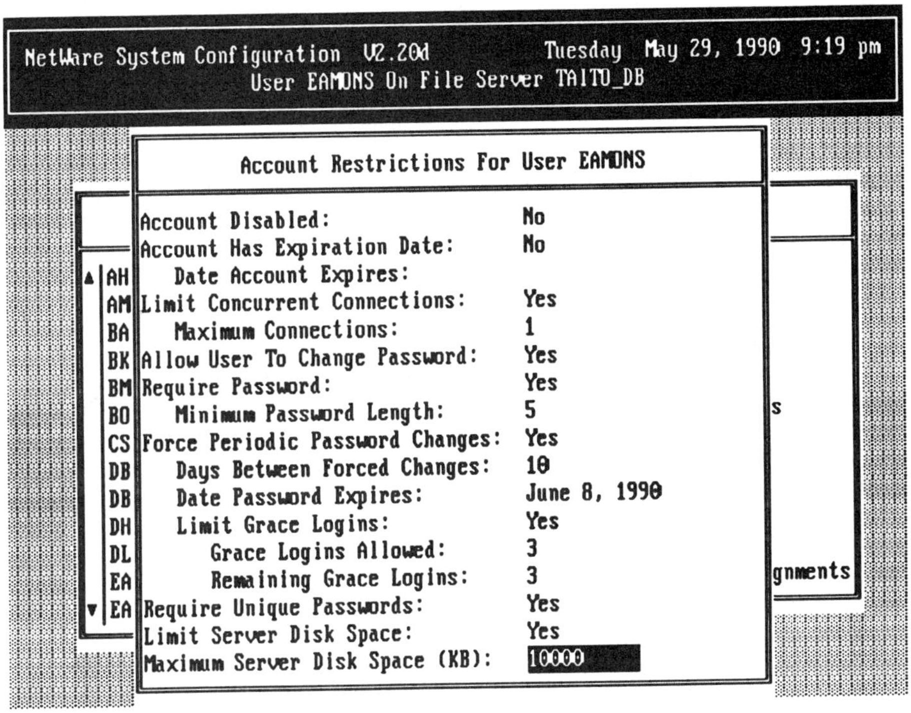

Figure 11.7 SYSCON Menu Utility, Account Restrictions for User (user name selected will appear).

Also, if you enable accounting, these should appear

allow unlimited credit,
low balance limit,
account balance.

Default Account Balance/Restrictions. The choices have been indented for a reason. The items furthest to the left are "Yes" "No" responses. If you answer "Yes" you must specify a variable on the line(s) below which have been indented.

NetWare's Account Balance restrictions settings give you the ability to control the resources utilized by the user. You can specify account balance, unlimited credit, low balance limit, password, and login restrictions.

> **NOTE:** Use these options with caution! For example, if you set up accounting and do not monitor the user's credit they can run out of funds. If the user is in the middle of a database sort when the account runs out of credit, the workstation will be cleared. This can result in datafile corruption.

Account Has Expiration Date: If you specify "yes" the user will be locked out of the network after the expiration date. For example, if you were asked to setup a contract employee on the system, you could set the expiration date for the projected end of their assignment.

> Date Account Expires: You will only be able to fill in this option if you have answered "Yes" to the one previous. NetWare will prompt you to enter the date.

Limit Concurrent Connections: With this option you can limit the total number of concurrent workstation(s) the user can LOGIN at. For example, if you have a careless user that logs in to a variety of workstations with out logging out from previous logins, you may wish to limit the user to one connection. They will be forced to logout from one station before logging in to another. If you answer "Yes," you will have to indicate the number of connections.

> Maximum Connections: Enter the number of the total concurrent logins that you wish the user to have, the minimum is one.

Require Password: If you wish to disable NetWare's password security set this to "No." If you choose "Yes," you have other options you can specify

> Minimum Password Length: Choose the number of characters required for a password between one and 20. The recommended length is at least five to insure network security.

Force Periodic Password Changes: Specifying "No" means that the user will never be required to change their password. When specifying "Yes" NetWare will track the date of the last password change, and compare it to the current file server date. If the date has expired when the user logs in, they will be prompted to change their password. If you answer "Yes," you will have to fill in the following variables.

Days Between Forced Changes: Enter the number of days here. When the time has expired, NetWare will force the user to change their password.

Limit Grace Logins: This option allows you to specify the number of times the user can ignore the prompt to change their password. Eventually the user will run out of grace periods and will be locked out of the system. If you enter "Yes" for Limit Grace Logins, you will have to specify the number of grace periods.

Grace Logins Allowed: Fill in the number allowed, three is recommended. This will allow a user to login three times without changing their password after it has expired.

Remaining Grace Logins: This tracks the setting you have specified in Grace Logins Allowed previously, and it automatically resets to the full number allowed after the password has been changed. This feature is designed to enforce password changes, and will not allow a user to login if they use up the grace logins.

Require Unique Passwords: If you choose "Yes," the system tracks the user's last eight passwords. A user must enter a unique password when changing the password at the command line, or when forced to change their password.

Limit Disk Space: This is specified when you install NetWare, and will only appear if you entered "Yes" at the time of installation. This option prevents users from using up the entire hard disk storage space.

Maximum Disk Space: Enter the number of blocks (of 4 KB bytes) in the blank beside this option.

Options That Will Only Appear if NetWare's Accounting Has Been Implemented

Allow Unlimited Credit: Like a charge account which grants "credit," users can be allocated allowable usage or access to the system, with no limit. Think of this as a gold credit card to the system.

Account Balance: This option allows you to specify a balance which operates the same as a spending limit. Operating the same as a bank statement, "Account Balance" tracks the descending balance of the limited credit you have allocated to a user.

Low Balance Limit: If "credit" is limited, the amount of credit granted will decrease as the user accesses the network. The same as overdraft protection at a bank, this option will allow a user to use more credit than they are allocated. A negative number will allow the user to spend more credit than they have been allocated.

How to Assign Time Restrictions

Time Restrictions is an option that allows you to specify the days and hours in a week that a user(s) can LOGIN to the network. To invoke this option, move to the TIME RESTRICTIONS option and press ←┘. Move your cursor to the day you wish to restrict and hold down the space bar. Notice how it removes the asterisks. Any blank spaces represent times they can not login to the system. If you wish to restrict multiple days, you can use your F5 key to mark the days and hours that you do not wish the user to login from. As with the account/password restrictions option, a template can be built in the Supervisors Options Window, or Multiple users may be selected from your user names window with the F5 key. Then time restrictions can be set up for multiple users (See Fig. 11.8.)

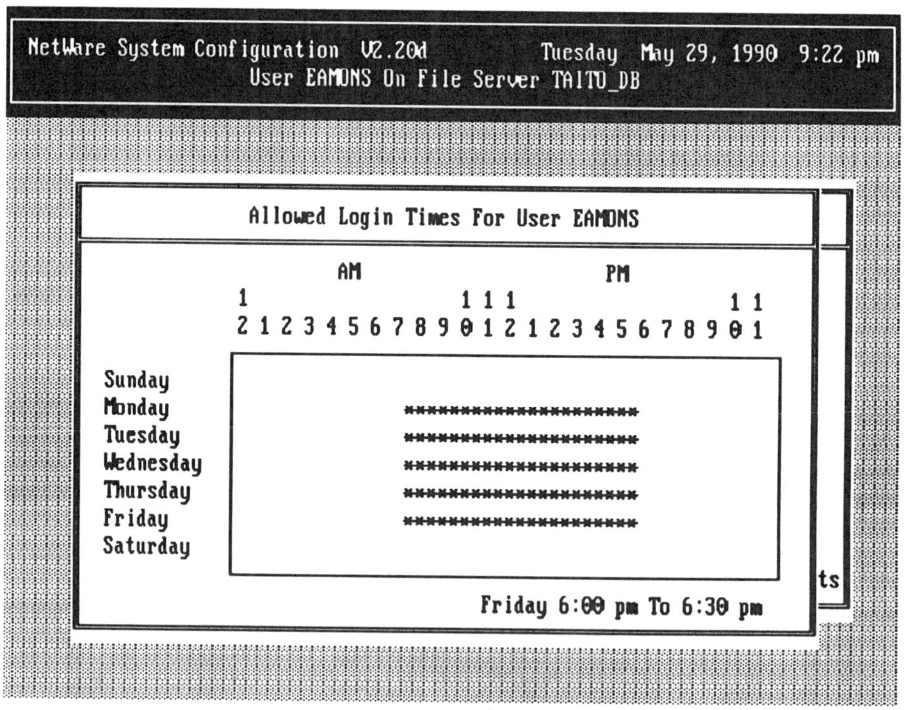

Figure 11.8 SYSCON Menu Utility, Allowed Login Times For User (user name selected will appear).

How to Assign Station Restrictions

Move to the STATIONS RESTRICTION option and press ↵.

This option allows you to limit the stations at which a user can login. To activate this restriction, you need to specify a network ID number (assigned to the file server NIC during installation), and a workstation address. Both addresses can be found using the USERLIST/E from the command line prompt at the workstation in question.

If you have not already found the addresses with the USERLIST/e command or another means, then exit SYSCON and type this command. Now go back into SYSCON, user information, user name, STATION RESTRICTIONS and press ↵. Now press <insert> and enter the network address. The system will prompt you to "allow login from all stations." You will need to answer no to this and then enter in the station address. You have now restricted this user to only logging in from the station you have specified (See Fig. 11.9.)

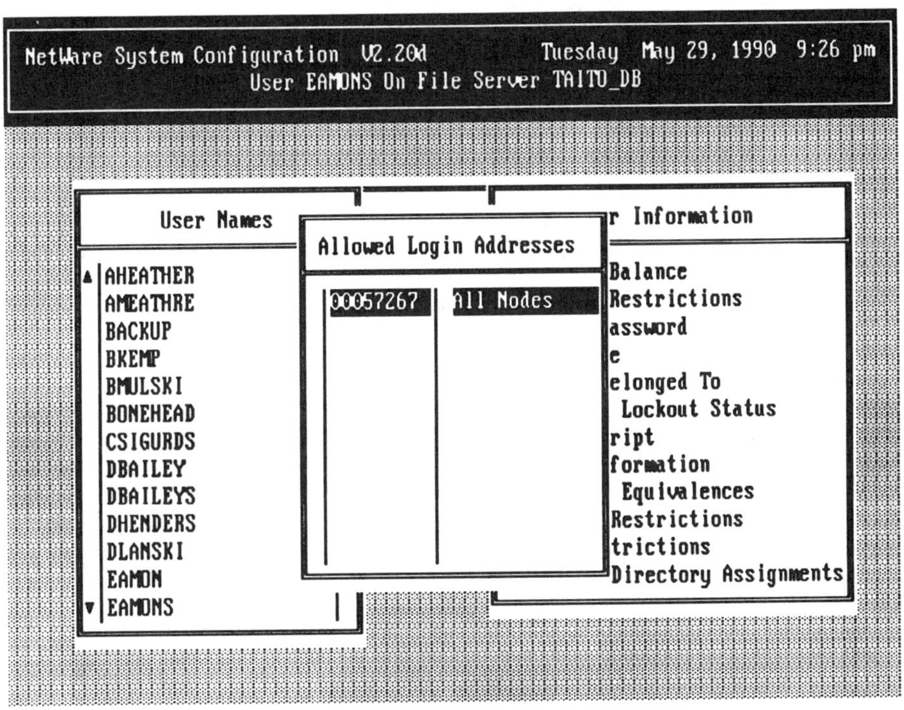

Figure 11.9 SYSCON Menu Utility, Allowed Login Addresses (per user).

Working with the Supervisor Options Window (See Fig. 11.10.)

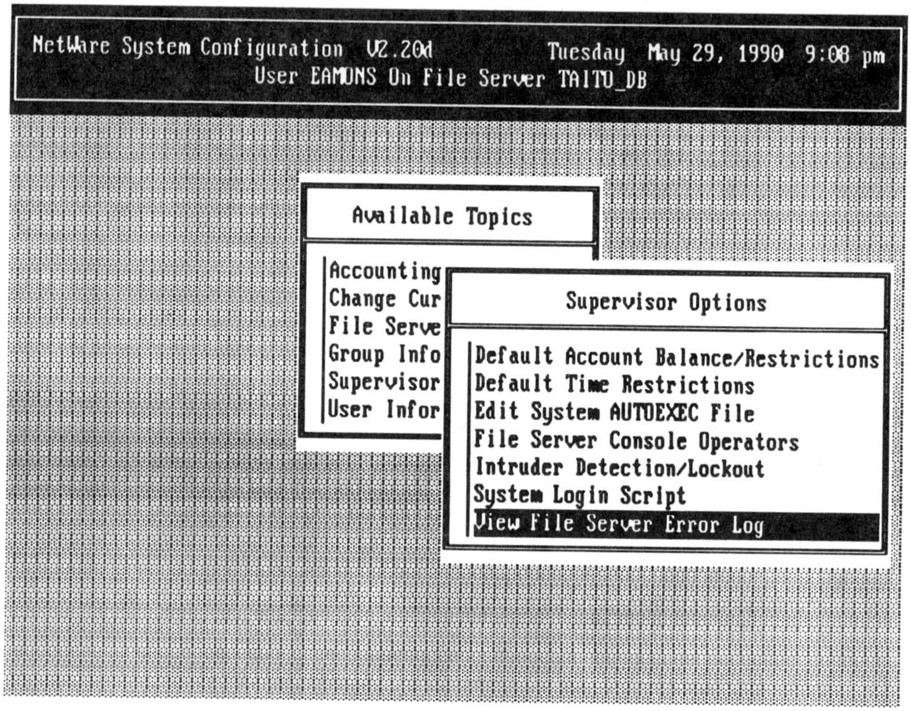

Figure 11.10 SYSCON Menu Utility, Supervisor Options.

The DEFAULT ACCOUNT BALANCE RESTRICTIONS menu (See Fig. 11.11,) is used to create a template of the account restrictions options that are discussed earlier in this chapter under user information. This is most useful if you have not created any of your users (a new system). Whatever you specify in this template will be assigned to any "new" users created after this template, automatically. For example, you may wish to force all users to have a password, with a minimum number of characters. A minimum of 5 characters are recommended to maintain security.

NOTE: Press the F1 (help) key for more information on each option.

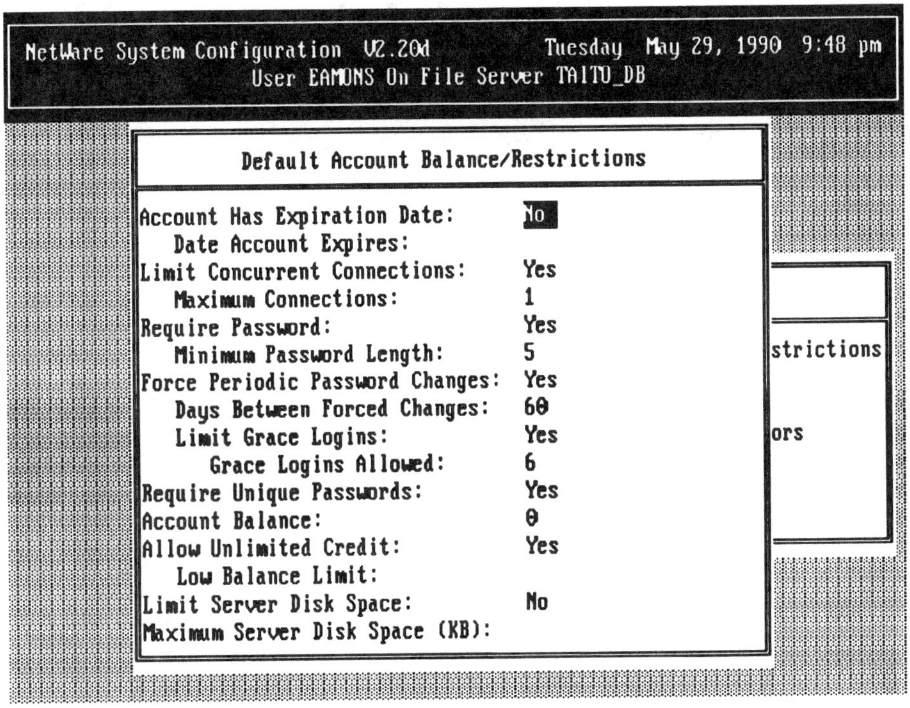

Figure 11.11 SYSCON Menu Utility, Default Account Balance/Restrictions.

The DEFAULT TIME RESTRICTIONS option is also a template (See Fig. 11.12.) Again, anything specified in this screen will be automatically assigned to any users created after this template. With this option you could restrict any of your users from logging in during your backup period or during weekends. The asterisks represent when you CAN login to the system.

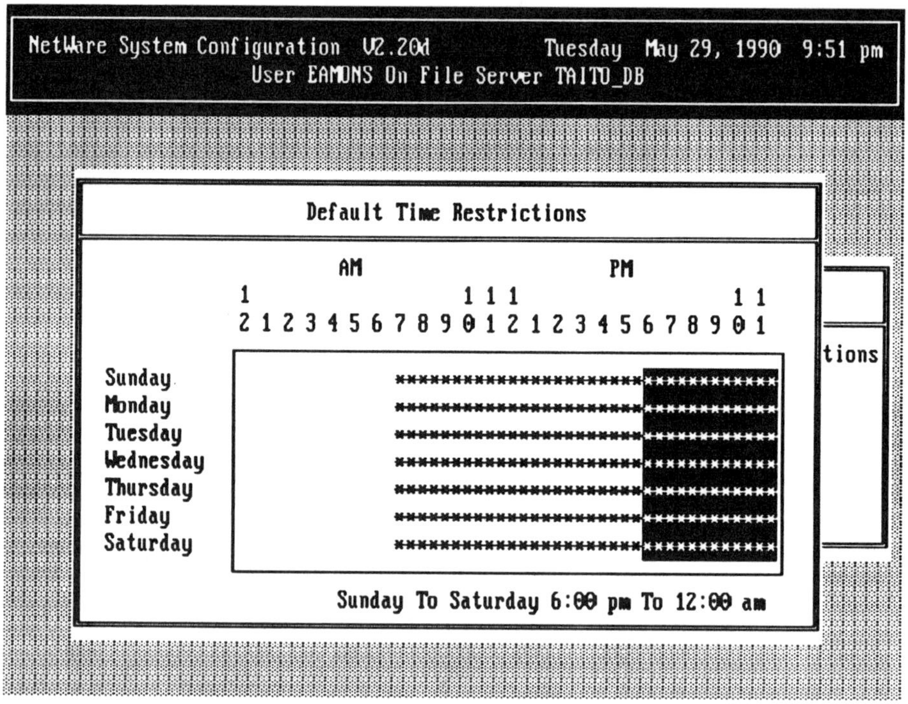

Figure 11.12 SYSCON Menu Utility, Default Time Restrictions.

The EDIT SYSTEM AUTOEXEC FILE option allows you to create an autoexec.bat file for your file server (See Fig. 11.13.) This is discussed in great detail in another section, (See Part 2, REFERENCE, Printing with NetWare). If you press F1 (help) you will get a sample autoexec file. Remember that unlike a DOS autoexec, this file must contain valid **console** commands. The escape key will save anything you type in this screen, if you answer "yes" to the prompt "save changes?"

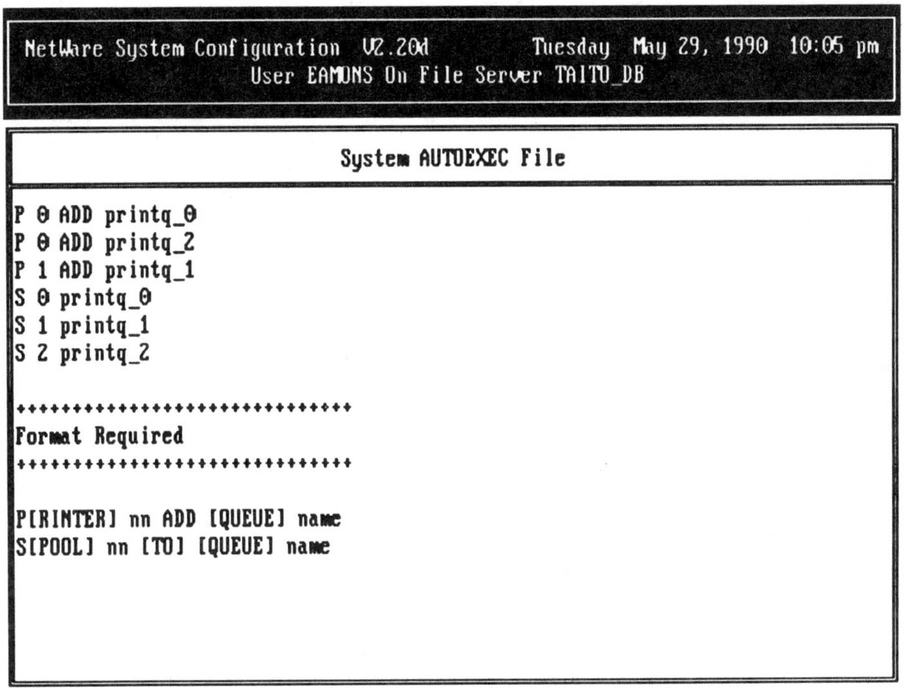

Figure 11.13 SYSCON Menu Utility, System AUTOEXEC File.

The FILE SERVER CONSOLE OPERATORS option allows you to create or view the console operators specified on your system (See Fig. 11.14.) Console operators are those users assigned in this window that can run the FCONSOLE utility. FCONSOLE allows a user to run the file server's many console functions from their workstations. Systems personnel and programmers are the users that you typically assign this status to. Supervisors and equivalence already have the right to run the FCONSOLE utility therefore you do not need to assign this status to these users. To grant a user console operator status hit your <insert> key. This will bring a list of all the users and groups on the system, to the screen. Use your arrow keys to move you to the user you wish to select and press ↵. If you wish to select multiple users, mark those you want with the F5 key and then press ↵ to save your selection.

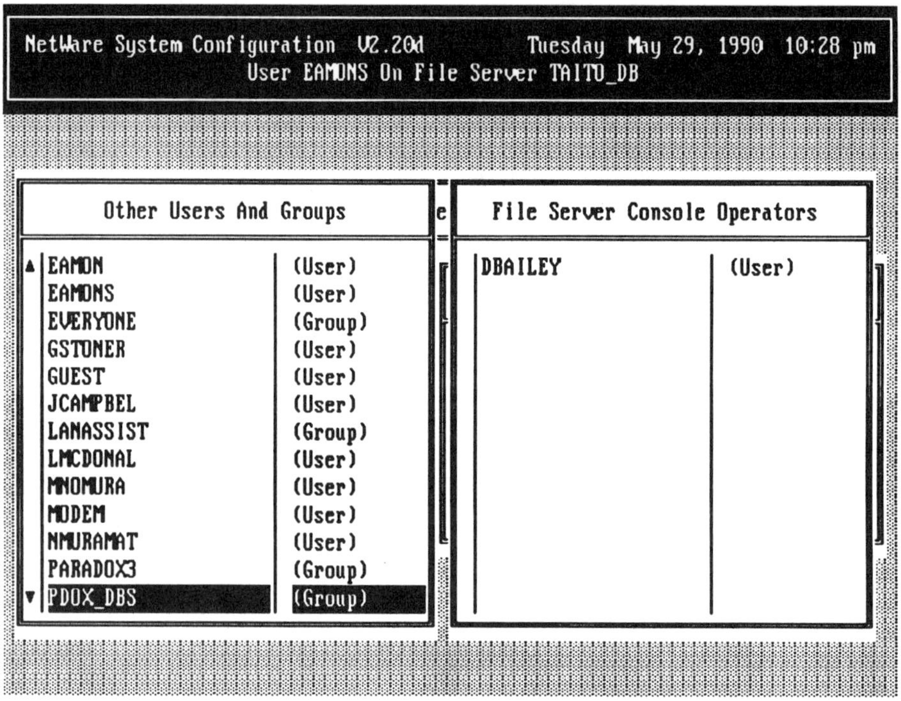

Figure 11.14 SYSCON Menu Utility, File Server Console Operators.

The INTRUDER DETECTION/LOCKOUT option is used to invoke intruder detection on your system (Fig. 11.15.) Intruders are detected by the monitoring of incorrect password attempts. As Supervisor, you can specify the number of attempts users have to correctly type in their password. You can also specify the amount of time their account will be locked if the number of attempts has been used up. To get into a system, hackers try random passwords until they are successful. By setting up this option, you can protect your system from this occurrence. You might want to specify 3 to 5 attempts at a password. After these have been tried the system will lock the user's account. It will send a message to the file server, write a message in the file server error log, and direct a response to the "view intruder detection option under user information." The account will then be locked for whatever time you have specified, this may be days, hours, or minutes.

Keep in mind that the intruder detection will lock out users who have forgotten or incorrectly typed in their passwords. If this occurs then Supervisor will have to enable the user's account.

> **NOTE:** Use with caution! An intruder can effectively lock the entire system if they attempt to LOGIN as all of the users, including Supervisor. Our recommendation is that you specify a relatively short time period to lock the system AND have a back door to Supervisor. This means another user who is Supervisor equivalence. This way only if both accounts were attempted, would they be locked.
>
> Unlike the templates discussed in the other options of SUPERVISOR OPTIONS window this option is set up for the entire system. We repeat, THIS IS NOT A TEMPLATE, ANYTHING SET UP HERE AFFECTS THE ENTIRE SYSTEM IMMEDIATELY.

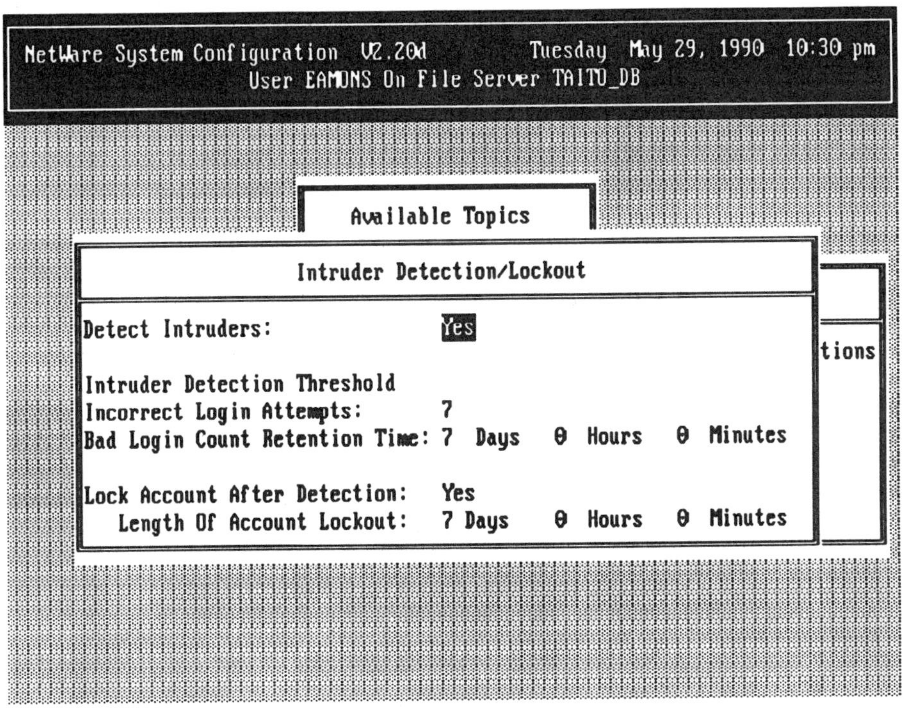

Figure 11.15 SYSCON Menu Utility, Intruder Detection/Lockout.

The SYSTEM LOGIN SCRIPT option allows supervisors to create a login script that will execute system wide. The login script is a set of instructions that directs workstations to perform specific actions when users log in to the network. As supervisor, you can create a system-wide login script (which is the same for all users on the network) that instructs all workstations to perform the same actions when users log in. Only supervisor/equivalent may create or modify the system login script.

> **NOTE:** Please refer to the Login Script explanation later on in this chapter, and review the examples.

The VIEW FILE SERVER ERROR LOG option allows you to view or delete the log of errors that have occurred on the system. Fragmented packets errors and intruder detections are the types of errors that will be listed in this file.

The FILE SERVER INFORMATION window informs you of the type and version of NetWare you have running. It displays the network and node address of the file server. The rest of the information in this screen has little value.

11.2 USING THE FILER MENU UTILITY

The FILER utility gets its name from its principal function of working with files. It is also useful for working with directories and subdirectories (See Fig. 11.16.)

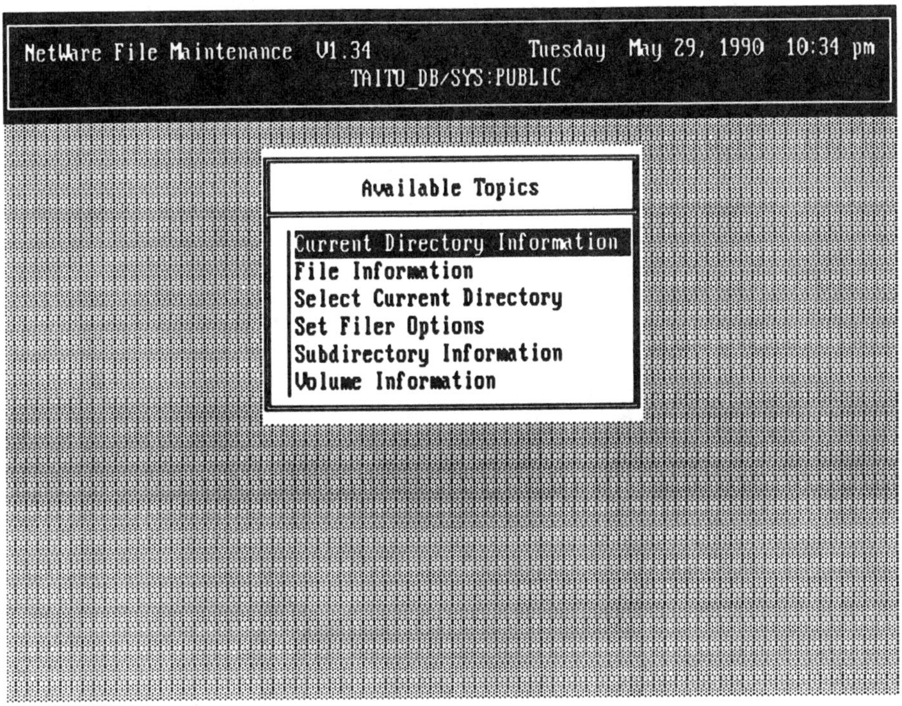

Figure 11.16 FILER Menu Utility, Available Topics (Main Menu).

Filer Options

FILER allows you to accomplish a variety of important functions. With the FILER utility, you can perform a variety of functions with directories/subdirectories, files, and volumes.

11.2.1 Directories/Subdirectories

FILER allows you to perform a variety of functions for directories/subdirectories, which allows you to

- **determine, and change the current directory/subdirectory path while working in filer,**
- **determine the creation date and time** of the current directory/subdirectory, as well as other directory/subdirectory information,
  - **view the "effective rights mask,"**
  - **determine the "maximum rights mask" directory rights,**
  - **determine the owner of the directory/subdirectory,**
- designate a directory include/exclude patterns.

11.2.2 Working With Files

FILER is especially useful in performing a variety of functions for files, which allows you to

- **list the files,**
- **determine the file attributes (flags),**
- **change or delete file attributes,**
- determine the file creation date,
- determine the file size,
- determine the owner (the specific user who created it) of the file,
- determine when the file was last accessed,
- determine the time and date that the file was last modified,
- determine the time and date that the file was last archived,
- designate that a file cannot be deleted without a confirmation, while working in filer,
- designate that a file cannot be copied without a confirmation, while working in filer,
- designate that a file cannot be overwritten without a confirmation, while working in filer,
- designate that a file will be an execute only file,
- specify to search for system and hidden files and designate a file include/exclude pattern,
- **index large files,**

NOTE: Bold items are those you will use most frequently.

11.2.3 View Volume Information

FILER will allow you to view volume information.

Directory Structure Exercise (using FILER)

A good grasp of directory structures is vital to working with NetWare. If you do not understand directory structures, either a DOS book, or a DOS course is recommended.

These exercises have been included to allow you a hands on practice, in which you will

- create directories,
- copy a file and rename files,
- assign trustee rights to a directory,
- view the volume information options,

Step 1. Access FILER by typing FILER at the command line, and pressing ↵ .

Step 2. Move to SELECT CURRENT DIRECTORY
(use the arrow keys and press ↵)

Step 3. Change the current directory to sys: and press ↵ .
Notice the change at the top of the window. You are now in the sys: volume which acts as the root directory.

Step 4. Now you are going to create a directory that will contain home (private) directories for your users. To do this, move to SUBDIRECTORY INFORMATION and press ↵ . Now press <insert> and add the word users.

Step 5. Now use your <escape> key to move you back to the main window "available topics." Move to the SELECT CURRENT DIRECTORY option and press ↵ . Change the current directory to sys:users and press ↵ . Move down to the SUBDIRECTORY INFORMATION window and press ↵ . Now press <insert> and add your name to create a private directory for yourself. Use the ↵ to save your entry. Exit FILER using the Escape <Esc> key. <Alt> <F10> will also allow you to escape from any NetWare menu utility, however you need to save your changes first.

Step 6. You are going to create a file in this subdirectory. You can do this with a DOS command or your favorite text editor. To use COPY CON, type COPY CON TEST at the command line in the subdirectory you have just created and press ↵ . Type any line such as test document, press ↵ , and enter a ^Z using the <Ctrl> and <Z> keys together, and press ↵ . When you have a document called TEST in the new subdirectory, return to FILER, as in step 1.

Step 7. Next you are going to copy the file you just created called TEST to the users directory. To do this, you will need to move to the correct subdirectory. Use the SELECT CURRENT DIRECTORY option on the main window "available topics" to move you there, if you are not there already. Then move to the FILE INFORMATION option on the available topics window and press ↵ . Find the file name "TEST" and press ↵ . Notice the option to copy files. Press ↵ on this option and it will ask you for the destination. This is when you specify SYS:USERS and press ↵ . At this point you can change the name of the file that is being copied into the users directory.

Step 8. Now check to make sure the file got copied. To do this, use the SELECT CURRENT DIRECTORY option on the "available topics" window. This will allow you to move into the user's directory.

Step 9. Now you will move to the FILE INFORMATION option and select it. You should see the file TEST. Rename the file TEST, using the <F3> function key.

Step 10. Now you are going to assign two trustees (users) to your sys:users subdirectory. Next, move to the CURRENT DIRECTORY INFORMATION option in the main window "available topics" and press ↵ . Move to the trustees option and press ↵ . Now press <insert> mark and add any two users.

Step 11. You are now going to assign these trustees ROSC to your directory. To do this press ↵ and then <insert>. Remove the rights that you do not want, with the delete key or mark and delete with F5. Normally you would not give rights at the users directory. Remember that trustee rights flow down. This means that the two users you gave rights to at sys:users would have those same rights at any directories below users, unless you specifically revoked them below.

Step 12. This is to familiarize yourself with the VOLUME INFORMATION option. Move to this option and press ←┘ . What information can you find that is of use to you as a supervisor?

Step 13. Unless you wish to keep this directory and the test files created, remove both the files and the new directory using FILER. Remember housekeeping is important to maintain an orderly directory and file structure.

Optional Filer Practice

This section has been included to give you some hands-on practice of the less used FILER features.

Step 1. Go to the File information option (Available Topics window). Press ←┘ and try some of the options.

Step 2. This is to familiarize yourself with the SET FILER OPTIONS. Move to that option and press ←┘ and now check the help (F1) key. Read the screens and try some of the options. The options in this window are only applicable while you remain in filer. In other words, the choices you make here are not permanent. Any changes invoked while in these window will be set back to the defaults when you leave filer. These options would only be used if you were doing a large clean up of your directory/file structure. The one you may use the most is the search attributes. This will allow you to search for system and hidden files while in filer.

12 LOGIN SCRIPTS

In this chapter

Utilizing Login Scripts, Identifier Variables.

12.1 UTILIZING LOGIN SCRIPTS

Login scripts are an extremely important tool you can use to structure the configuration and environment your users will need to operate efficiently on the network. The login script is a set of instructions that directs workstations to perform specific actions when users LOGIN to the network.

SYSTEM: As supervisor, you can create a system-wide login script that instructs all workstations to perform the same actions when users LOGIN. Only supervisor or equivalent may create or modify the system login script.

USER: Supervisor or individual users may also create a user login script. User login scripts specify drive mapping's and other information needed only by the individual user. (Login scripts are only executed when users login to the first file server. Users do not access a second login script when they attach to another file server.) Users have rights to modify their own login scripts.

There are four different login scripts, and each has a distinct purpose

Default Login Script

- created by NetWare when the system is installed,
- executes when a user script does not exist,
- sets up basic mappings for the system,

- cannot be edited.

NOTE: Contained in the login file located in SYS:LOGIN directory.

System Login Script

- a system wide script,
- created in syscon under Supervisor Options,
- executed when any user logs in.

NOTE: Contained in the file NET$LOG.DAT in SYS:PUBLIC.

User Login Scripts

- created in syscon under User information,
- contains mapping's and commands that are customized for that user

NOTE: Login Scripts are stored in a file called login located in SYS:MAIL/USER_ID.

NetWare uses the following logic questions to determine which login scripts will execute

Is there a system login script?
Is there a user login script?

In response to these questions the four following possibilities exist

DEFAULT	SYSTEM DEFAULT	SYSTEM USER	USER
N/N	Y/N	Y/Y	N/Y

The Default Script

```
WRITE "Good %GREETING_TIME, %LOGIN_NAME."
MAP DISPLAY OFF
MAP ERRORS OFF
Remark: Set 1st drive to most appropriate directory.
MAP *1:=SYS:; *1:=SYS:%LOGIN_NAME
IF "%1"="SUPERVISOR" THEN MAP *1:=SYS:SYSTEM
```

```
Remark:  Set search drives (S2:machine-os dependent).
MAP S1:=SYS:PUBLIC; S2:=S1:%MACHINE/%OS/%OS_VERSION
Remark:  Now display all the current drive settings.
MAP DISPLAY ON
MAP
```

To understand the default script, refer to the sections that follow "Identifier Variables," and "Most Common Login Script Commands."

12.2 IDENTIFIER VARIABLES

Following are the variables that can be used in Login scripts to designate

HOUR	Hour of day or night (1-12)
HOUR 24	Hour (00-23)
MINUTE	Minute (00-59)
SECOND	Second (00-59)
AM_PM	Day or night (am or pm)
MONTH	Month number (01-12)
MONTH_NAME	Month name (January, February etc.)
DAY	Day number (01-31)
NDAY_OF_WEEK	Weekday number (1-7, Sunday = 1)
YEAR	Year in full format (1983, 2016)
SHORT_YEAR	Year in short form (83, 16, etc.)
DAY_OF_WEEK	Day of week (Monday, Friday, etc.)
LOGIN_NAME	User's unique login name
STATION	Workstation number
P_STATION	Physical station (12 hex digits)
GREETING_TIME	Morning, afternoon, or evening
SHELL_TYPE	Shell type number (0, 27, 3, etc.)
NEW_MAIL	Yes or No, indicating whether or not new mail has arrived from NetWare's mail program. Your mailbox is checked automatically when you log in, and the correct value is assigned.
OS	The workstation's operating system, that is MSDOS
OS_VERSION	The version number of the workstations's DOS
MACHINE	The machine which the shell was written for, that is, IBM_PC
SMACHINE	Short machine name ie: IBM
ERROR_LEVEL	A value; for example zero = no errors or any number other than zero = errors

MEMBER_OF_GROUPNAME . . . Name of group

Most Common Login Script Commands

Listed are the commands you will use most often in Login Scripts. While this is not a complete list, you will probably need only those we have explained.

MAP: This command is the most important one used in login scripts. It is used in much the same way as in the command line. In a login script, however, a variable (identifier) may be substituted (see list of identifiers).

```
MAP F:=SYS:USERS/%LOGIN_NAME
MAP G:=SYS:DATA/SALES
MAP S1:=SYS:PUBLIC
MAP S2:=SYS:PUBLIC/DOS/%OS_VERSION
MAP S3:=SYS:APPLIC/WP
```

NOTE: You must have a search drive to public, and a comspec command in the login scripts.

ATTACH: Used to connect to additional file servers without interrupting the current execution of the login script. You can specify file server, username, and password. We recommend that you do not include the semicolon (;) and password in the attach command but rather have the system prompt the user on attachment. If the password is in the login script this file will have to be changed every time the user changes their password.

```
ATTACH FS3/KIM;LAND
```

COMSPEC: You must tell NetWare how to find the correct DOS directory and version for each workstation and DOS version. To do this, you must create a search drive in the system login script and use the COMSPEC command to have the COMMAND.COM file reloaded properly in workstations. (Some application software will write over COMMAND.COM in memory, and therefore, the system will need to find it when exiting an application.)

```
COMSPEC=A:COMMAND.COM      (OR)
COMSPEC=C:\COMMAND.COM     (OR)
MAP S2:=SYS:PUBLIC/%MACHINE/%OS/%OS_VERSION
COMSPEC=S2:COMMAND.COM
```

NOTE: It is always easier to use only one DOS version network wide whenever possible.

DISPLAY: Display the contents of a specified text file on your workstation screen during the login process. This file might contain system messages or company messages for the day (someone's birthday, meetings scheduled, board room schedule, etc.). Suppose the supervisor puts messages in a public "bulletin board" file, (SYS:PUBLIC/BULLETIN/NEWS.TXT) this command would be necessary in the login script.

DISPLAY SYS:PUBLIC/BULLETIN/NEWS.TXT

NOTE: If the directory does not exist or the file is not found, no error message will appear on users screens when they log in.

FDISPLAY: FDISPLAY is used as a filter. The previous example is the same, only the command is now FDISPLAY. This means printer or word processing codes will not be displayed on the screen, otherwise, they would appear as "garbage characters."

DOS SET: Used to SET a variable in the DOS workstation environment to a specified value.

SET PROMPT ="PG"

DRIVE: Used to specify a default drive other than the first network drive, for the user to exit to, from the login script.

DRIVE J:

EXIT: Used to terminate the execution of the login script. This command allows you to execute BATCH files and also DOS commands such as DIR.

EXIT "GOMENU"

EXTERNAL PROGRAM: Executes a program that is external to the login script. This command can be used to execute applications such as mail from within your login script. The first character of this command must be a # sign. The file it is executing must be a .com or .exe. This command can also be used to redirect printing to the network printers with the capture command. This command must appear after your search drives have been mapped, otherwise, NetWare will not know where to find the .exe or .com files.

```
#CAPTURE P=1
```

FIRE PHASERS: "Treckie" fans this one is for you! This command activates the beep the number of times you specify. Nine is the maximum times that phasers can be fired in one command. It can be used to alert users of the existence of new mail (Novell's mail system only). The mail package no longer ships with NetWare but is available separately.

```
IF NEW_MAIL ="YES" THEN FIRE 9
```

IF . . . THEN . . . END: The IF . . . THEN command is available to perform logical checks and processes with your login script. These checks are only executed if they are true. The AND qualifier is a valid condition. The OR qualifier is not valid. Nesting of IF statements is not valid. The greater than (>), less than (<), equal to (=), and not equal to (<>), are valid comparatives that can be used in the conditional statements. The identifier variables listed at the beginning of this section can be used in a conditional statement.

```
IF NEW_MAIL ="YES" THEN FIRE 5
IF NEW_MAIL ="YES" THEN BEGIN
FIRE 5
WRITE "YOU HAVE NEW MAIL"
END
```

PAUSE: This stops operation until any key is pressed.

WRITE: This will replace any of the identifier variables with the appropriate text and display any text that is in quotes. This is used to display messages on the screen, or blank lines.

```
WRITE "SYSTEM MAINTENANCE IS OCCURRING TODAY"
WRITE "Hi %LOGIN_NAME"
WRITE "Good %GREETING_TIME John"
```

System Login Script Example

```
MAP S1:=SYS:PUBLIC
MAP S2:=SYS:PUBLIC/%OS/%OS_VERSION
COMSPEC=S2:COMMAND.COM
MAP S3:=SYS:APPLIC/WORD
MAP S4:=SYS:APPLIC/MAIL
#CAPTURE P=1
FDISPLAY SYS:PUBLIC/BULLETIN/MSG.TXT
IF MEMBER OF "SALES" THEN FDISPLAY SYS:SALES/MSGS.TXT
IF NEW_MAIL="YES" THEN #MAIL
```

User Login Script Example

```
MAP DISPLAY OFF
MAP F:=SYS:USERS/%LOGIN_NAME
MAP G:=SYS:SALES/WORD
MAP H:=SYS:SALES/DFLEX
WRITE "GOOD %GREETING_TIME %LOGIN_NAME"
WRITE
WRITE
WRITE
FIRE 4
WRITE "SMILE...TODAY IS A NEW DAY"
PAUSE
SET PROMPT="$P$G"
EXIT "START"
```

User Login Script Practice

This practice has been included to give you a hands-on session creating a login script for yourself. This will help you become familiar with some of the possibilities of the user login script.

> **NOTE: Be sure to create a user login script not a system login script.** System scripts affect all users and this might not be recommended for an exercise in a live network. The directories used in this example must be created in filer or DOS in order for this exercise to work.

Enter SYSCON, go to USER INFORMATION and press ↵. Find your user name (not SUPERVISOR) and press ↵. Move to login script and press ↵. You now have an on-screen editor available to you. To save press <escape>. Enter in the following lines.

Step 1.

```
MAP S1:=SYS:PUBLIC
MAP F:=SYS:USERS/%LOGIN_NAME
MAP G:=SYS:USERS
MAP
```

Save changes and exit
LOGOUT and LOGIN again to notice changes. A LOGIN is an implied LOGOUT.

Step 2.

```
WRITE "GOOD %GREETING_TIME, %LOGIN_NAME"
WRITE
WRITE
WRITE "I THINK YOU ARE GREAT!"
WRITE "THUS I AM HERE TO SERVE YOU"
```

Save changes and exit.
LOGIN again to notice changes.

Step 3.

```
IF DAY_OF_WEEK = "replace this with the day" THEN BEGIN
WRITE "STAFF MEETING TODAY!"
WRITE "IT IS IN BOARDROOM A AT 12:00 NOON SHARP"
WRITE "DON'T BE LATE....WE WILL BE OFFERING LUNCH"
END
```

Save changes and exit.
LOGIN again to notice changes.

13 USING NETWARE'S MENUS

In this chapter:

Creating User Menus, A Sample Menu, How to Create a Menu, Using Variables in Commands, Working with Subwindows, Running the Menu, Sample Menu.

13.1 CREATING USER MENUS

NetWare has a menu utility that allows users and supervisors to create windowed menu programs. These menus are ASCII text files that may created with any ASCII text editor. The text files may not contain formatting characters of any kind.

13.1.1 A Sample Menu

```
%MAIN MENU
A) WORD PROCESSING
   F:
   WORD
   G:
B) SPREADSHEET
   H:
   123
   G:
C) MAIL
   MAIL
D) FUN
   NCSNIPES
E) LOGOUT
   !LOGOUT
```

NOTE: The exclamation mark (!) in front of the logout command is necessary. In this sample menu, Titles, such as Word Processing, and Fun are options, and WORD, 123, etc. are the commands for starting the applications.

13.1.2 How to Create a Menu

1. You will need to create this file with an ASCII text editor. The file must have an extension of .MNU.

2. There are a few types of statements that the menu must contain. They are

Title	(%Main Menu) % identifies a title
Options	(Word Processing) displayable statements
Commands	(WORD) Executable commands-indented

3. Title: You can also position your windows and set the color through IBM's color palette. This is part of your title statement.

   %MAIN MENU,5,10,2

   This would place the center of the window on row five, column ten with the color palette two, if using a color monitor. If you do not include any of these parameters, the default is to the center of the screen vertically and horizontally with the color palette set to zero.

   Vertical placement: Lines are measured from the top of the screen to the center of the menu. The line value you specify should equal the number of lines you want above the menu plus half the length of the menu.

   Horizontal placement: Columns are measured from the left edge of the screen to the center of the menu. The value you specify should equal the number of columns to the left of the menu plus half the width of the menu.

4. Options: These statements allow the user to see a displayable option on the screen from which to choose. These may be for word processing, mail, games, DOS commands, and so on.

   WORD PROCESSING

5. Commands: Commands follow the options statement. The command is what gets executed when the user presses ↵ on the option displayed. These commands must be indented at least one position

```
WORD PROCESSING
        WORD
MAIL
        MAIL
```

13.1.3 Using Variables in Commands

Command lines in the DOS (ASCII) text file are not limited to single commands. Several parameters can be combined to expand the command. DOS's COPY command is an example of this. Parameters such as source directory and destination directory can be used to create a "string."

By numbering the variables (such as a destination drive or a filename) as @1, @2, @3, and so on, will enable you to keep the value and repeat it in a further command. By doing it this way, the command does not need to be repeated. Every time you include that variable (@1, @2, etc.) in the command string, it will automatically keep the same value. Any command not indented is recognized as a new command and will reset the values of variables until they are again redefined.

EXAMPLE

```
COPY
     COPY @1 "ENTER SOURCE DRIVE/FILENAME" @2"ENTER
     DESTINATION"
     DIR/W @1
     DIR/W @2
     PAUSE
```

In this example, the program copies a file from one drive (directory) to another and then displays the directory for each drive. The following displays the process.

1. The variable @1 displays the message "Enter source drive/filename" on the screen. The user then enters the appropriate drive and filename and presses ←┘.

2. The variable @2 displays the message "Enter destination." The user enters the destination drive and presses ←┘. This creates a string for the menu system: COPY C:sam f:.

3. The COPY command then copies the file sam from drive C: to drive F:.

4. The program then proceeds to the next command in the string, DIR/W. Before executing this command, the program needs to know which drive to list. It finds this information through the value for @1 that was specified earlier for "Enter source drive." Therefore, the user does not need to enter a drive letter.

5. The program displays a directory listing of only the file sam for drive C:. Because you specified a filename in the @1 variable, only that file will be displayed.

6. The program then displays a directory listing of the destination drive (from the DIR/W command). Because the variable @2 is included after the second DIR/W command, the program knows that it should use the same value for @2 specified earlier for "enter destination" (drive F). Therefore, the user does not have to enter the drive letter. A directory of drive F is then displayed.

7. When the user presses any key, the program continues.

13.1.4 Working with SubWindows

You may want more than one window of options available for your user. You can group applications together in a separate window from your menu's main window. Your main window can have an option called APPLICATIONS which, when chosen calls up an additional window that the user would make their selection from. Your menu program would need to have a submenu (or subwindow) command in it.

Example

```
%JULIE'S MAIN MENU,5,10
APPLICATIONS
   %APPLICATION SELECTION
FUN
   NCSNIPES
LOGOUT
   !LOGOUT
%APPLICATION SELECTION
WORDPERFECT
   g:
   WP
   f:
PARADOX
   h:
   PARADOX3
   f:
LOTUS
   i:
```

```
        123
        f:
    MAIL
        MAIL
```

NOTE: The percent sign (%) has been used to identify the title of the main menu, it also indicates a submenu. The system then begins searching through the rest of the menu for an "exact" match for text following the percent sign (%). When it finds this symbol, the submenu is then brought to the screen with its displayable options. The exclamation point (!) in front of LOGOUT is necessary.

13.1.5 Running the Menu

There are two ways to execute a menu

- From the DOS prompt
  MENU filename (MENU Julie),
- From the login script
  EXIT "batch file" (EXIT "start").

NOTE: The batch file will be stored in a common directory or in a users home directory. It will contain

```
MENU filename
```

13.1.6 Sample Menu

```
%SAMPLE MENU,2,8
APPLICATIONS
    %APPLICATIONS
FUN
    NCSNIPES
MAIL
    MAIL
LOGOUT
    !LOGOUT
NETWARE UTILITIES
    %UTILITIES
%APPLICATIONS,20,10
```

```
WORDPERFECT
   F:
   WP
   G:
DBASE III
   H:
   DBASE
   G:
LOTUS
   I:
   123
   G:
%UTILITIES,15,10
NCOPY
   NCOPY @1"ENTER SOURCE" @2"ENTER DESTINATION"
   DIR/W @2
   PAUSE
DOS COMMAND
   @1 "ENTER DOS COMMAND"
   PAUSE
USERS LOGGED IN
   USERLIST
   PAUSE
WHO AM I
   WHOAMI/A
   PAUSE
```

NOTE: The user must have the rights ROSWCD in the directory from which they will be running the menu. The menu creates and deletes two temporary files (RESTART.000, and GO000.BAT). The error message if this is not set up correctly will be "File: MENUPARZ.EXE not found."

TEST IT . . . . LOGIN AS THE USER YOU HAVE STORED IT UNDER.

14 Optional Account Restrictions (Limiting Hard Disk Space)

In this chapter:

Introduction, Installation, Assigning Disk Space Restrictions to Users.

14.1 INTRODUCTION

Disk space on your network hard drive must be carefully managed for optimum usage. One of the tools provided by SFT NetWare V2.1x is the ability to limit the amount of hard drive space users can utilize. This is known as "disk resource limitation."

The default in NetWare is set to "not limit" hard drive space. This means that if you do not set limits, one user can conceivably use up the entire file server hard drive space. If you wish to utilize this option, you must activate it during installation of NetWare (NETGEN), miscellaneous maintenance.

Once you have activated this option through NETGEN, it will now appear in the SYSCON utility under Supervisor or User windows, as "Limit Disk Space." You can set this up for multiple users or just one user.

> **NOTE:** If you do not activate this during the installation of NETGEN, then the "limit disk space" option will not appear in SYSCON. This means that you would have to re-run NETGEN if you changed your mind.

14.2 INSTALLATION

After you have linked the NetWare operating system and file server utilities, the available options menu will again be displayed. If doing a hard drive install, you will need to exit NETGEN at this point. The installation must be continued at the file server and required files downloaded to floppies. NETGEN will prompt you for this. If doing any of the other choices of installation, carry on. Now you will select "Install with Custom Options." This option will allow you to do the following: modify the partition table on the system hard drive, modify the size of the hot fix redirection area, reinitialize the disk with new NetWare volumes; **change the default system configuration parameters and volume parameters (miscellaneous maintenance)**, change the network addresses and the number of communication buffers, and change the network printer configuration.

We are only interested at this time in "**Miscellaneous Maintenance**." You will now be changing the system configuration parameters (from the default settings). The option to limit disk space is the one we are addressing in this chapter. If the "Limit Disk Space" is set to "No," then the "Number of Bindery Objects" field will be blank. If the "Limit Disk Space" option was previously set to "Yes," the maximum number of bindery objects will be displayed.

Bindery objects are the users and groups defined on the file server. Limiting these objects allows the limitation of hard drive space. The number of bindery objects must be between 500 and 5000, inclusive. We recommend that you do not go with the default but raise it slightly. The larger the installation the larger the number of bindery objects that you should specify. This number can always be changed by going back through NETGEN, Miscellaneous Maintenance.

Change the limit disk space field to yes. To activate editing the bindery objects field, press the Enter key. Erase the default number of objects with the Backspace key and enter your choice.

14.3 ASSIGNING DISK SPACE RESTRICTIONS TO USERS

When assigning disk space for each user, two options are available, either when a user is being created, or later on

a. At initial setup of your system, you can modify a default template that will apply to all users created after this template. Do this in SYSCON, Supervisor Options, Default Account Restrictions window. Here any limit you specify, that is, 10 MB, will be applied to any user created after this screen,

b. If you have not already created your users or do not want the same amounts for all users, you can specify this either on an individual basis or mark a list of users to select. This is done in SYSCON, User Information. Either hit return for individual restrictions or use your F5 (mark) key and select any number of users. Then hit return on Account Restrictions.

NOTE: An error message indicating insufficient disk space will appear for any user who has reached the limit of their drive space allocation.

15 NETWARE'S ACCOUNTING

In this chapter:

Setting up NetWare's Accounting, Setting Up Charge Rates, Charge Rate Example, Using NetWare for Billing Purposes, Associated Commands.

15.1 SETTING UP NETWARE'S ACCOUNTING

The Accounting feature is not automatically installed, you must activate (install) it in SYSCON. Here is a list of the options that you have available through this utility

- You can track when each user logs in and out of the file server. This option is automatically initiated if you install accounting. An entry is placed in the file server's audit file each time a user logs in or out of the server. No charges are made to users by this option.

- Charging each user's account for resources consumed. You can decide which resources you want to charge for. They can be file server, print servers, job servers, or gateways.

- Tracking and charging users for services performed on the network.

- Charging users for the amount of file server disk space they are using. To charge for this use, you specify the amount that should be charged for each block of disk storage. You will also have to specify how often and at what times the file server should measure the disk space users are using and charge their accounts.

- You can also charge users for the amount of time they use the file server, as well as the amount of work they ask the file server to do. These are measured by the file server in four ways. They are

  the time the user is logged in,

  the amount of requests (reads) for data (programs and/or information) the user makes,

  the amount of data (write) requests (programs and/or information) made by a user,

  the number of requests the user makes of the file server.

All of this information is stored in a file called NET$ACCT.DAT.

15.2 SETTING UP CHARGE RATES

BLOCKS READ — This option allows you to set up charges for the amount of data users read. The charge is assigned per block read. One block is equal to 4096 bytes or 4 KB. You can charge different rates for different times of the day in ½ hour increments.

BLOCKS WRITTEN — Here you set up the charges for the amount of data written to the drives. Again this can be specified in ½ hour increments with the block size at 4 KB.

CONNECT TIME — This allows you to charge users for the amount of time they are logged in to a server. Also specified in ½ hour increments. The charge is assigned per minute.

DISK STORAGE This allows you to charge for each block (4 KB) that is stored on the drive for one day. The charge is assigned per block-day (the number of blocks stored in a day).

SERVICE REQUESTS These charges are for any service requests made. Again, multiple rates are supported in ½ hour increments, it is assessed per request received.

15.3 CHARGE RATE EXAMPLE

The main reason to implement NetWare's accounting is to monitor users network utilization. NetWare's accounting will track usage, if you want to produce billings, purchase a third-party billing program. These programs will allow you to bill users for their network usage. This management option will enable you to recover the capital cost of a network installation, or it can be used to allocate network costs by department.
You might decide to do this in either of the following situations

- You could charge other departments for their usage and recover your investment when many departments use the LAN and each has its own budget,
- If you have a shared office environment where many firms share the reception and secretarial pool, you could also share a LAN and provide billing for this service. This means that a firm could start a document and the secretarial pool could finish it and print it leaving the document in the firms directory, and you could bill for all of the time used for this project.

Once you have made the decision to implement accounting, you will need to determine the amount of money you wish to recover on a monthly basis.

First you should give all of your users "unlimited funds" on the network. This is the same as giving them a gold credit card to the system. This way you do not need to calculate their spending requirements. Then you will install accounting through SYSCON and set up charge rates of 1/1. The multiplier represents the total units to be charged back. The divisor represents the total estimated usage. The moment this option is installed, it will start accumulating some charges.

> **NOTE:** The charge rate of 1/1 will be used for monitoring the network usage and will not have any effect on actual charge rates. If you are using accounting only to monitor the system and not bill, this is sufficient and nothing else needs to be done.

15.4 USING NETWARE FOR BILLING PURPOSES

After the procedure described previously has been operating for about a month, you should run the supervisor command ATOTAL. This command is run from the SYS:SYSTEM directory and you must be logged in as supervisor, or equivalent. ATOTAL will give you for that month, a break down of the total connection time used, the total blocks read, and the total blocks written on the system. It will also give you the total disk storage used, and the total service requests. Now you will have some real figures to work from. Therefore, you can calculate new multipliers and divisors and give the users balances and low balance limits on their accounts.

EXAMPLE: You wish to recover an initial capital outlay of $54,000 within three years. This translates to a recovery requirement of $1500 per month, which must be considered when pricing out the options charged for each

- block read,
- block written,
- block-day of disk storage,
- service request,
- minute of connect time, or
- any combination of the options listed.

We are going to generate $1500 per month as follows:

- $500 from connection time,
- $500 from blocks read,
- $500 from blocks written.

You will need to apply this information and the totals generated by ATOTAL to the following formula suggested by Novell in their manuals to complete your billing calculations:

$$\frac{\text{(Total to be charged for service)}}{\text{(Estimated total usage of service)}} = \frac{\text{(Charge rate multiplier)}}{\text{(Charge rate divisor)}}$$

The result will give you the appropriate charge rates that you can set up in SYSCON. Novell gives you some excellent examples in their Supervisor Reference Manual-SYSCON: System Configuration section.

> **NOTE:** Keep in mind that usage will change from time to time so you will need to manage this based upon the figures given by ATOTAL.

15.5 ASSOCIATED COMMANDS

PAUDIT This command automatically sends all of the accounting information in the audit file NET$ACCT.DAT to the screen. This output can be redirected to a printer or a file, and edited using an appropriate editor.

After NetWare's accounting is installed, it tracks all login and logout transactions, as well as denied logins. Denied access can be as simple as a user making a mistake in his or her password, or it can be a record of NetWare refusing access to an intruder. In addition, it will give you a breakdown of your charges per user. This file collects a large amount of data so you may wish to delete it from time to time. If you have a billing program that is reading this information, deletion should not occur until after your billing period.

ATOTAL This utility will summarize the contents of the PAUDIT file NET$ACCT.DAT. ATOTAL generates a report compiling NetWare's accounting information and lists the following totals:

- blocks read,
- blocks written,
- connection time in minutes,
- service requests,
- disk storage in blocks per day.

16 Transaction Tracking System (TTS)

In this chapter

Introduction, Logical Record Locks, Physical Record Locks, Transactions, Explicit and Implicit Transactions, Setting up TTS, Setting the TTS Flag (File Attribute).

16.1 INTRODUCTION

Transaction Tracking System (TTS) available with SFT NetWare 2.X. tracks every transaction that has been marked (flagged) TTS, from its initiation to completion. Files with the TTS flag or attribute are referred to as "transactional files." It is usually not necessary to flag work and report files created and used by an application software package with the TTS file attribute. An example of a transaction could be an update to an inventory database. For example, a customer orders a part. This part is shipped thus removing it from the stock-level database file, and a packing slip is generated and kept track of in another file, while an invoice is produced for this customer affecting the customer's account and the accounts receivable file. All of this could be defined as a single transaction.

TTS ensures an "all or nothing" situation. In other words, all of the transaction would have to be completed and written to the file, or none of it is written. This prevents corrupted database files. TTS tracks all files that have been flagged and in the event of a workstation failure or a file server failure, during a transaction, the file server will request a "back out" to the last wholly completed transaction. This transaction would have to be re-entered but your database would remain intact including all system information and tables.

TTS accomplishes all of this through physical and logical record locks and the TTS attribute.

16.2 LOGICAL RECORD LOCKS

Record locking is an approach to limiting access of a specific portion of a file to one user at a time (See Part 1 CONCEPTS, Chap. 3 Software, Sec. 3.2 Software Basics for Stand-alone Workstation, Multiuser Software Basics.)

This is accomplished through the use of logical record locks, which is utilized differently by each application software package. Database programs for example will assign a "name" to each section of data when the datafile is accessed. Another user cannot access this named section until the first user is finished, and has closed the section of the datafile.

16.3 PHYSICAL RECORD LOCKS

A physical record lock prevents access to a range of data in a file. This physical lock operates even if the file is not open when an access attempt is made. If an unauthorized user attempts to open the locked data, they will get an error message such as "access denied."

16.4 TRANSACTIONS

To maintain file and database integrity, all writes whether single or multiple are regarded as a single "transaction." TTS ensures that each transaction will be tracked to ensure that

- either all of the write request will be written to the datafile on a drive, or
- none of the data will be written to the datafile.

TTS is designed to ensure database integrity. Without TTS it would be almost impossible to determine the status of a datafile after an interruption such as a power failure, a hung workstation, a file server failure, and so on. After an interruption, TTS will allow you to back out without affecting the file. For example in the case of a file server failure, when you bring the system back up you will get this message from TTS:

"Do you wish to roll back incomplete transactions? (Y/N)"

16.5 EXPLICIT AND IMPLICIT TRANSACTIONS

There are two ways to identify the start and end of a transaction to the file server:

Explicit Transactions: These occur when the application software issues any one of the three extended NetWare functions called

- explicit begin transaction,
- explicit end transaction,
- abort transaction.

Explicit transactions are recommended over implicit transactions for the following reasons:

- the application software can determine when the updates contained within the transaction were actually written to the datafile on disk,
- placing BEGIN and END transaction calls within the application forces the programmer to clearly identify the beginning and the end of the file update sequences,

The BEGIN and END transaction calls encourages grouping of file updates, and correct record locking practice. Locking and unlocking of records is done as a group to avoid a potential deadlock, or to avoid leaving records locked pending keyboard input.

Implicit Transactions: These occur automatically from the operating system level when a workstation completes its first logical record lock, or first physical record lock to a transaction file. When all records are unlocked, the file server concludes that the transaction should be ended. The NetWare utility SETTTS is provided which can alter the number of locks it takes to start and end an implicit transaction (the default is on the first lock). Some multiuser software applications may keep one or more records always locked, and the SETTTS utility allows them to work with implicit transactions.

> Implicit transaction tracking is designed to work transparently with existing multiuser software that uses record locking (physical or logical, NETWARE or DOS). When a user FLAGS the files as transactional everything else is automatic. However, implicit transactions are *not* guaranteed to work with all multiuser applications. In particular, applications that do not synchronize file updates exclusively with record locks or which synchronize the updates improperly, may not work. To be certain, check the application software documentation, or call their support line (if one is available) for confirmation.

NOTE: Beware that some application software packages will generate errors when their datafiles are flagged TTS. For example, the Paradox database program will be unable to sort a table that is flagged TTS, since part of the sort process is to delete the original file. NetWare will not allow a TTS file to be deleted.

During a transaction, logical and physical record locks are normally held by the file server until the end of the transaction, even if they are unlocked by the workstation before the transaction is completed. There is, however, one exception. If there were no file writes while the lock was in force, then the unlock request is honored. If the lock is held by the file server, the station requesting the unlock gets the normal "record successfully unlocked" completion code and is unaware that the lock is actually being held pending transaction completion.

Any records written during a transaction will be physically locked by the file server if they were not already physically locked by the application software. These physical locks remain in force until the transaction is completed. Physically locking the written records is an added protection that keeps other workstations from examining or modifying them. If an application writes to a physically locked record and then unlocks it, the actual unlocking of the record is delayed until the transaction is complete.

Record unlocks are delayed by the file server because the data they are controlling access to could still be changed by a transaction back out. By delaying the record unlocks and by physically locking all records that were written, the file server guarantees that other workstations will not see the data until the end of the transaction. Normally multiuser software will synchronize and keep other workstations from examining records while they are being changed. In a non-TTS environment, it is valid however, to unlock some updated records in the middle of a transaction, if they have been completely updated. In a TTS environment those records can still be changed, not by the application software, but by a transaction back out. That is why the file server delays the unlocking of records until the transaction is complete.

16.6 SETTING UP TTS

When you install SFT NetWare using NETGEN you will be given the option of adding TTS, or not (See Part 2 REFERENCE, Chap.8 Installation Overview, Sec. 8.1 Step-by-Step). This is one of the first things you must specify in NETGEN-SFT with TTS or without. Once this has been set, TTS has been invoked. Next you will need to flag all of your database files with the TTS file attribute.

16.7 SETTING THE TTS FLAG (File Attribute)

Transaction Tracking will only take place on files that have been flagged as TTS. This file attribute can be set

- from the command line using the NetWare FLAG utility,
- through the use of the FILER utility,
- by the application software program.

NOTE: NetWare will not allow a file flagged TTS to be deleted. Obviously if you wish to delete the file, or if a software program operation requires file deletion you will have to alter the file attributes using either FLAG or FILER.

Using FLAG: At the command line, type FLAG (file name) TTS.

Using FILER: The FILER menu utility will allow you to set the file attributes (See Fig. 16.1).

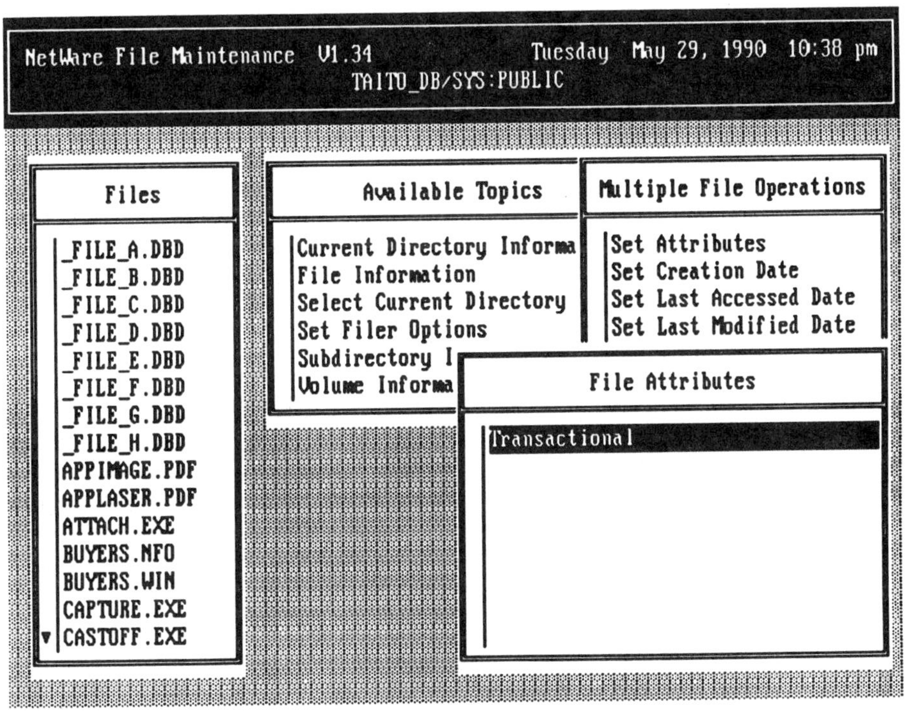

Figure 16.1 Use FILER Menu Utility, to determine or set file attributes.

Position the movable lightbar to "Select Current Directory," select the directory you wish to work in, then the "File Information" window. To select more than one file use the F5 function key and mark each file you wish to add the TTS file attribute to. After you have marked the selected files, hit the enter key, and move to the TTS attribute option, and hit the enter key again to add the attribute to the marked files. As with all NetWare menu utilities, you exit FILER using the Esc key or with ALT F10 after saving your changes.

TTS File Attribute Settings by the Application Program: Depending on the programming of the original source code for a software package, the file attribute flagging could be accomplished automatically.

17 APPLICATION INSTALLATIONS

In this chapter:

Wordprocessors, Accounting Packages, Spreadsheets, Databases.

Once the network has been installed and set up properly, it is necessary to ensure that this work does not come to naught when the application software is added. It is equally important to correctly install any application software package(s). Unfortunately, many installation manuals avoid this issue entirely with the simple phrase, "See your Network Administrator." If you are the administrator, these instructions do not contribute a great deal to your peace of mind during installation and setup.

This chapter deals with important considerations for installing a word processor, accounting package, spreadsheet, and a database. The packages chosen for detailed consideration have been included for several reasons

- WordPerfect was chosen because it recognizes NetWare requirements such as logical drives, multiple printers, and user's private directories. It also utilizes NetWare's search drives,
- ACCPAC was chosen because it is an atypical installation with very specific requirements. ACCPAC does not implicitly recognize NetWare. It requires the use of the DOS share command for local data. Setup and configuration is **very specific** for both workstations and file server(s),
- EXCEL has been included as a spreadsheet example operating in a WINDOWS environment. WINDOWS or another type of graphic user interface is becoming common. WINDOWS has some very specific considerations to correctly operate on your network,
- PARADOX was chosen as a database example, because it truly "interacts" with NetWare and is considered well behaved on a network. It recognizes both logical and search drives. NetWare user names are recognized and can be used in Paradox Application Language (PAL) scripts. The PARADOX program is a true self

contained multiuser program, and does not require the DOS SHARE TSR at the workstation.

To set up a package correctly and to ensure efficient network operation, you must consider each item on this checklist

- GROUP and USER trustee rights required,
- file attributes,
- configuring the application software,
- user configuration or setting files,
- workstation environment configurations,
- paths or mapping required,
- creation any customized batch files,
- network printer redirection (CAPTURE).

17.1 WORDPROCESSORS

One of the most common application software packages on any LAN is a word processor. While there are hundreds if not thousands of packages, not all of them are suitable for the network, as true multiuser packages (See Part 1 CONCEPTS, Chap. 3 Software, Sec. 3.2.2 Single User Software Basics, and Sec. 3.2.3 Multiuser Software Basics).

It is recommended that only one word processor be used on a network if at all possible. The choice of the package is a management decision, whether it is made casually, or through a special management committee. In reality, emotion and interoffice politics often enters into the equation when in fact, the package should be assessed on its technical merits, and the ease with which users can operate the package.

The most popular packages are WordPerfect, MS Word, Multimate Advantage II, IBM's Display Write, and Wordstar. This book was written using WordPerfect, which has a large market share, that is one reason it was chosen as the package to be explained in this chapter.

Installing Wordperfect on the Network

Create a directory for the WordPerfect Software that will clearly indicate what is in the directory

For WordPerfect 5.0, there is an optional install program INSTALL.EXE, or use the DOS command MD to create the directory WP50, move to the directory and use the DOS command

COPY A:*.*, or follow the standard procedure outlined in the installation manual.

For WordPerfect 5.1, the INSTALL.EXE program, part of the WordPerfect package must be run for the installation. It will create the directory called WP51.

> **NOTE:** This directory name can be changed during the install.

Prior to the 5.1 release, the network package was separate. With 5.1 only one package is shipped, which is both for stand-alone and networks. The INSTALL program provides a menu with choices (See Fig. 17.1.)

```
Installation

     1 - Basic        Perform a standard installation to L:\WP51.

     2 - Custom       Perform a customised installation.  (User selected
                      directories.)

     3 - Network      Perform a customised installation onto a network.
                      (To be performed by the network supervisor.)

     4 - Printer      Install updated Printer (.ALL) File.

     5 - Update       Install updated program file(s).

     6 - Copy Disks   Install every file from an installation diskette to a
                      specified location.  (Useful for installing all the
                      Printer (.ALL) Files.)


Selection: 0
```

Figure 17.1 WordPerfect Version 5.1 Install menu, which shows Network Installation as a choice.

It's a wise management decision to keep the old version on the network, until both you and the users are convinced that the new software is fully operational. With both versions having different directory names, you have the flexibility to add the new version, and to create batch files to load the application software.

File Attributes

By default, any files created in or copied to any directory are Nonshareable, Read-Write. To enable multiple users concurrent access to the application program files, the file attributes must be changed or FLAGged to indicate shareable status.

Every application software wordprocessing package might have different file attribute requirements, for details consult your installation manual, or call your software manufacturer.

Establish Drive Mappings for Users

While some network administrators use batch files to create distinct drive mappings, the most effective way system wide, is to change the system LOGIN script.

To enable users to "run" the software from their data directories you must put a search drive mapping in place such as

```
MAP S3:=SYS:WP51
```

> **NOTE:** This search drive should be added to the system LOGIN script, to put this in place system wide.

Trustee Rights Required

Trustee rights required for the directory containing the application software should be assigned to a GROUP which users are then a member of. For example, a group called "WP" would have the required rights for the wordprocessing package. Ideally these rights should be Search, Read, and Open, unfortunately, not all packages will operate with these restricted rights (WordPerfect will).

User's Private Directories

User's private directories are required for many reasons. They will contain any configuration or setup files (including video type, printer type, and port) that are user specific and also many packages require private work or temporary files, best located in these private directories. These need to be accessible by only one user (these files cannot be shared). Private directories will also create a "comfort zone" for your users, a private area of the network, which contains only their files.

Each user should have a separate private directory such as on the Volume SYS: with the logical drive G:, the mapping to be added to the SYSTEM login script would be

MAP G:=SYS:USERS\%LOGIN_NAME

The login script command that would be added to the individual User's login scripts would be

DRIVE G:

This would take your user to their own directory immediately after login.

Set Files and Configuration Suggestions

With the network version of WordPerfect, each user has a custom configuration as in the illustration (See Fig. 17.2) stored in a file with the extension SET. If you have experienced difficulty with users changing these files, and creating problems, change the rights in this directory to ROSC (Read, Open, Search, and Create). The paths shown are suggested as a way to solve many problems.

Special Printing Considerations

WordPerfect has the capability to address network printers from within the application with no prior setup required. The CAPTURE, ENDCAP commands are therefore not required.

```
Setup: Location of Files

     1 - Backup Files                     L:\WP51

     2 - Keyboard/Macro Files             L:\WP51\MACROS

     3 - Thesaurus/Spell/Hyphenation
                        Main              L:\WP51\SPELL
                        Supplementary     L:\WP51

     4 - Printer Files                    L:\WP51\PRINTERS

     5 - Style Files                      L:\WP51\STYLE
               Library Filename           L:\WP51\LIBRARY.STY

     6 - Graphic Files                    L:\WP51\GRAPHICS

     7 - Documents



Selection: 0
```

Figure 17.2 WordPerfect will allow you to specify directories and subdirectories for auxiliary files.

Adding Font Capability to Enhance the Printed Page

One of the most vital considerations with word processors on a network is the quality of the printed output. This can be greatly enhanced by utilizing available fonts (see your printer documentation) which can be

- built into the printer (i.e. HP LaserJet III), called resident fonts,
- added as a hardware font cartridge which is installed or "plugged into" the printer,
- software fonts, installed as a software package and added to the file server hard drive.

NOTE: Software fonts use a portion of the printers memory, hardware fonts do not. To lessen the impact on network traffic, the most commonly used software fonts should be downloaded once and stay resident in the printer's memory. If the printer is turned off, they will have to be reloaded.

What is a Font

A basic understanding of fonts is required to make the decision of what font cartridges if any, are required.

A font is a design for a set of alphabetic letters, numbers, and symbols. One of the most popular, Times Roman (sometimes called "Modern") was designed almost 200 years ago, and is the one used for this book. Another popular design, Helvetica is an example of "sans serif" type and is popular because the design is clean and simple, however, Times is often considered easier to read. Other sans serif types are News Gothic and Futura. All letters, numbers, and symbols of a certain font (originally called a typestyle) were originally designed to harmonize on the printed page, so fonts should not be mixed.

17.2 ACCOUNTING PACKAGES

Networks provide an environment for the operation of multiuser accounting packages. When adding an accounting package to the network, you should consider

- the number of users the package must support,
- whether the package is fully multiuser in all of its modules, and if not will this cause a problem,
- the amount of available RAM required on the workstation.

Most accounting packages are modular, with a variety of modules each designed to suit a specific accounting requirement. The most common modules are: general ledger, accounts receivable, accounts payable, inventory, order entry, payroll, and job costing. There are many less common modules, and some specifically tailored to individual municipal, state, provincial, and federal tax requirements.

We have chosen ACCPAC PLUS from Computer Associates International, Inc., for the install detailed in this chapter.

Installing Accpac on the Network

Similar to many application software installations, ACCPAC does not require that you create a directory for the package, this will be handled by their INSTALL program. Before changing to the floppy (A:) and running the installation programs, ensure that you are in the root directory of the drive into which you wish to install the ACCPAC program. You will first install the windowing system manager, then you install the ACCPAC plus program, and then you activate the network (using the disk included with LanPak).

The ACCPAC INSTALL copies all of the main program files to the root of a volume. With NetWare, rights flow down (See Part 2 REFERENCE, Chap. 10 Network Security (SYSCON and FILER). That means that if you install the ACCPAC program in the root directory, which requires that users have all rights in order to operate the software, by definition users will have rights to the entire volume. If you only have one volume on your network, they will automatically have rights to all directories and files. To solve this, ACCPAC suggests that you install the program in a separate volume. To do this you must bring down the file server, reinstall NetWare, and run NETGEN to specify a separate volume.

> **NOTE:** Ensure that you have backed up your complete file server before you initiate this procedure.

The ACCPAC documentation describes a method by which you can install ACCPAC in the root directory, and then move it to a directory of choice.

DOS Workstation Setup

Included in your ACCPAC package is a utility called NOVSET, which is used to create or modify a SHELL.CFG for your workstation. It will also increase the value of Files = (file handles) in your CONFIG.SYS, so that the total file handles does not exceed 253 for NetWare and DOS. The files = number is the maximum number of file handles which can be used concurrently by a workstation. File handles are stored in a work space as identifiers, which are used by the operating system to keep track of open files.

> **NOTE:** One file handle requires 48 bytes of memory, therefore, the maximum for ACCPAC utilizing 10 windows and requiring 230 file handles would be 11,040 bytes or just over 11 KB of memory (workstation RAM).

ACCPAC tracks the "unit" total currently running at any one time. One unit is required to run one program module at one computer. The original installation of LanPak includes four network units. Each LanPak diskette provides you with four units.

File Attributes

By default, any files created in any directory are NonShareable, Read-Write. To enable multiple users concurrent access to the application program files, the file attributes must be changed or FLAGGED to indicate shareable status. A utility called NOVSHAR is supplied by ACCPAC, which changes the file attributes of the programs you have just installed to shareable.

Each application software accounting module can have different file attribute requirements. For details, consult your LanPak administrators manual. If you are unsure about the installation, Computer Associates has a "Qualified Installer Referral Service," so that their customers may obtain "professional assistance in the installation and support" of their software. It is highly recommended that you read the LanPak administrators manual.

Establish Drive Mappings for Users

You must map a search drive to the location of the PLUS.EXE program located in the root of the dedicated ACCPAC Volume.

MAP S5:=PLUS: (where PLUS is the name of the volume)

To enable users to "run" the software from their data directories you must put a search drive mapping in place

MAP S5:=PLUS:

> **NOTE:** This search drive should be added to the system LOGIN script, to put this in place system wide.

Trustee Rights Required

Trustee rights required for the directory containing the application software should be assigned to a GROUP which users are a member of. For example, a group called "ACCPAC" should be given rights to all program and data directories. Another group perhaps called "ACCPAC2" may be the only one with access to payroll files, and be able to use a different printer and utilize an additional "start list." A start list is a list of the ACCPAC data sets you have on your system. You choose the data set you are going to run. This can be a common list for a user group. For further details, See the ACCPAC documentation, section for Installing on Novell NetWare, which lists all default directories and the recommended rights.

Users Private Directories

Users private directories are not required with the ACCPAC package.
You should establish any configuration or setup required that is user specific (including video type, printer type, port, and other options), and place these in a common location.

> **NOTE:** When you have determined what directory you wish to use for these variables, you must indicate their location to ACCPAC with environment variables, to start the windowing system manager with a particular printer, a start list, and user options using the DOS SET command.

This syntax can be used in the workstation Autoexec.bat file, or can be included in a Login Script, or in menu batch files. These are DOS SET variables for ACCPAC

- set plus print = drive:\pathname (points to appropriate printer list for the user),
- set plus start = (enter appropriate start list),
- set plus user = (appropriate user options),
- plus /sdrive:\pathname (this will give you a specified path).

For more information refer to the network administrators LanPak manual.

Shared Data Directory

Multiple users have access to this directory. For example, in PLUS:ASP\DATA, the trustee rights to this directory should be assigned to a group such as ACCPAC. Users must have all trustee rights to data directories for ACCPAC to operate correctly.

You must FLAG all datafiles added to PLUS:\ASP\DATA after the initial installation. The attributes required are Read Write Shareable (RWS). Subsequent files created by ACCPAC

PLUS are assigned RWS by ACCPAC. If you have created directories other than the default ones suggested, you must also ensure the datafiles in these other directories have RWS attributes.

Special Printing Considerations

In a network printer situation, you might be forced to create a batch file with modified capture commands specific to ACCPAC requirements. This will be necessary when generating reports where ACCPAC requires a longer timeout than your flag has indicated otherwise, you will end up with one line per printer page.

Two possible solutions are to increase your timeout to a workable time (try 10 to 20), or disable the autoendcap. For more information on the CAPTURE command (See Part 2 REFERENCE, Chap. 18 Printing with NetWare.)

Transaction Tracking (TTS) and Backup Consideration

ACCPAC is not compatible with TTS available with SFT NetWare. TTS conflicts with the ACCPAC file protection method. TTS can be used with other packages on the network, however ACCPAC files **should not be flagged "Transactional" under any circumstances.** For more information on TTS (See Part 2 REFERENCE, Chap. 10 NetWare Security (SYSCON and FILER), and Chap. 16 Transaction Tracking System).

ACCPAC recommends that you do complete data backups. Do not backup modified files only. For more information refer to the ACCPAC documentation on backup.

For more information on backup procedures (See Part 1 CONCEPTS, Chap. 5 System Maintenance, Sec. 5.3 Backups.)

17.3 SPREADSHEETS

Many networks are utilized by single or multiuser spreadsheet applications.

The more common network packages installed are: Lotus and clones, Excel, SuperCalc, and MultiPlan. There are many others, however, we have listed the more popular.

Installing Excel on the Network

The first EXCEL install decision you must make is, will you be running WINDOWS Runtime (included in the package), or a full version of WINDOWS (must be purchased separately for every workstation), and which version(s) will you require?

The examples that follow will assume that you are adding the full WINDOWS package to your system.

WINDOWS includes an install procedure, to begin, use the instruction A:SETUP. The WINDOWS Setup procedure copies all of the main program files into the directory you specify during setup.

EXCEL includes an install procedure, to begin, use the instruction A:SETUP. Excel's setup program will recognize any previous WINDOWS installations and will ask if you wish EXCEL to be installed in the WINDOWS directory. If you indicate no, Setup will prompt you for the name of the directory to install the EXCEL program and support files. Installing EXCEL in the WINDOWS directory, (the default procedure) will make system maintenance and setup simpler.

Neither WINDOWS nor EXCEL tracks the number of concurrent users. Therefore, it is your responsibility as System Manager to correctly identify your user totals and to ensure that these comply with your Licensing. For more information (See Part 1 CONCEPTS, Chap. 3 Software, Sec. 3.3 Software Basics for LANS, Sec. 3.3.3 Network Licensing)

File Attributes

By default, any files created in any directory are NonShareable, Read-Write. To enable multiple users concurrent access to the application program files, the file attributes must be changed or FLAGGED to indicate shareable status. You must flag all the WINDOWS and EXCEL program files in the WINDOWS directory as Shareable.

Each spreadsheet package may have different file attribute requirements. For details, consult your installation manual or call the manufacturer.

Establish Drive Mappings for Users

You must map a search drive to the WINDOWS directory containing the WINDOWS and EXCEL program files.

Similar to the procedure described in the word processor application installation section, drive mappings for WINDOWS and EXCEL should be included in the system LOGIN script.

To enable users to "run" the software from their data directories, you must put a search drive mapping in place

MAP S6:=SYS:WINDOWS

NOTE: Microsoft recommends that the search drive should be one of the first on the list of search drive mappings. This is a management decision depending on the number of users per application program, and which has been assigned a higher priority. The lower the search drive number assigned, the faster the program will load and run for your end users.

Trustee Rights Required

Trustee rights required for the directory containing the application software should be assigned to a GROUP which users are then a member of. For example, a group called "EXCEL" would have the required rights for WINDOWS and the spreadsheet package. Ideally these rights should be Search, Read, and Open, unfortunately, not all packages will operate with these restricted rights (WINDOWS and EXCEL will not). WINDOWS requires all rights except Parental for all users. You must remember to protect your program files by FLAGging them as Read Only and Shareable.

WINDOWS also requires all rights to a TEMP directory for temporary print files created by WINDOWS to enable your users to print. The location of this directory must be indicated to WINDOWS by using the DOS SET command which can be added to the Autoexec.bat on the workstation

SET TEMP=F:\TEMP

If this environment variable is not set, WINDOWS will attempt to put these files in the root of the volume that WINDOWS is installed on. Your users will receive a message indicating that they have a PRINTER problem!

User's Private Directories

User's private directories are used by WINDOWS to store the file called WIN.INI (Windows initialize). This file includes information on the printer type and port(s) available, and the name(s) and locations of any screen and printer fonts, as well as many workstation specific configurations.

> **NOTE:** EXCEL has a section in the WIN.INI file specific to its requirements See your EXCEL documentation.

Shared Data Directory

This is a directory that multiple users have access to. For example, SYS:XCELDATA, the trustee rights to this directory should be assigned to a group such as XCELDATA or added to the group EXCEL. Users should have all trustee rights to this directory to allow them to "house clean." WINDOWS will not allow multiple users to access the same spreadsheet concurrently, it will indicate this with an error message stating that the requested datafile is locked and unavailable for use.

Special Printing Considerations

You should indicate in the users WIN.INI file that spooler = no to disable WINDOWS internal spooler. If you do not have this spooler flag set to no, your job will still print, however, it will take longer, as WINDOWS will spool the job, then send it to the NetWare Spooler. Using spooler = no, cuts out one step, printing your job faster (See your WINDOWS documentation).

In a network printer situation, you might be forced to create a batch file with modified capture commands specific to Excel requirements. This can be necessary for two reasons

- where Excel requires a longer timeout than your CAPTURE flag has indicated, you will end up with sections on separate pages for spreadsheet printouts
- the same situation occurs when sending graphs or charts to a network printer.

Two possible solution are to increase your timeout to a workable time, or disable the autoendcap. For more information on the CAPTURE command (See Part 2 REFERENCE, Chap. 18 Printing with NetWare.) If you encounter printing problems, check to ensure that you have fulfilled the WINDOWS requirement for temporary print work files as detailed.

17.4 DATABASES

Many networks are installed to handle a multiuser database application. Often these are preprogrammed packages such as point of sale or order entry database applications.

The more common network packages installed are: Dbase and clones, Paradox, Revelation, and Oracle. There are hundreds of others, however we have listed the ones with an impressive market share.

We have chosen to detail the Paradox Installation, because it is considered "well behaved" on a network, and it has above average documentation.

Installing Paradox on the Network

Create a directory with the suggested title of PARADOX3.

Paradox includes an install procedure, and to begin, use the instruction A:INSTALL. The Paradox Install procedure copies all of the main program files into the directory you have created. You will then be asked to create a password, which will grant you access to the NUPDATE program. This program is used to update or modify installation information, for example you can increase your count of registered users, when adding "Node Paks."

> **NOTE:** If you lose track of your password, you must re-install the program.

Depending on the version of Paradox, you may also need to run

- NINSTALL instead of INSTAL, followed by,
- PINSTALL to load the Paradox Personal Programmer,
- SINSTALL to load the Paradox sample tables and tutorial files,
- AINSTALL installs the Paradox sample applications,
- DINSTALL which installs the Data Entry toolkit.

For clarification refer to the Paradox Network Administrators Guide, included with Network Node Packs.

Paradox is one of the network packages that maintains a dynamic count of all users currently running Paradox. Therefore you need not be concerned about being in violation of your license agreement. For more information (See Part 1 CONCEPTS, Chap. 3 Software, Sec. 3.3 Software Basics for LANS, Sec. 3.3.3 Network Licensing.)

To update your user count and add new package registration numbers, you need to run a PARADOX program called NUPDATE, included with your network version of PARADOX.

File Attributes

By default, any files created in any directory are NonShareable, Read-Write. To enable multiple users concurrent access to the application program files, the file attributes must be changed or FLAGGED to indicate shareable status. You must flag all the PARADOX program files in the PARADOX directory as Shareable.

Each database package can have different file attribute requirements. For details, consult your installation manual or call the manufacturer.

Establish Drive Mappings for Users

You must map a search drive to the Paradox directory containing the Paradox program files.

Similar to the procedure described in the word processor application installation section, drive mappings for Paradox should be included in the system LOGIN script.

To enable users to "run" the software from their data directories, you must put a search drive mapping in place

```
MAP S4:=SYS:PARADOX3
```

> **NOTE:** This search drive should be added to the system LOGIN script, to put this in place system wide.

Trustee Rights Required

Trustee rights required for the directory containing the application software should be assigned to a GROUP which users are then a member of. For example, a group called "PARADOX" which would have the required rights for the database package. Ideally, these rights should be Search, Read, and Open, unfortunately, not all application software packages will operate with these restricted rights (Paradox will).

Users Private Directories

Users private directories are required for many reasons. Any configuration or setup files (including video type, printer type, and port) that are user specific reside in the Users Private Directory. Many packages also require private work or temporary files.

These private directories need to be accessible by only one user and are also a location for that user's nonshareable files. PARADOX requires a PARADOX2.CFG, or PARADOX3.CFG (depending on the version) file for each user. PARADOX also uses this private directory, as specified in the PARADOX.CFG file to store each users temporary work files or answer tables (objects).

> **NOTE:** PARADOX recommends that the available work space be four times the size of your largest table.

Each user should have a separate private directory such as on the Volume SYS: with the logical drive G:, the mapping in the SYSTEM login script would be:

```
MAP G:=SYS:USERS\%LOGIN_NAME
```

The login script command that would be added to the individual Users login scripts would be

```
DRIVE G:
```

This would take your user to their own directory immediately after login.

Shared Data Directory

This is a directory that multiple users have access to. For example, SYS:PDOXDATA the trustee rights to this directory should be assigned to a group such as PDOXDATA or added to the group PARADOX. Users must have all trustee rights because PARADOX keeps track of all file locks, in a FILENAME.LCK file, for every active open table. PARADOX does not require the datafiles to be FLAGged as shareable, that is handled within the program.

> **NOTE:** If a user has ROS rights only, they will not be able to access or view any tables.

PARADOX.NET: This file tracks the total number of concurrent active users. Borland recommends that this file be placed in the shared data directory. Better performance can be achieved if you place PARADOX.NET in its own directory, such as, SYS:PDOXNET. All users must have all trustee rights except parental to this directory.

The location of the shared data directory, the PARADOX.NET file, and the users private directory all must be indicated in the PARADOX.CFG configuration file. This file also specifies your printer types, video types, and setup configurations. The PARADOX.CFG file is created or modified by running a script called CUSTOM.SC located in the PARADOX program directory.

Special Printing Considerations

In a network printer situation, you might be forced to create a batch file with modified capture commands specific to PARADOX requirements. This can be necessary for two reasons

- for reports where PARADOX requires a longer timeout than your flag has indicated, you will end up with one line per printed page,
- the same situation occurs when sending graphs to a network printer.

Two possible solution are to increase your timeout to a workable time, or disabling the autoendcap. For more information on the CAPTURE command (See Part 2 REFERENCE, Chap. 18 Printing with NetWare.)

18 PRINTING WITH NETWARE

In this chapter

Printing in the NetWare Environment, Overview, Default Features, Custom Features, Commands and Utilities, Capture and Endcap, NPRINT, PRINTDEF, PRINTCON, PCONSOLE, Printer Mappings: Console Commands/AUTOEXEC.SYS, Steps to Setting Up the Printing.

18.1 PRINTING IN THE NETWARE ENVIRONMENT

18.1.1 Overview

First you must understand that NetWare can only recognize printers that are directly connected to the file server. This means that NetWare does not allow you to share printers at users' workstations. If you wish to do this, you must purchase third-party "print server" software. An example of this is LANSpool. NetWare runs the print server software in the file server. This is known as a VAP (Value Added Process). This software then redirects the printing to the designated printers.

When you install NetWare with NETGEN, you must tell it that you will be using the Lpt or Com ports on the file sever. If you fail to do this or set it up incorrectly, then your printing will not function.

NetWare allows you a total of five printers connected to the file server. If you require more, then you must purchase a third-party print server package. The five possible printers are: three parallel and two serial. This means that you can use Lpt 1, 2, or 3, and Com 1 and 2.

Regardless of the printers (parallel or serial) that you will be using, you must initialize the printers through NETGEN. If you are using serial printers you will need to specify the baud rate, parity, protocol, and so on. If any of this information is incorrect your printers will not work.

NetWare will not tell you this until after you have finished the installation and are testing the printing.

Once you have told NetWare the information it requires, a queue is established for each printer you have selected. This is a system default, one queue for every network printer. You can change this if you wish.

A queue is a holding area or line up of print jobs waiting to be sent to the printers buffer (See Part 1 CONCEPTS, Chap. 2 Hardware, Sec. 2.1 Hardware Basics for Stand-alone PCs, Sec. 2.1.5 Printers). This queue is created on the file server hard drive in the SYS:SYSTEM directory. It might be called something such as 040015, and so forth. All jobs sent to the queue are printed on a first come first serve basis unless otherwise specified. By default all users can send jobs to all of the queues unless modified.

To manage these queues, NetWare sets the supervisor as a "queue operator." A queue operator is responsible for managing and customizing the queues as required. You may establish any of your users as queue operators if you wish.

To print on the network, you must first redirect your jobs from the workstation's local printer port to the file server. The command to do this is CAPTURE (explained further in this chapter). Once you have redirected your printer port, you can use any of the following to print: PCONSOLE menu utility, the NPRINT or CAPTURE/ENDCAP command line utilities, the printing commands of your particular application, or any of the DOS printing commands and redirection methods.

Once you have printed your file, NetWare places it in the print queue. When the printer is ready to print the file, NetWare sends it from the queue to the printer. This printer and queue relationship is known as printer mapping. The process to accomplish this is called the spooler (see console commands explained further on in this chapter).

NetWare 2.1x allows you to assign multiple queues to one printer or multiple printers to one queue. The reasons for doing this are respectively: you can have one queue set to a higher priority for rush jobs thus they are printed ahead of the other queue, or you have a lot of files printing to one queue and two printers working to speed up the process.

In addition you can specify the users that will be allowed to place jobs in each queue.

18.2 DEFAULT FEATURES

The system defaults are

- each printer is assigned one queue,
- each queue is assigned one spooler process,
- the group EVERYONE is assigned as a queue user to all queues created by the system during NETGEN. As a result all users can print to these system created queues. (Users/Groups must be designated as queue users in any queues "you" create, in order to print,)
- the SUPERVISOR is assigned as a queue operator to all queues created by the system during NETGEN. The queue can be manipulated by queue operators through the PCONSOLE utility. Normally printing occurs on a first come, first-served basis. However, as a queue operator you can change the order of the jobs in the queue, put the job on hold, or delete the job,
- all files are printed according to the parameters set on the printer, that is, condensed, landscape, portrait, and so on. A default print job configuration is created that will print the file with a banner page specifying the users name and file name.

18.3 CUSTOM FEATURES

You can customize the printing in a variety of ways

- new queues and spooler mappings can be created. This is done through PCONSOLE, CONSOLE COMMANDS, and the AUTOEXEC.SYS file for the file server,
- users can be assigned to specific print queues. You can also change the system created queues default of allowing the group EVERYONE to print. This is done through PCONSOLE,
- print queue operators can be assigned to manage specific queues. This is done through PCONSOLE,
- the printer's default parameters can be changed (electronically) by creating printer definitions to configure jobs as required. This allows you to have a user print to a spreadsheet definition which will automatically: reset the printer, change the font, change the bin, and so on. This is done through the utilities PRINTDEF and PRINTCON.

18.4 COMMANDS AND UTILITIES

18.4.1 CAPTURE and ENDCAP

CAPTURE redirects the printing from your local printer ports to the network queues. You can specify which local printer port you wish to redirect. This command should be executed before going into your application software. Often it is placed in the login scripts. Capture has many options that can be specified.

SHOW is used to display the file server, queue, and the printer that your local printer port has been redirected to. This option should not be used with any other capture option.

CAPTURE SH

AUTOENDCAP is used to automatically print the file after 30 seconds if it does not receive further print requests during this time. It leaves the local printer port (LPT) redirected to the network. This command is automatically enabled by default.

CAPTURE A

NOAUTOENDCAP is used to stop a file from being printed until you specifically close the capture file.

CAPTURE NA

TIMEOUT is used to specify the number of seconds between the print command (defined by your application) and when the file is placed in the queue. You can specify 1 through 1000 seconds. You will need to do this if your application is having trouble printing or if you are printing large files. For example, when using WordPerfect you should specify a timeout of 7 through 15. You will have to test this until you get the most efficient results.

CAPTURE TI=7

LOCAL is used to indicate which local printer port (LPT) you wish redirected with the capture command (LPT1 is the default). The number you specify represents the local printer port.

CAPTURE L=2

SERVER is used to specify the file server to which you are send your print jobs.

CAPTURE S=servername

JOB is used to specify the print job name (configured using the PRINTCON utility) to be used.

CAPTURE J=jobname

PRINTER is used to specify the network printer destination of a print request. The number (0, 1, 2, 3, or 4) that you specify represents the network printer (default is P=0).

CAPTURE P=1

QUEUE is used to specify the queue to which your printing is to be directed. The name (PRINTQ_0) represents the queue.

CAPTURE Q=queuename

FORM is used to specify a "form" number that represents a type of paper. As an example, form 0 could represent checks, form 1 regular bond paper, and form 2 letterhead. Forms are setup in PRINTDEF. The number you specify represents the paper you wish loaded in your printer. When utilizing this feature NetWare will send a message to the file server screen requesting you to mount the requested form. All printing to this printer is halted until you enter the appropriate file server command to mount the form requested.

CAPTURE F=1

COPIES is used to specify the number of copies of the job you want printed. The number of copies can be up to a maximum of 256.

CAPTURE C=2

TABS is used to specify a custom tab configuration if your application does not automatically specify tabs. Most applications do. It will replace all the tab characters with the number of spaces you indicate. You are allowed 0 through 18.

CAPTURE T=5

NOTABS is used to specify that all the tabs in your print job arrive at the printer unchanged. This must also be used for any graphic printing since it indicates to NetWare the file contents are "Byte Stream" and not "Text."

CAPTURE NT

NAME is used to specify the users name (default is your login name) on the banner page of your print job.

CAPTURE NAM=name

BANNER is used to specify the message to print on the banner page. This can include any phrase up to 12 characters (LST: is the default).

CAPTURE B=message_to_print

NOBANNER is used to specify no printed banner.

CAPTURE NB

FORMFEED is used to specify a form feed, after your print job.

CAPTURE FF

NOFORMFEED is used to specify no form feed.

CAPTURE NFF

CREATE is used to send data directly to a file rather than the network printer. You can include a path where you want the file saved.

CAPTURE CR=path/filename

KEEP is used to protect your captured print data in the event of a workstation failure. The file server will retain all the data sent from your workstation, and 15 minutes after the failure, the file server will send the captured print data it did receive to the network printer. If this option is not included the file server will automatically discard any partial print data it received.

ENDCAP ends the capture of a local printer port and returns the local printer port to its original status. Therefore you can use this command if you wish to print locally. In addition this command can be used to force a close of your print file and send it to a network printer. This is automatically done through AUTOENDCAP (default) which automatically prints the file after 30 seconds if it does not receive further print requests during this time. The ENDCAP command will force the print job to be sent to the queue immediately if it is executed prior to the "autoendcap" taking effect.

18.4.2 NPRINT

This is NetWare's equivalent to the DOS print command.

The same options can be specified with NPRINT that are available with the CAPTURE command.

18.4.3 PRINTDEF

The PRINTDEF (Printer Definition) utility is used for two purposes. The first is to create forms. With this option you can specify a form name, number, width of your paper in characters, and the number of lines on your page. When this feature is utilized it will send a message to the file server screen prompting you to change the paper on your printer. You will then need to enter in a console command to notify the server when the form has been mounted (See Fig.18.1.)

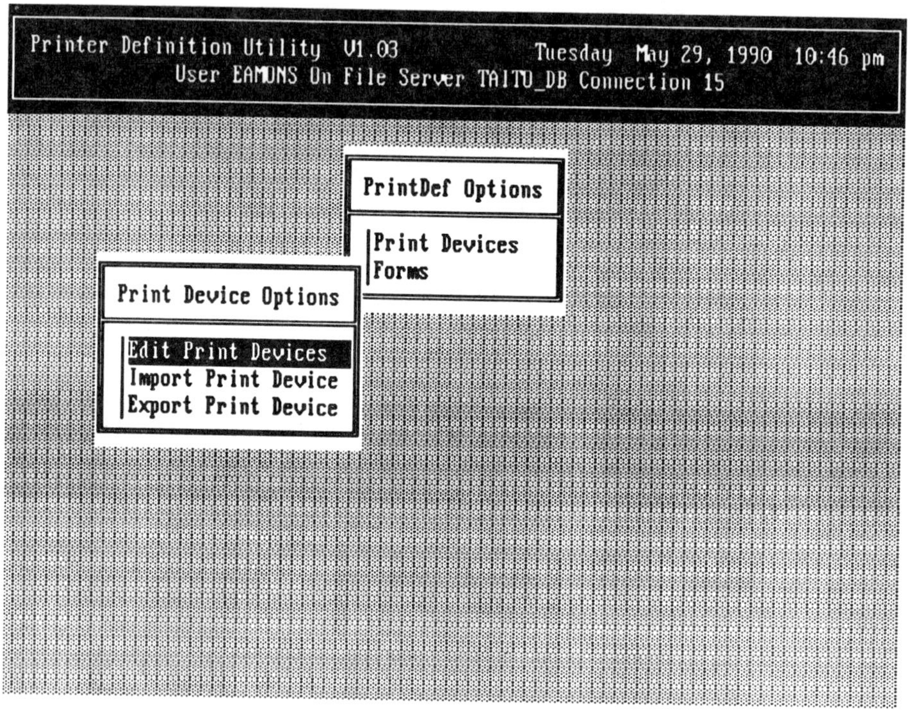

Figure 18.1 PRINTDEF Menu Utility, Print Device Options.

The second purpose for PRINTDEF is to define printers. With this option you can create a printer name and list all of the possible escape sequences that the printer will use. These escape sequences can usually be found in the printer's manual. You then assemble these escape functions into modes. For example, a mode called SPREADSHEET can automatically reset the printer, print in landscape, near letter quality and with a particular font when the job is sent. Without this option you would have to specify this physically at the printer or with application software. Using PRINTDEF allows you to automate this process from your workstation. Your printer must support the features specified (See Fig. 18.2.)

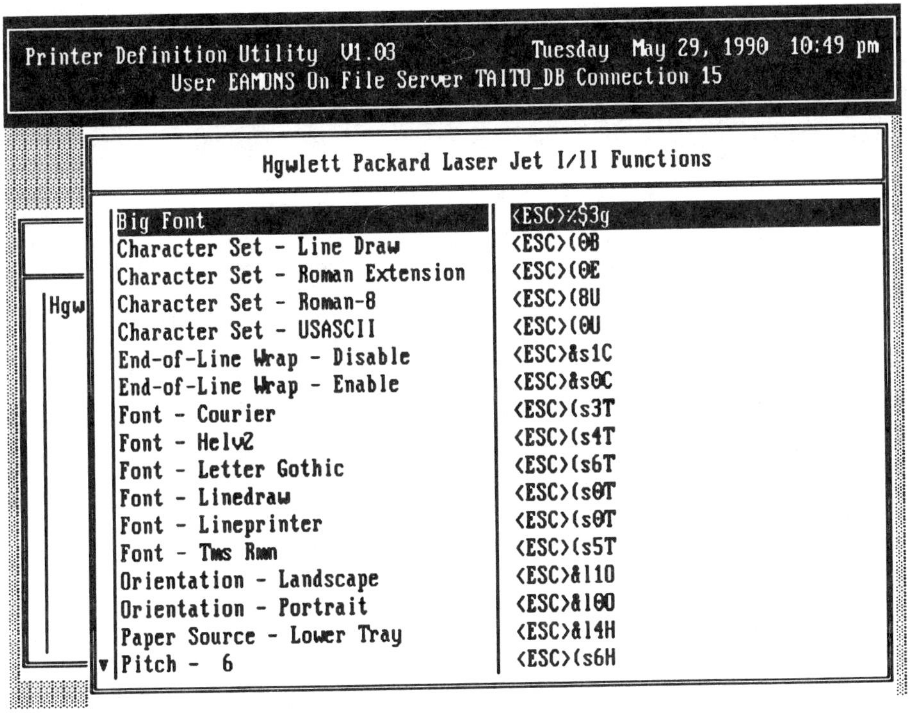

Figure 18.2 PRINTDEF Menu Utility, Printer Device Functions.

NetWare gives you some printer definitions for more commonly used printers. These are found in the PUBLIC directory and have a file extension of PDF (See Fig. 18.3.)

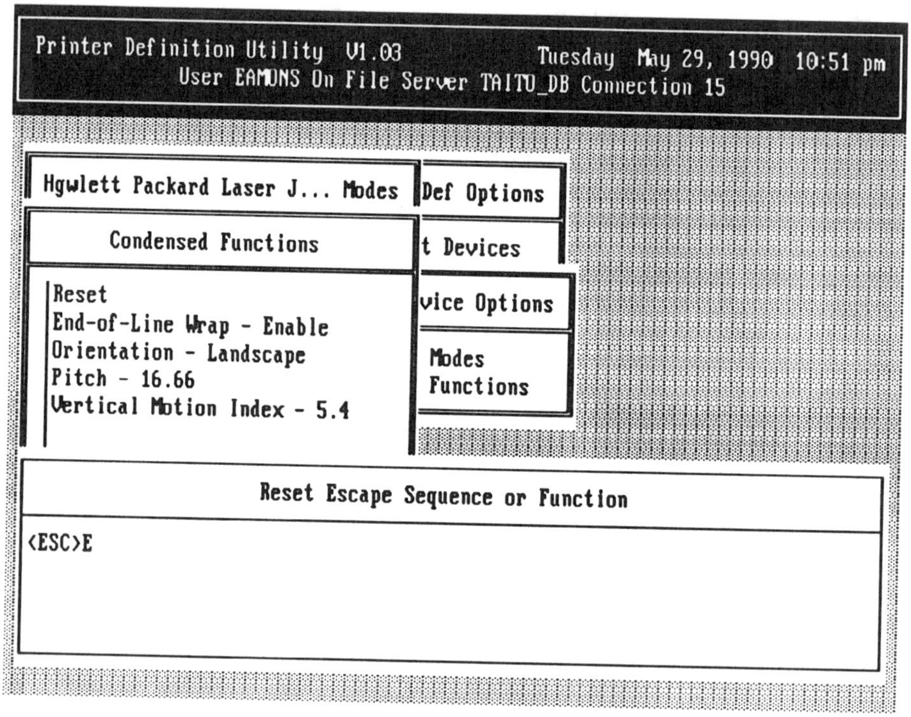

Figure 18.3 PRINTDEF Menu Utility, Reset Escape Sequence or Function (for Printer Device)

Once you have setup PRINTDEF, you can export this configuration to any other file servers you have on your inter-network.

> **NOTE:** Each file server can only have one PRINTDEF file. Only SUPERVISOR has access to this utility.

18.4.4 PRINTCON

The PRINTCON utility (printer configuration) is used to create configurations for individual users. These print job configurations will control the way a users printing will occur. Individual users or Supervisor create print job configurations by selecting from the modes and forms previously set up in PRINTDEF. Also options found in the CAPTURE command (Banner, copies, etc.) can also be specified (See Fig. 18.4.)

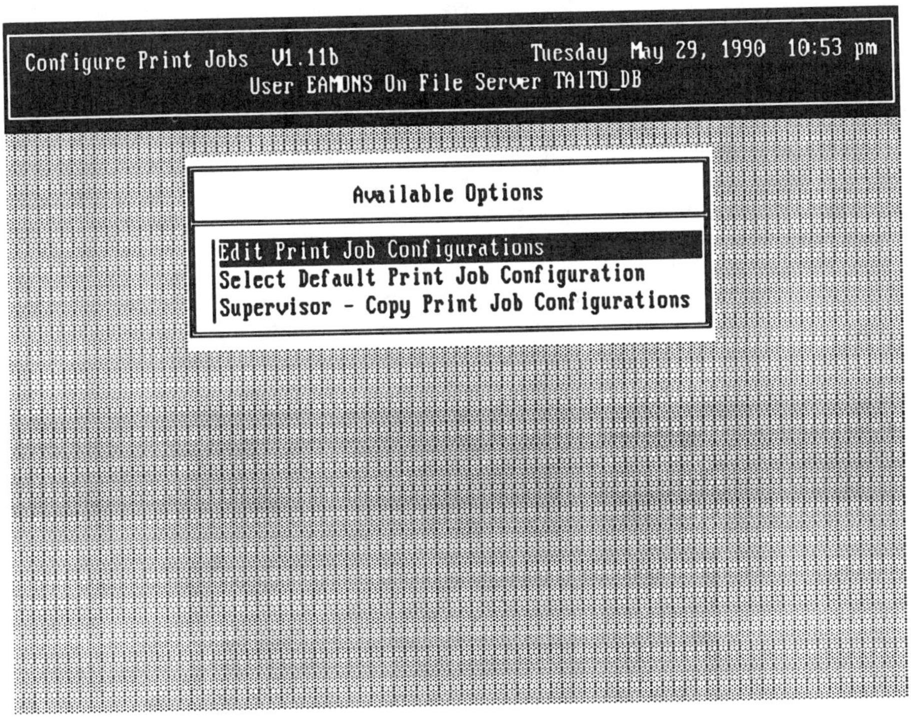

Figure 18.4 PRINTCON Menu Utility, Main Menu.

For example, you can set up a "job" called SPREADSHEET. Then instead of having to set up the printer for landscape, near letter quality, no banner, form number, and so on, the user simply needs to specify the name of the "job" and this will occur automatically. This can be specified with the CAPTURE command in the login script or through batch files (See Fig. 18.5.).

CAPTURE J=SPREADSHEET

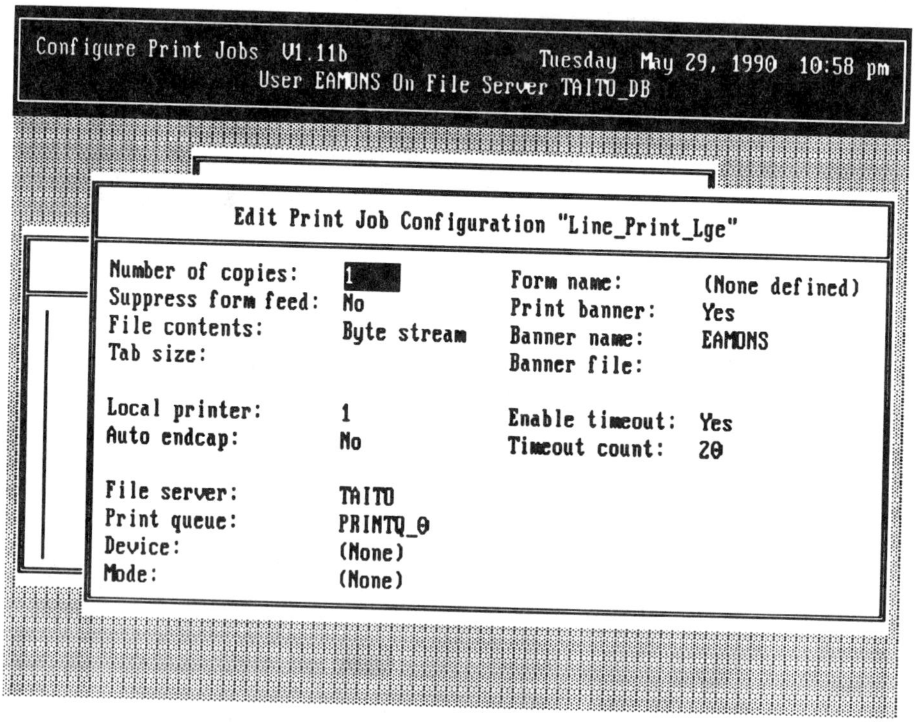

Figure 18.5 PRINTCON Menu Utility, Edit Print Job Configuration.

In addition you can specify a default job configuration through this utility. When you have set up print job configurations you will need to exit this utility and it will prompt you to save. Save and then go back into the utility and copy this configuration to any users as required. This saves the job configuration in the users mail box (USER ID).

18.4.5 PCONSOLE

The PCONSOLE (print console) utility is used to

- print a file (See Fig. 18.6,)

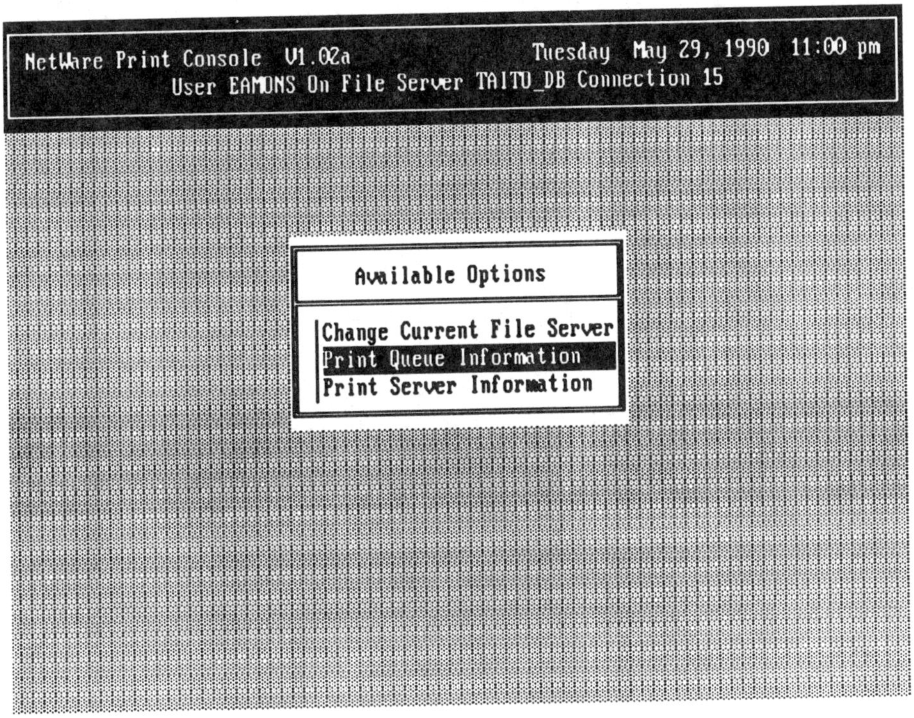

Figure 18.6 PCONSOLE Menu Utility, Main Menu.

- assign queue users and operators, for example as SUPERVISOR you may restrict users queue access, or queue operators can be assigned to share the SUPERVISOR workload (Fig. 18.7.) Queues created in PCONSOLE have no users/queue operators assigned, they must be added. Newly created queues must also be mapped to a printer using the ADD QUEUE TO PRINTER console command, or included in the AUTOEXEC.SYS file,

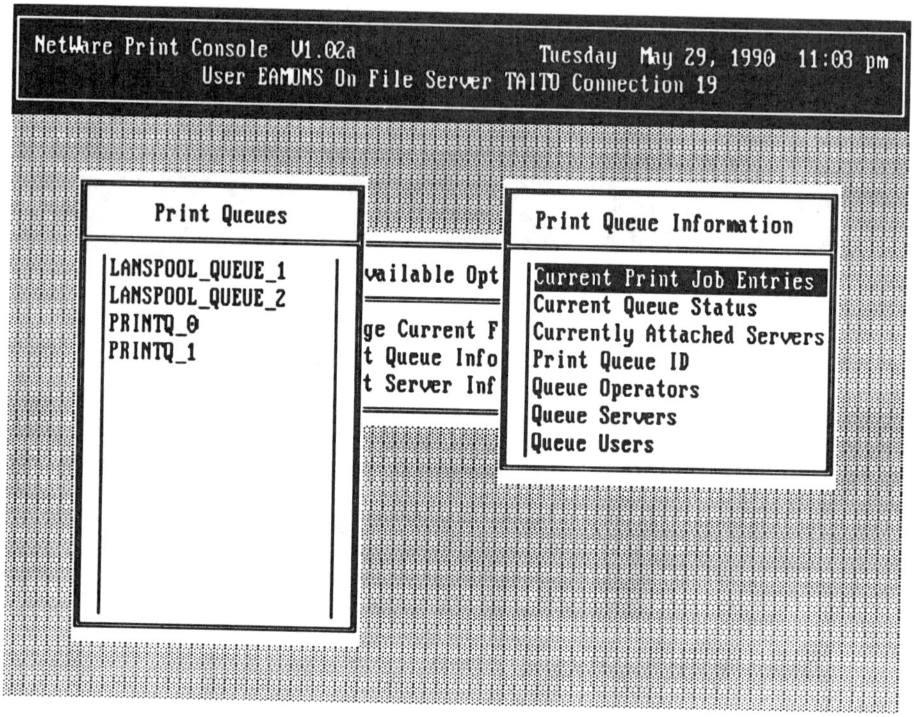

Figure 18.7 PCONSOLE Menu Utility, Print Queue Information.

- create/delete print queues, which can be restricted for use by designated users, and queue operators,
- delete print jobs from a queue,
- change the status of a queue,
- change the order of jobs in a queue,
- choose from the job configurations created in PRINTCON.

18.5 PRINTER MAPPINGS: CONSOLE COMMANDS / AUTOEXEC.SYS

NetWare's AUTOEXEC.SYS (AUTOmatically EXECute) file functions on the file server, in the same way that DOS's AUTOEXEC.BAT file on a stand-alone. When the file server first comes up, it looks for the AUTOEXEC.SYS. If it does not exist, NetWare creates the defaults.

If you create new queues either through PCONSOLE or the file server command CREATE NEW PRINT QUEUE, you must map these queues to a particular printer. In addition, if you want these queues to continue to exist after the server is down you must create an AUTOEXEC.SYS for the file server (Sec Fig. 18.8.) The AUTOEXEC file is created in SYSCON under SUPERVISOR options. In this file you can setup new queues and specify queue priorities. This file must contain valid console commands. You can also create this file using DOS's COPYCON command. If you create an AUTOEXEC.SYS file, be sure to include your default print queues and spooler mappings.

> **NOTE:** Any queues and mappings not placed in this file will no longer exist after the file server is booted. Also the system will not generate any default queues if an AUTOEXEC.SYS file exists, so be sure to include them.

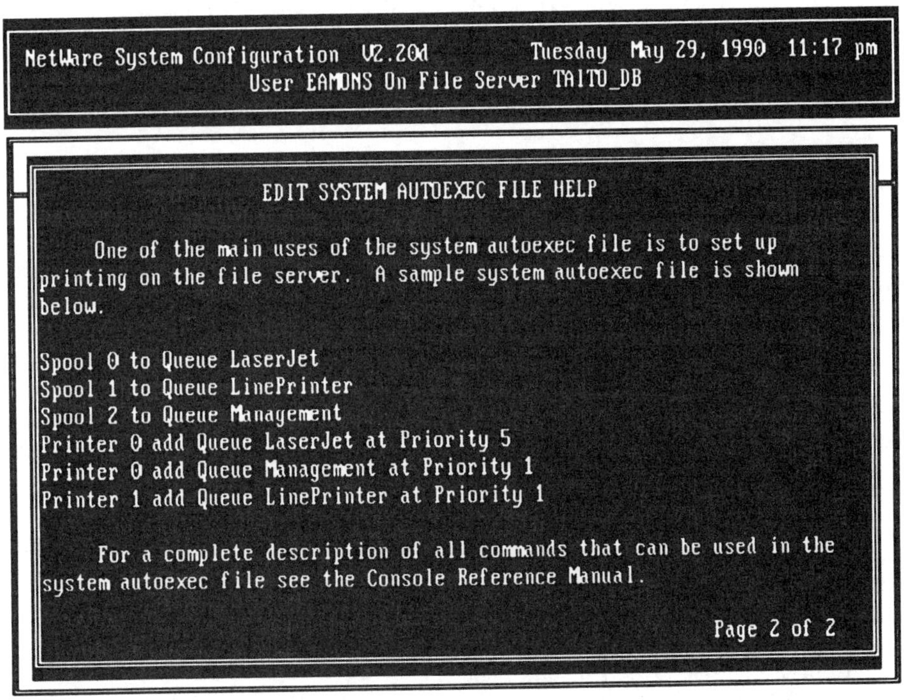

Figure 18.8 SYSCON Menu Utility, Edit System AUTOEXEC File Help. A sample AUTOEXEC.SYS file has been included.

CONSOLE COMMANDS: These commands must be entered at the file server. Here are the important printing commands

- printer queue mapping command syntax:
  P[RINTER] nn ADD [QUEUE] name
  or
  P[RINTER] nn = [QUEUE] name
- list of printers connected to the server:
  P[RINTER]
- list of queues that are servicing a specified printer:
  P[RINTER] nn [Q[UEUE[S]]]
- list of all the queues:
  Q[UEUE[S]]
- command syntax to create a new queue:
  Q[UEUE] name CREATE
- command syntax to change a form:
  P[RINTER] nn MOUNT [FORM]
- command syntax to assign (map) the spooler to a specified queue:
  S[POOL] nn = name
- list of all the spooler mappings:
  S[POOL]

Setting Up Network Printers

One of the main advantages of networks, is the ability to share expensive resources such as laser, postscript, high speed line printers, and plotters. When they are set up properly so as to be completely transparent to the end user, it can be a dream. Most times, however, it's more like a nightmare.

Ideally the end user should only have to know how to print from each application software on the system. For example, in the following applications this should be the process to print for the end user

- in Wordperfect, Shift + F7, and print choices should be all that an end user should have to do,
- from Lotus, the end user should be able to go to the main menu, highlight print, and hit ↵,
- from Excel/Windows, File and Print,
- from Ventura Desktop Publisher (it can be configured to run on NetWare), move the highlight bar with the mouse to "Print," and click.

It should be that easy!

This is the basic print process:

Application software
is told to print

↓

Software printer device driver (if any)
interprets print job for
printer of choice and sends to printer port

↓

CAPTURE redirects print job
to the file server

↓

At the file server, the
job is added to the
Print Queue (spooler)

↓

The spooled print job is downloaded
to the printer buffer (memory), as
fast as the printer can print.

Naturally nothing is ever that simple. Software can call for special fonts which the printer cannot support or the printer can be configured incorrectly. All printing options can be manipulated through PRINTDEF, PRINTCON, PCONSOLE, CAPTURE/ENDCAP, NPRINT, and BATCH files. In addition some printer manufacturers offer compiled Basic programs to set and reset the printer electronically to various print emulation modes. If such a program does not exist from the manufacturer you can specify the code, if you wish in PRINTDEF. However you might find your time better spent utilizing what NetWare has to offer combined with some good batch files, and printer support will not be such a major issue.

18.5.1 Steps To Setting Up The Printing

1. Create print queues and assign priorities, spooler mappings and assign to printers

   SYSCON (AUTOEXEC),
   CONSOLE COMMANDS (file server)

2. Define printer definitions and forms (forms, printer name, functions and modes)

    PRINTDEF

3. Create a printer configuration

    i.e., spreadsheet, normal, etc.

    NOTE: this means you are configuring the printing for a user to automate their printer needs.

    PRINTCON (create, assign a default and copy to a user)
    (creates a PRINTCON.DAT file in the user's MAIL directory)

    a. Edit print configuration

    <INSERT> will add a new one. Create a configuration for every requirement for your users.
    i.e., spreadsheet, normal, draw, letter, etc.

    b. Assign the default that the user would (will) use most often.

    c. Exit PRINTCON and save database.

    d. Re-enter PRINTCON and copy to 1 user to test it on.

4. Log in as that user and test this.

5. If it works, OK! Then go back to PRINTCON and copy the configuration to your other users.

6. Set up BATCH files to further automate the process, or add it to the users' menus (if you are using them).

7. If you want to assign different queue users and operators, go into PCONSOLE and edit these two options.

8. Test it.

19 SYSTEM MANAGEMENT

In this chapter

Backup, House Cleaning, Monitoring NetWare's Accounting, Documentation, Package Name, Source (developer), Support and Sales Lines, FCONSOLE, Broadcast Console Messages Option, Change Current File Server Option, Connection Information Option, Down File Server, File/Lock Activity, LAN Driver Information, Purge All Salvageable Files, Statistics, Summary, Supervisor Commands, Console Commands.

19.1 BACKUP

This text places an emphasis on backups (See Part 2 REFERENCE, Chap. 5 System Maintenance, Sec. 5.3 System Maintenance, Backups). We feel backup is the most important network issue and the primary responsibility of a System Manager or network Administrator, a sentiment shared by most management.

To ensure that backups are done and logged on a daily basis, a backup procedure must be developed **and adhered to**. It's important that the backup be as simple as possible, in case the personnel generally in charge of the process is unavailable. If the process is simple the backup will be done, if it is complex nothing will be done, and you will end up without a current backup.

Backups must be simplified to a point that any user can follow very simplistic instructions for a successful backup.

19.2 HOUSE CLEANING

Hard Drives on stand-alone systems become cluttered with old documents, unused software applications, backup, and temporary files (usually created without the users knowledge). This problem is the same on a network, only the magnitude of the problem is directly proportional to the number of users and files.

In many network situations, free drive space only results from "crisis management." Commonly nobody deletes anything until the network runs out of drive space. If that volume is the SYS: volume you can crash your network. Monitor your system, establish and enforce maintenance procedures.

> **NOTE:** A network volume should have a minimum of 10 percent free space for temporary work files, printer spooler files, and automatic backup files.

On the majority of networks, a weekly cleaning is highly recommended. This can be accomplished by creating a batch file that has in it commands required to delete all temporary and backup files on all volumes in all subdirectories. In this example, the three logical drives F:, J:, and K: are cleaned of temporary files, backup files, and leftovers from Novell's menu system.

```
F:
cd\
xx del *.bak
xx del *.tmp
J:
cd\
xx del *.bak
xx del *.tmp
xx del restart.*
xx del go*.bat
K:
cd\
xx del *.bak
xx del *.tmp
xx del restart.*
xx del go*.bat
```

This example uses a utility called XX, which will allow you to delete the specified files listed (using letters and wildcard characters) from the logical drives root directory, and all subdirectories. This network compatible XX public domain program (short for Trans Directory Execute Utility) allows you to execute a command (DIR, DEL, TYPE, etc.) in each directory and subdirectory matching the path and filespec.

It is recommended that you call this batch file something such as WK_CLEAN.BAT or any file name that will allow you to readily identify the file, and its purpose.

> **NOTE:** For details on creating and using batch files, and wildcard characters refer to your DOS manual.

On a monthly basis, produce a printout of any shared data directories utilizing a network utility such as LT Stat, or LOMAX Utilities. This report lists the file name, date last modified, date last accessed, and the owners name. Copies should be distributed to all users, and they should be encouraged to delete any old or unused files (documents, Christmas mailing lists, unused spreadsheets, etc.).

Every six months produce these same reports for the complete network. The reports should be distributed as necessary to ensure that your system contains only current and timely datafiles and software versions.

19.3 MONITORING NETWARE'S ACCOUNTING

Enabling NetWare's accounting package allows you strict management control of your network's resources (See Part 2 REFERENCE: Chap. 10 Network Security (SYSCON and FILER), and Chap. 14 Optional Account Restrictions.)

NetWare's Accounting will track all system usage. Third party utilities such as LOMAX and LT Stat allow you to analyze NetWare's data and produce reports as required. For example, you might have a clerk in accounting that requests a 386 workstation. These reports will tell you if this is a reasonable request, compared to other users usage on the network. You will then will be able to make an informed management decision.

19.4 DOCUMENTATION, PACKAGE NAME, SOURCE (developer), SUPPORT and SALES LINES

As a network grows, it quickly becomes impossible to keep track of the software on the system, and the relevant product information required for support.

It is highly recommended that you establish either a hard copy or an electronic file using a database, word processor and so on, that has current information in one place.

Easy access to this information can be gained using an electronic format. To ensure that you can receive timely technical assistance from the technical support, you should have on hand at a minimum, the **bolded** information listed below. The recommended fields and the field sizes and types (for a database) can include:

Field Name	Type and Size	Information
Name	A20	Your name for the Package
CName	A20	Manufacturers Package Name
S/W Type	A5	Classification of the software package, for example, WP-Word processor
Company	A50	Manufacturer name
Address1	A30	The first line of the mailing address
Address2	A30	The second line of the mailing address
City	A25	
State/prov	A2	
Country	A6	
Zip/postcode	A14	
FName	A20	First name of a contact person
LName	A20	Last name of a contact person
Phone Tech	A20	Technical support phone number
Phone Sales	A20	Sales information phone number
Phone BBS	A13	Bulletin board phone number (if any)
Fax	A13	Fax phone number
CIS	A10	Compuserve Forum Name (if any)
First Installed	D	Date of original installation
Last Update	D	Installation date of last update or upgrade
Current Version	A20	Current version number and letter
Serial Number	A30	Registered serial number
Machine(s) Installed On	A20	Location of software programs
# of Registered Users	N	Legal user count
FS Space Used-Progs	N	File server space used for the program and supporting files
FS Space Used-Data	N	File server space used for any data generated by this package
FS Space Used-Date	D	Date of space usage compilation

With this kind of information current and literally at your fingertips, your job becomes easier and more efficient.

19.5 FCONSOLE

The FCONSOLE menu utility is one of the best tools available with NetWare for managing your network on a daily basis. FCONSOLE stands for file server console. This menu utility allows the supervisor or a user with "console operator" status, to obtain information regarding the file server and modify various parameters from a workstation. Previous to Version 2.1x this information was only available through console commands executed at the file server. This was inconvenient when the file server was located on a different floor or remote to the system manager.

Common uses of FCONSOLE on a daily basis are

- to allow the System Supervisor or equivalent to DOWN the file server remotely,
- to check the file server statistics summary for overall peak usage,
- to check connection information about a user currently on the system,
- use the status screen to alter the file server time or enable/disable login.

FCONSOLE provides a variety of information, starting from the main menu screen:

Each menu item has additional submenus, that perform necessary functions, and provide valuable information and status reports to help you manage your network.

19.5.1 Broadcast Console Messages Option

Use the broadcast option to send a message, of up to 55 characters, to all stations logged into the current file server. This option is useful when you want to inform the users of any system changes, including downing the file server. You can accomplish the same function using the Console command "BROADCAST."

19.5.2 Change Current File Server Option

Use the change current file server option to select another file server on your internetwork. You may wish to use another server as your default server. This option will provide you with a list of available file servers, to which you can attach.

19.5.3 Connection Information Option

The connection information option operates in much the same way as the "USERLIST" command. It will provide you with a list of all the logical connections attached to the file server. It also provides the following options on each of these listed connections

Broadcast Console Message
Clear Connection
Logical Record Locks
Open Files/Physical Records
Other Information
Semaphores
Task Information
Usage Statistics

Broadcast Console Message: Use the broadcast option to send a message, of up to 55 characters, to all stations logged into the current file server. This option is useful when you want to inform the users of any system changes, including downing the file server. You can accomplish the same function using the Console command "BROADCAST." You will notice that this option appears both on the main window of FCONSOLE and within the Connection Information Option.

Clear Connection: If a workstation "hangs" you will want to use this option to close the workstations files and disconnect it from the network. This can also be accomplished with the console command "CLEAR STATION."

Logical Record Locks: All logical record locks, and the type and tasks utilized by connections, are listed by this option. Generally, this information is only useful to programmers. Most system managers will never use the information provided in these screens. Nevertheless we have provided you with a list of the statuses that can apply to locks, and a definition of each.

STATUS	DEFINITION
Logged	Records are locked as sets by a workstation requiring their useage. This prevents other stations from trying to lock the same records.
Locked shareable	Records can also be locked as shareable without being exclusive, to a workstation.

Locked exclusively	This status is used with data that is changing to prevent another workstation from locking the record.
Being held by the transaction tracking system	Any file being updated that has been flagged "TTS" is held with an exclusive lock, enabling TTS to back out smoothly as required.

Open files/physical records: This option provides a list of all files currently in use by a workstation. The status, task, and physical record locks of a file are listed. We have provided a list of statuses and an explanation of each. Command.com is always identified as Task 1.

STATUS MESSAGE	DEFINITION
Open	This status message indicates that the file is not flagged shareable, and it is currently open.
Open in share mode	This status message indicates that the file is flagged shareable and it is currently open.
Not open	This status message indicates that the file is locked or logged but not open.
Open for read only	This status message indicates that the workstation has requested read access but not write.
Open for write only	This status message indicates that the workstation has requested write but not read file access.
Open for read and write	This status message indicates that a request has been made for both read and write file access.
Allow read and writes	This status message indicates that other workstations are authorized to read and write to the file.
Deny reads, but allow writes from stations	This status message indicates that other workstations are not authorized to read from a file but they can write to the file.

Allow reads, but deny writes from other stations	This status message indicates that other workstations are authorized to read but they cannot write to a file.
Deny reads and writes from other stations	This status message indicates that a workstation is preventing other workstations from reading or writing to a file.
Locked by shared file set transaction	This status message indicates that the "file locked" belongs to a shared file set transaction. After the shared file set transaction is completed, the file is detached preventing further access until the workstation locks the file again. This is not the same as a TTS tracked transaction.
Locked by file lock	This status message is self explanitory.
File is detached (no I/O is permitted until the file is locked	This status message indicates that a previous shared set file transaction has occured on this file. The workstation has now unlocked the file, but it must relock it before further access is permitted.
File is logged	This status message indicates that a workstation wants to simultaneously lock several files.
Held open by TTS	This status message indicates that TTS is holding a file open until the transaction is completed. This occurs if a file has been closed that has an active transaction occuring.
TTS holding file	This status message indicates that TTS is holding a file until its transaction is completed. This occurs if the file lock has released the file during a transaction.
File detach is being held by TTS	This status message indicates that TTS is holding a file open until its transaction is completed. This occurs if the file is closed while the transaction is taking place.

P) Explicit transaction tracking in process	This status message indicates that a workstation has issued an explicit "begin transaction" function call, but has not issued an "end transaction" call and the file has been flagged as transactional.
(P) Implicit transaction tracking in process	This status message indicates that a workstation has locked a physical or logical record on a file that is flagged transactional. This causes an implicit "begin transaction" function call to occur. The transaction is completed when the workstation unlocks the records.
Transactions will be tracked by the TTS	This status message indicates that a file has been flagged as transactional, thus any changes made to this file by a workstation will be tracked. This enables the sytem to back out the transaction in case of a failure before it has reached its completion.

Semaphores: Semaphores have two main purposes. The first is to limit the number of tasks that can be used or changed by a resource simultaneously. The second is to limit the number of workstations that can run an application software program or command at the same time. Semaphores are assigned an open account and a value. The open account is used to track the number of workstations using (open) a particular semaphore. The value is used to assign a limit to the number of resources that can be used at a particular time by a workstation.

Task: The task option lists the status of various tasks, being utilized by workstations, as follows

workstation is not waiting
workstation is waiting on physical record lock
workstation is waiting on a file lock, etc.

Usage Statistics: Total disk I/O and packet requests are displayed for specified users. The users usage is tracked from the time of login.

19.5.4 Down File Server

You will use this option to close all of the files opened at the file server, write all information in file server RAM to the hard disk, and prepare the system for shutdown. This can also be accomplished at the file server through the console command "DOWN."

19.5.5 File/lock Activity

If you wish to see information on files, locks, and semaphores on a directory/file basis, use this option. The same information is available on a per connection basis through the connection information option.

19.5.6 Lan Driver Information

This option is useful to retrieve information regarding the Network Interface Cards (NICs) in your file server. A list is displayed of the NICs and their address settings. This information can also be found with the file server console command "CONFIG."

19.5.7 Purge All Salvageable Files

This option will seldom be used. If you are running out of hard disk space you can purge all salvageable files on the server. Bear in mind that files are automatically purged when users delete or create a new file.

19.5.8 Statistics

This can be the most important information available through FCONSOLE. We recommend that you use the F1 help key and read through the screens, because of the sheer volume of information that is made available to a system manager through the use of these options. The information provided however, is comprehensive, and fairly straight forward. As a result the focus that follows is on the summary option which you should be viewing and documenting monthly. Information on file server RAM, hard disks, directory entries, hot fix redirection area and more, is provided to help you manage you LAN. This management tool is invaluable to system managers.

Cache Statistics
Channel Statistics
Disk Mapping Information
Disk Statistics
File System Statistics
LAN I/O Statistics
Summary
Transaction Tracking Statistics
Volume Information

19.5.9 Summary

The summary option contains much of the information needed for monitoring network performance.

File Server Up Time: This item on the summary screen is the amount of time (updated every second) the file server has been continuously operational with no down time.

Number of File Server Processes: This item on the summary screen indicates the number of processes that the file server can service simultaneously. The number indicated will vary depending upon the LAN, disk, drivers, and the version of NetWare in use.

Current Server Utilization: This item on the summary screen is used as an indicator of the need for either additional memory in your server, or possibly the requirement for a second server. It displays the percentage of time that the file servers CPU is being used. A percentage in excess of 80 percent is cause for concern. You will notice that this number will vary anywhere between zero to 100 depending on CPU utilization.

Disk Requests Serviced from Cache: This item is an indicator of the percentage of time that your request was able to be serviced from the RAM cache buffers as opposed to the hard disk. Cache buffers, service requests faster than disk access. You will need to add additional memory to the file server if this item is displaying a percentage of less than 80 percent.

Packets Routed: This item indicates the number of packets routed from one NIC to another within the file server to reach their destination.

Total Packets Received: Packets include file service requests, packets to be routed, packets destined for IPX or any other file server socket. This item is an indicator of the number of packets received by the file server within the last second.

File Service Packets: This item specifically indicates the number of file service request packets that the file server has received within the last second.

Total Number of Cache Buffers: This item indicates the number of cache buffers in memory remaining after initilization of the operating system. To increase this number add more memory.

Dirty Cache Buffers: This item indicates the number of cache buffers that contain information that has been updated, but has not been written to the hard disk. Information within these buffers is sent to the hard disk when the buffers are full or every three seconds whichever comes first. If this item indicates a percentage above 50 you will need to add additional memory to your file server.

Total Server Memory: This item indicates the amount of memory that you have installed in your file server. Memory that is fragmented (not large enough to be used), is recorded under unused server memory.

Routing Buffers: This item is also referred to as communication buffers. It is assigned during NETGEN installation utility, and is dependant upon the type of NIC used. Routing buffers are used to store incoming packets from users when the file server has no service processes available. It is a good practice to maintain a number between 15 to 20 above your peak used.

Open Files: This item indicates the maximum number of files that the file server can have open simultaneously. Each user can have approximately one to 25 file open at the file server, depending on the application software package in use. Applications like databases tend to open more files than wordprocessing packages. A rule of thumb is to divide the peak used column by the number of workstations connected to the file server. This calculation gives you an average number of open files. Multiply your average by the total number of users on the system to get a maximum estimate. Bear in mind that open files affect dynamic memory pool.

Indexed Files: Indexed files are used for databases or large files over one to two megabytes in size. This item indicates the number of index files that are open and active at the same time at the file server.

Transactions: The numbers indicated under transaction represent the maximum alowed, peak used, and currently in use by the Transaction Tracking System (TTS), the maximum allowable is 200. If you require memory in your file server to be available you may wish to set this maximum to a lower number. This will not prevent TTS from functioning, but it will slow down the process. You will notice that your maximum allowable will be ten numbers less than you specified. Don't panic, these are used for other purposes.

Bindery Objects: Bindery objects can be users, groups, print queues, print servers and file servers. This item is an indicator used to track and limit (thru NETGEN and SYSCON) the amount of disk space that any object can utilize.

Connections: This item indicates the number of objects that have been connected to the file server during the period that the file server has been up.

Dynamic Memory 1: The Dynamic memory one pool is used for disk drive mappings, and file service requests. It is represented in bytes. There are two ways to alter this number, add more memory to the file server, or remove unnecessary drive mappings from users login scripts.

Dynamic Memory 2: This pool is used to track open files, file locks and record locks.

Dynamic Memory 3: This pool is used to track other file servers, routers, and bridges.

19.6 SUPERVISOR COMMANDS

The commands listed are located in the SYS:SYSTEM directory. Only commands judged important for daily operation have been included in this list.

BINDFIX

This command line utility is used to purge previously deleted users, trustee assignments, groups, and passwords. You would use this command if: you get an error in the bindery indicated by the inability to create, delete users/groups, or a specific bindery error message. It also will prompt you to delete mail boxes of users that no longer exist and trustee rights to directories that no longer exist.

The NetWare 2.15 bindery consists of two files, NET$BIND.SYS and NET$BVAL.SYS. This is NetWare's internal database of all of the user, group, and security information. If for some reason this becomes corrupt, BINDFIX should fix it.

BINDREST

This command line utility is run after BINDFIX. BINDFIX creates a backup of the bindery files with an .OLD extension. BINDREST will restore these files back to the previous bindery information.

HIDEFILE

This command line utility is used to hide specified files so that they cannot be seen with the DOS DIR command. Hidden files cannot be deleted or copied over.

SHOWFILE

This command line utility will allow you to make hidden files visible.

PAUDIT

This command line utility prints (to screen, file, or printer) all accounting transactions from the audit file, NET$ACCT.DAT, which contains a record of all accounting functions in a chronological order. When accounting has been activated, entries are placed in the file server's audit file every time a user logs in or out, intruder lockouts are also recorded. After printing this data you should delete the NET$ACCT.DAT file since it will continue to grow, a new file will be generated automatically.

ATOTAL

This command line utility provides a summary of the NET$ACCT.DAT file. Compiles and lists the totals of the following

- blocks read,
- blocks written,
- connect time in minutes,
- service requests,
- disk storage in blocks/day.

SECURITY

This command line utility is one of the most useful supervisor commands. It checks for any potential breaches in your network's security structure. Prints (to screen, file, or printer) details by user, login script existence, grace login status, periodic password changes, password length requirements, requires password-Yes/No, if password is assigned, and any rights in root directories of volumes. Items that the security command monitors follow.

Objects with no password assigned: All users should have a password, or anyone will be able to login under the name of an object (a user is one of many objects).

Objects with insecure passwords: Passwords that are easily guessed are not sufficient to maintain system security (e.g., username, first name or spouses name). This command line utility checks for passwords that equal the username, and also for accounts not requiring password of a minimum of five characters.

This command line utility also checks for, require change passwords at least every 60 days, unlimited grace logins after password expiry, and the requirement to use a unique password each password change.

Objects with security equivalence to the supervisor: This command line utility lists and users that have supervisor equivalency.

Objects that have privileges in the root directory of a volume: This command line utility lists any users that have been granted access privileges in root directories of a volume. Remember "security flows down," and also a user with "parental" rights in a root directory can grant themselves or others all rights to that volume.

Objects that do not have a login script: User's login scripts are kept in their mail directory. As a result, it is possible for other users to create this file if it does not exist.

Objects with excessive rights in the standard directories: This command line utility checks NetWare's default directories for trustee rights. The trustee rights established by NetWare during installation to the group everyone are listed.

SYS:SYSTEM [________]
SYS:PUBLIC [___O_RS_]
SYS:MAIL [C______W]

SECURITY checks that the only object possessing rights greater than Create and Write in a user's mail directory is it's owner.

19.7 CONSOLE COMMANDS

Console commands can only be issued from the file server console keyboard, some of the resulting information can now be accessed from the FCONSOLE menu utility.

BROADCAST

This command allows you to send a message to all stations logged in or attached to the file server. For example you may want to send a message like "Server going down in 10 minutes, please log out."

CLEAR STATION

This command removes all allocated file server resources of a specific station. This command is used when a station has somehow "crashed" and inadvertently left some files open on a server.

CONFIG

This command lists all Network Interface Cards located in the file server, and the address settings that have been specified during the NETGEN installation.

CONSOLE

This command allows you to switch a nondedicated file server from local DOS mode into the console mode. This enables you to use console commands.

DOS

This command allows you to switch a nondedicated file server from console mode into the local DOS mode.

DISABLE LOGIN

This command allows you to prevent additional workstations from logging into the current file server. Any users currently connected, will remain connected.

ENABLE LOGIN

This command reverses the results of the DISABLE LOGIN command.

DISK

This command is used to list the status of the network hard drives. With Disk Coprocessor Boards (DCBs) installed in your file server, the channels to which the DCBs are connected are listed.

> **NOTE:** You can run duplexed drives with third-party drive controllers.

DOWN

This command will write the cache buffers to the hard drive, and close all open files.

DOWN also logically shuts down the NetWare operating system processes prior to the file server being powered down.

MONITOR

This command displays a monitor screen showing a maximum of six workstations at a time. It lists open files, server utilization, and the NetWare OS version. To view the next six workstations type MONITOR 7, and so on.

NAME

This command shows the file server's name.

OFF

This command is used to turn the monitor display off.

UNMIRROR

This command is used to shut down a mirrored drive. While UNMIRRORed, the other drive in the mirrored pair will continue to function with Hot Fix, but will lack mirroring or duplexing protection.

REMIRROR

This command restores SFT mirroring or duplexing protection to a pair of disk drives after one of the drives in the pair has failed or has been UNMIRRORed.

SEND

This command is used to send a message to a specified workstation connection.

SET TIME

This command is used to set the date and time of the file server.

TIME

This command is used to show the file server's time and date.

VAP

This command lists all Value Added Processes (VAPs) that are currently loaded onto the operating system.

PART 3 DATA COMMUNICATIONS

This part has been provided to introduce you to Novell's communication products. Communications are divided into four categories: remote access (PC to LAN), wide area networking (LAN to LAN), and host connections (PC to Host and LAN to Host). The host communication sections are divided into asynchronous (X.25) and synchronous.

20 DATA COMMUNICATIONS

In this chapter

Communication products covering PC to LAN, LAN to LAN, PC to Host, and LAN to Host connectivity.

20.1 PC to LAN CONNECTIVITY

When connecting remote PCs there are two types of connections: local and remote execution. All processing in a remote execution environment, occur at the remote PC. Users dial in to networks via modems and communications software. Similar to all Novell's communications products, the connection is transparent. This type of connection is designed for companies that require infrequent file transfer/access. It is not for CPU intensive applications because communication occurs at telephone line speeds which are slower than LAN speeds. To help get around this potential bottleneck, remote users should have the software application programs and utilities installed in their workstation and in this way only data is transferred down the line.

All processing in a local execution environment occurs at a workstation on the LAN. This workstation acts as a host machine to the remote PC. No processing occurs on the remote PC, only screens updates and keystrokes are sent back to and from the remote PC. Once your communications software has made the connection these two PCs act as one PC. The LAN workstation acts as the processor, while the remote PC mirrors the screen and keyboard. This type of connection has the advantage of better performance since only keystrokes and screen updates are sent over the telephone lines. The disadvantage of this type of connection is the necessity of a workstation on the LAN to be dedicated for the duration of the connection. You may use this type of connection when frequent remote access to the LAN is a requirement.

You will be faced with two issues when making a purchasing decision for your type of connection. First decide on the number of users who require remote access. Then decide on the type of applications they will be using. If you anticipate a large number of remote users access to the network, you might consider a product such as the NetWare Access Server. If you anticipate a small or infrequent number of remote users access to the network, then you can use the NetWare AnyWare (used with Novell's Asynchronous Communications Server-NACS) product. You might decide that you require a store-and-forward electronic mail service and may consider the NetWare MHS (Message Handling Service) server product.

20.1.1 NetWare Anywhere

This software product is a solution that allows remote PCs to access the LAN and all of its services. It is used in conjunction with the Novell's NetWare Asynchronous Communications Server (NACS). NetWare AnyWare and NACS uses the local execution method of connection.

This type of connection requires a workstation on the LAN, running NetWare AnyWare, to process the data for the remote PC. A remote PC will dial into the network using a communications package with terminal emulation capabilities. The connection is made through the NACS which handles the redirection to the LAN workstation running NetWare AnyWare. In addition, the NACS handles all the modem pooling and protocol requirements. The NACS uses a Wide NetWork Interface Module (WNIM+) adapter card to connect the modems. Up to four WNIM+ cards can be installed in a single NetWare Asynchronous Communications Server. As mentioned previously under local execution types, this type of connection appears to the remote PC as fast as if they were directly cabled on the LAN. It is sold in a four-user license configuration.

The following is a list of this products features

- virtually any LAN application can be run by remote PCs,
- remote users are restricted by LAN security,
- high speed error correcting modems are supported along with most standard modems,
- restriction of access to the LAN through NetWare AnyWare can be configured on a group or user basis,
- batch or menu commands can be used for file transfer,

- any host services such as gateways are accessible by remote PCs,
- printing can be redirected dynamically to either the remote or LAN side of the connection.

20.1.2 NetWare Access Server

This product allows you to connect up to 15 remote PCs or terminals to your NetWare LAN. The communications software required by a remote PC or Macintosh are included with this package. This product has the features of NetWare AnyWare, the difference between these two products is that this product gives you multiple NetWare AnyWare sessions. The main advantage of the NetWare Access Server (NAS) is you do not have the additional cost of a dedicated workstation required per connection. Asynchronous, direct connection or connection through multiplexers by remote users, is supported.

You will require a 80386 Industry Standard Architecture (ISA) bus machine to support the Deskview 386 multiuser, multitasking abilities. This provides you with multiple 640 KB virtual machines, one session is required per user with the ability of a connection to use multiple sessions. One session is reserved for managing the remote connections, by the network supervisor.

> **NOTE:** The NetWare Access Server may be accessed by workstations on a remote LAN with communications capabilities.

To enable all 15 connections, you will need the NETWARE Access Server software, a 386-based computer with up to 12 MB of memory, and four WNIM+ boards.

The NAS has the following features

- a total of 15 remote users or sessions, and one supervisor session are supported,
- multiple local network workstations are not required to support this product for heavy dial-in use,
- all levels of network security are enforced,
- dial-back capabilities provide extra security on a user basis,
- operations can be reviewed through audit trails,
- server, session, and modem statuses can be monitored and controlled through utilities by the supervisor,
- sessions can be left running allowing the user to disconnect and reconnect later to follow up their job,
- printing can redirected to network or remote printers,
- wide varieties of modems are supported,
- batch and menu utilities can be used for file transfer.

20.1.3 NetWare Asynchronous Communications Server (NACS)

This product mentioned with NetWare AnyWare can be used for PC to LAN, LAN to LAN, and LAN to HOST communications, depending upon the communication interface used.

The NACS software runs on a dedicated IBM PC, AT, or compatible machine which becomes your asynchronous communications server. This enables up to 16 simultaneous network local workstations to initiate or receive calls in or out of your LAN. It is a modem pooling device which can support multiple types and speeds of modems.

If you wish to connect a workstation on your LAN to an asynchronous host, you can utilize this product in conjunction with terminal emulation software, such as Novell's ASCOM IV.

In addition, the NACS handles all the modem pooling and protocol requirements. The NACS uses a Wide NetWork Interface Module (WNIM+) adapter card to connect the modems. Up to four WNIM+ cards can be installed in a single NetWare Asynchronous Communications Server. A WNIM+ has an on-board processor, memory, and four asynchronous ports.

Included in the NACS are the following features

- up to 16 asynchronous connections are supported,
- up to 19.2 Kbps speeds per port are supported,
- a single network can have multiple NACS installed,
- connections can be made available to users requiring host and/or public data networks,
- multiple asynchronous communications packages are supported,
- user/communication package has full access to modem control, including hardware flow control,
- inactive sessions are timed out and unused ports are released.

20.1.4 NetWare ASCOM IV

This product is a communications package which allows you to emulate asynchronous display terminals required when connecting to a asynchronous host through the NACS. It also supports dialing into a NetWare Access Server (NAS) session. Users can utilize ASCOM IV for file transfer to and from an asynchronous device. The package is available as a four-user license.

ASCOM IV has the following features

- most ASCII terminals are supported,
- file transfer is available,
- most modems are supported, including those with high-speed error correcting modes,
- dialing directory can be customized on an individual basis.

20.2 LAN to LAN CONNECTIVITY

Multiple remote LANS can be connected to create a wide area network (WAN). The remote LANS may be located in different cities or countries and still access each other's resources. The connection between these remote LANS can be accomplished, depending on your needs, through voice grade dial-up lines, public, or private packet switching network services (PDN), direct digital services, or T1 lines. The following products allow you to connect multiple LANS: NetWare Link/Async, NetWare Link/X.25, NetWare Link/T1, and NetWare Link/64.

20.2.1 NetWare Link/Async (previously NetWare Async Remote Bridge)

This product utilizes COM1/COM2 ports and/or WNIM+ adapters (through external (router) or possibly internal bridging (router)), to give you up to six connections into/from a LAN. It has been designed for the company that requires transfer of small to medium sized files, electronic mail, and possibly host connection. If you are configuring this with the WNIM+ adapter, you can only use a maximum of two in a single machine.

ELS NetWare Level II v2.15 is bundled with Link/Async configured using COM1 or COM2. Advanced and SFT NetWare v2.15 are bundled with Link/Async configured with COM1/COM2 and/or WNIM+ (external or possibly internal bridged). NetWare 386 v3.0 is bundled with Link/Async configured as an external bridge only.

This product has the following features:

- simple to install and use,
- inactive connections can be configured to time-out,
- an inexpensive solution utilizing asynchronous modems and voice-grade telephone lines,
- simultaneous connection to remote networks is available to multiple users.

20.2.2 NetWare Link/X.25

This product allows you to connect multiple LANs through private or public X.25 networks using an X.25 adapter card (or X.25 extended adapter-PS/2) and router software.

Up to 11 remote LANs can be connected simultaneously through one NetWare Link/X.25. This is accomplished by mixing (multiplexing) the 11 connections over one line. This is referred to as a virtual circuit.

This product is installed in an dedicated/nondedicated external bridge (router). Similar to all the Novell communication products, the connections are transparent to the users. The NetWare Link/X.25 includes the following features

- one X.25 link will connect up to 11 remote LANs,
- dedicated or nondedicated external bridge installation is used for this connection,
- dial-up and leased lines are supported,
- can access remote 3270 hosts,
- topology independent.

20.2.3 NetWare Link/T1

This product allows multiple LANs to be connected via synchronous lines which will give you speeds from 9600 bps to 2 Mbps. In the USA, the T1 is limited to 1.544 Mbps and 2.048 Mbps in Europe. To accomplish this connection, you will require the Link router software, Novell's Synchronous/+ Adapter (supports V.35, RS422, or RS232), Data Service Unit/Channel Service Units (DSU/CSU), and a data switch or multiplexer at each end.

Fractional T1 links are available and are supported by this product. This means that you can divide a T1 line into multiple channels for voice, video, and data.

The NetWare Link/T1 can be configured to run in either the file server or in a dedicated/nondedicated external bridge. All communications are automatically routed over the shortest most efficient path with inactive links bypassed. Novell's IPX/SPX and NetBIOS protocols are supported for communication.

Like all the Novell communication products, the connections are transparent and security is based on NetWare's operating system. The NetWare Link/T1 has the following features:

- completely transparent connections,
- installation, on-line troubleshooting, load testing, and error rate checking diagnostics are included,

- RS232, RS422, and V.35 interfaces are supported,
- topology independent.

20.2.4 NetWare Link/64

This product is the same as the Link/T1 but has speed limitations of up to 64 Kbps. It has the following features

- completely transparent connections,
- installation, on-line troubleshooting, load testing, and error rate checking diagnostics are included,
- RS232, RS422, and V.35 interfaces are supported,
- topology independent.

20.2.5 Host Communications

Connections into a host environment can be accomplished through stand-alone, multiple stand-alones (on or off a LAN) or LAN connections (through a gateway). In all cases the PC can emulate a host terminal or printer. The connection between PCs and a host can be accomplished through a remote or direct connection into a cluster controller, multiplexer, or front end processor. When a remote connection is required, the PC can emulate the cluster controller.

20.2.6 Types of Connection

If you are installing a gateway you have a choice of three types of connections: Systems Network Architecture (SNA), asynchronous, or X.25. The type of connection decided upon depends on the host and the availability of ports. In addition your decision will include the distance and speed requirements.

20.3 PC to Host Connectivity

20.3.1 3270-CUT Workstation

This product allows a IBM PC, PS/2 or compatible to directly connect to a 3x74 cluster controller, and emulate an IBM CUT (Control Unit Terminal) display terminal. It is a single station package. The NetWare 3270 CUT Workstation product encompasses many features including: file transfer, multiple APIs, low workstation memory usage, Model 2, 3, 4, and 5 full display sessions support, and keyboard remapping utilities.

20.3.2 3270-Multi Workstation

This product is a terminal emulation package allowing a single station (IBM PC, PS/2 and compatible) to support emulation of up to five IBM display terminals and printers. The connection is accomplished directly in one of three ways: coaxial, Token Ring, or Synchronous Data Link Control (SDLC). This is available as a per-user license.

Coaxial: To establish a coaxial connection to a 3x74 or compatible cluster controller (SNA or non SNA), a coaxial adapter is required for each PC. The cluster controller must be configured for Distributed Functional Terminal (DFT) mode. The following types of adapters can be used: Novell's coax adapter for PC or PS/2, a IBM 3278/79 adapter, a IBM 3270 connection adapter, or an IRMA I prom based adapter (with PROMS from Novell).

Remote: To establish a remote connection to an IBM 37xx cluster controller, a remote communications adapter is required. The connection is through externally clocked synchronous modems via SNA/SDLC lines. The following types of adapters can be used: Novell's Synchronous adapter for PCs and ATs, the IBM Multiprotocol adapter/A for PS/2s.

Token Ring: To establish a stand-alone Token Ring connection, you will need an IBM or compatible Token Ring adapter. For this connection one of the following devices must be located on or bridged to the Token Ring network: a 3174 cluster controller (using a Token Ring network gateway feature), a 3720/25/45 front end processor (using either a Token Ring Interface Couple (TIC) or Token Ring Adapter (TRA)), or a 937x (using the IBM Token Ring Subsystem Controller Option).

20.3.3 5250-SDLC Workstation

This is used to remotely connect IBM PCs or compatible, PS/2 model 25 and 30 to an IBM System 3X minicomputer. It is a single user package that emulates the 3X's 5250 terminals and 5251 Model 12 and 5294 cluster controllers.

You have available to you through an SDLC connection, a total of nine concurrent host sessions, up to five of these utilized by either serial or parallel local printers.

The NetWare 5250 SDLC Workstation offers may features including: a user interface that is menu driven, sequential file transfer software, and 5250 terminal tools including status line.

20.3.4 5250-Twinax Workstation

This single user emulation product allows you to connect your IBM PCs and compatible, PS/2 Model 25 and 30 to IBM's System/3X and AS 400 minis. It emulates the following terminals: IBM 5250 and 3180. As the product name implies the connection occurs over twinax cable.

You have available to you a total of seven concurrent host sessions and a single DOS session, any or all of these sessions can be dedicated to local serial or parallel printers.

The NetWare 5250 Twinax Workstation product provides many features including: sequential file transfer software, support for all IBM System/3X applications and utilities, 5250 terminal tools including status line, and automatic command entry.

20.4 LAN to Host Connectivity

20.4.1 SNA Gateway Products

Novell's SNA connectivity is available in the following products: NetWare SNA Gateway ELS, the NetWare SNA Gateway, and NetWare 3270 LAN Workstation software.

20.4.2 NetWare SNA Gateway ELS

This product provides an entry level solution into the SNA environment. It provides support for either the remote SDLC (offering 16 sessions) or Coax (offering 5 sessions) options.

20.4.3 SNA Gateway

This product is used to connect PC LAN workstations to an IBM SNA host. An adapter can be installed in any workstation to create the gateway, and the terminal emulation software is run at the users stations. Up to 97 PC LAN workstations can access the host through the gateway depending on the type of host connection used. Keep in mind that the number of sessions running does not match the number of workstations because a station can run more than one session.

Novell's SNA gateway utilizes a PC LAN workstation to emulate an IBM cluster controller. This workstation then becomes a gateway. The gateway is connected to the host through any one of three connectivity options: coaxial, SDLC, or Token-Ring. There are a number of connection options available for this product.

Coax: Coax provides you with support for up to five sessions through a coaxial connection replacing a modem. If you connect to a DFT port on the cluster controller speeds up to 2.3 Mbps can be achieved.

Remote: Remote provides you with support for up to 16 sessions through SDLC externally clocked modems at speeds of up to 19.2 Kbps, to a 37xx front end processor.

Coax Mux: Coax mux provides you with support for up to 40 sessions through a coaxial connection to a 3299 port on a 3174 or 3274 cluster controller at speeds up to 2.3 Mbps. These connections can consist of a total of eight multiplexed, five session Distributed Function Terminal (DFT) lines through a single connection.

Token Ring: Token Ring provides you with support for up to 128 sessions over 97 workstations connecting to a 3174, 937X, or 37xx processor. Considering the processing required, an 80386 based machine is recommended with two Token Ring adapters installed in the gateway machine.

High Speed Remote: High speed remote provides you with support for up to 128 sessions over 97 workstations, through SDLC externally clocked modems, at speeds of up to 64 Kbps, to a 37xx front end processor.

20.4.4 3270-LAN Workstation

This product is used when you wish to connect PC, PS/2s or specified compatible to a SNA host through a gateway connection. It is an IBM 3270 terminal and 3287 printer emulation package that is used with the NetWare SNA Gateway or SNA Gateway ELS product.

You have available to you, a single DOS session and up to five host display and printer sessions per workstation. It is sold on a per server license basis and is bundled in with SFT or 386 NetWare. The NetWare 3270 LAN Workstation product provides you with many features including: file transfer, multiple APIs, low workstation memory usage, Model 2, 3, 4, and 5 full display sessions support, over 30 languages supported, and keyboard remapping utilities.

20.4.5 5250 Gateway

This product is used to connect PC LAN workstations to an IBM System/3X through a gateway server, over remote SDLC connection. This is used in conjunction with your 5250 terminal emulation software running at the users workstations. The gateway provides the connection to the host through either a modem or modem eliminator. Up to nine concurrent terminal or printer sessions can be accessed by the users. Five of these can be running concurrently in any one workstation. If you require more sessions for users you connect multiple gateways to your LAN.

20.4.6 5250-LAN Workstation

This product is to be used with the 5250 gateway. It provides the terminal emulation for your PC LAN workstations. The primary benefit of this package is its multisession support. The NetWare 5250 LAN Workstation has many other features including: five host terminal and printer sessions per workstation, a DOS session with hot key access, and 5250 terminal tools including status line, and automatic command entry.

GLOSSARY

In this chapter

Computer and Local Area Network Terms, referring to Novell's NetWare Operating System.

Access: This is the process of data retrieval from the permanent computer magnetic storage, into Random Access Memory (RAM). Data must be in the electronic memory, for computers to manipulate it.

Access time: A measure of time from sending a command to receiving and answer.

ACK (Affirmative Acknowledgement): Used in block transmission, indicates that the previous transmission block was accepted by the receiver and that it is ready to accept the next block of the transmission.

Active hub: This device amplifies transmission signals in certain network topologies. An active hub can be used either to add additional workstations to a network or to lengthen the cable distance between workstations and the file server. See also Passive Hub.

Add-in board: An optional circuit board that modifies or enhances a microcomputer's capabilities. See also network interface card.

Address: An identifying number for a location in computer memory. Also a unique number that identifies a particular network or network station.

Algorithm: A calculation method or formula used in problem solving. For example, an algorithm can be used to reschedule data transmissions after there has been a data collision.

AM (Amplitude Modulation): A way to transmit data or sound. A sine wave (the carrier) of high frequency (500,000 cycles per second (hertz) or higher) is made.

Amplitude: Peak voltage of a wave.

Analog: Used to describe voltage or current values, based on a continuous ratio system. See also Analog Transmission, Modem.

Analog transmission: A data communications scheme utilizing a continuous signal, varied by amplification. For example, analog transmissions are used by Broadband networks. The type of data transmitted over telephone lines, opposite of digital. See also modem.

Application (software): A software program (or package) that has a user interface and makes calls to the operating system to manipulate datafiles, thus allowing a computer user to perform a specific job (such as database, spreadsheet, accounting, or word processing).

Archive: To backup datafiles. See Backup.

Architecture: This term, when applied to computers describes the component and interface types, and the physical interfaces the system utilizes in its design.

ARCNET: This acronym stands for: **A**ttached **R**esource **C**omputer **Net**work, which is a LAN scheme designed by Datapoint. The communication rate of 2.5 Mb/sec + is achieved between network devices by ARCnet.

ASCII (American Standard Code for Information Interchange): A standard code that represents characters in a computer, that is, the letters A thru Z, a thru z, the digits 0 thru 9, punctuation marks and various control functions. This character set is used internally by the IBM PC and most other microcomputers. The standard character set uses a 7 bit code to create 128 characters. IBM PC-compatible computers use an extended ASCII character set, which adds an eighth bit to the code, doubling the number of characters to 256. Each bit pattern determines the appearance of a character. ASCII characters form the computer's text display and control such features as back space, line feed, carriage return, and so on.

Asynchronous (async): Data sent in a series, one bit at a time. Asynchronous modems are satisfactory for accessing most BBS or time-sharing systems. A method of data communication in which transmissions are not synchronized by a clocking signal. Each character has a start and stop bit to synchronize signals between the sending device and receiving device. This allows a character to be sent at random after the preceding character has been sent. Asynchronous transmission is used by Local Area Networks.

Attach: To gain access to a file server with a username/password, particularly to access any additional file server(s) after being currently logged in to one file server. The term also can refer to physically connecting components, often by cable.

Attenuation: Loss of signal strength.

Attributes: See File attributes.

Auto answer: Used to describe a modem when it is set to automatically answer incoming calls on a phone line.

Automatic rollback: A feature of the TTS (Transaction Tracking System). Returning a database to its original (uncorrupted) state, abandoning the current transactions. This occurs when a file server or work station running under TTS fails in the middle of a transaction. The database is "rolled back" to its most recent complete state, preventing corruption from the half-complete transaction. See also Backing Out and TTS.

Background task: Performed in a subordinate status to those tasks in the foreground. For example, a nondedicated file server can operate as both a workstation with application software in the foreground, and as a network file server with NetWare in the background. Foreground, being the software package the user currently "sees," and background being the software which is running "behind" that package.

Backing out: Used to describe one of the functions of NetWare's Transaction Tracking System (TTS). For example, a series of database changes is a single transaction, that must be either fully written to the database, or "backed out" (not written at all).

backup: This term refers to the process of creating a copy of files, or to describe the copy created, (diskette, tape, etc.) Backups are made to ensure data recovery in case of system failure. Off premises backups are kept to ensure data integrity in case of fire or catastrophic problems affecting the system and the premises such as fire, theft etc.

Bad block table: A list of physical storage locations (addresses) kept on a hard drive, that are physically unable to reliably store data. The bad block table is usually duplicated on a printout that is shipped with the hard drive. This list is also called "Media Defect List." See also Hot fix, Read-after-write verification.

Bandwidth: The maximum capacity or range of frequencies between the highest and lowest of a communications channel, typically stated as bits per second (bit/sec) or cycles per second (Hertz). Bandwidth indicates network speed, because it measures the highest rate at which the network can pass information.

Banner: An optional first page of a network printer printout. It provides information on the current print job such as, the user, the workstation connection number, the file name (if available), the source directory of the file, the print queue, the file server, and the time and date of the printout.

Baseband coax: Short for Baseband Coaxial Cable, which is a single channel medium used to carry baseband transmissions. See also Baseband system.

Baseband system: A communications method in which the transmission is placed directly onto the cable in digital form. No translation is necessary in a baseband system at the sending or receiving end because the I/O of the microcomputer is also digital.

Base memory address: The beginning address of a block of memory. A network interface card (NIC) uses the base memory address as a buffer where both the computer and the NIC can leave information and signal each other for information pickup.

Base I/O address: The start point or beginning address of an I/O device. The base I/O address allows a CPU to find the correct port to communicate with a particular device.

Batch mode: An instruction or a series of instructions which run without user interaction. When multiple files are downloaded from a file server, or a host Mainframe Computer, they are referred to as "batch transfers."

Baud rate: Data transferred over a serial interface and/or modem is transferred at an imprecise unit of speed, roughly equivalent to bits per second, called the "baud rate." For example, a device that transmits 300 bits of information per second is said to transmit at 300 baud. This is roughly equivalent to 30 characters per second. Typical baud rates are 300, 1200, 2400, and 9600.

Binary: Pertaining to a choice, or condition in which there are two possibilities (usually 0 and 1).

Bindery: Datafiles maintained by NetWare's O/S and used to monitor network resources. These files contain a dynamic list of "objects" (users, groups, file servers, etc.) and their "properties" (rights, passwords, network addresses, etc.).

BIOS (Basic Input/Output (I/O) System): A set of programs, usually in firmware, that enables each computer's central processing unit to communicate with printers, disks, keyboards, consoles, and other attached input and output devices.

Bisynchronous (bisync): Binary synchronous. This is a serial data transmission protocol, controlled by a clocking signal, developed for mainframes by IBM.

Bit: A contraction of "Binary digIT." It is the smallest unit of information and must indicate one of two states, "off" (0) or "on" (1). See also byte.

Bit rate: The rate at which bits (binary digits) are transmitted over a communications path. The bit rate is not the data signaling rate (Baud) which measures the rate of signal changes being transmitted.

Bit stream: Refers to a continuous series of bits being transmitted.

Block: A unit of stored data. In NetWare, a block is 4 kilobytes (KB), or 4096 bytes, of data. For example, a 40 MB hard drive contains roughly 10,000 blocks of data storage area.

BNC: This cabling term is a short form for Bayonet Nut Connector.

Boot: To load a computer's operating system into RAM. After the operating system has been booted, applications can be loaded into the computer. See also Bootstrap, remote reset and warm boot.

Bootstrap (bootstrap loader): A program that starts a "cold" computer. Generally, the bootstrap program tells the computer where to find the operating system software so that the computer can load the operating system.

Boot up: See Boot.

bps (bits per second): The basic unit of data communications rate measurement.

Bridge: This device matches circuits and connects local area networks using routing buffers to check addresses and which may regulate bandwidth. A software and hardware connection between two networks, usually of similar design. There are two types of NetWare bridges, internal and external. If a bridge is located in a file server, it is an internal bridge. If a bridge is located in a workstation, it is an external bridge.

Broadband (wideband): A analog communications system characterized by a large split, or multiplexed bandwidth providing multiple communications channels. Modems are required at either end of the transmission cable to convert the digital signals to and from analog signals.

Broadcast: NetWare uses this transmission technique in which all logged in stations receive these message transmissions.

BSC (Binary Synchronous Communications): See Bisynchronous (bisync).

Buffer: A storage area in RAM where data that is being transferred may be stored temporarily. Data is placed in buffers when the devices handling the data process it at different speeds. For example, a printer may not be able to process information as fast as a file server can send it.

Any information the printer is receiving but cannot process immediately is placed into a buffer until the information can be processed.

Burst error: A series of consecutive errors in data transmission. Refers to fact that errors are prone to occurring in groups on communication lines.

Bus: An electrical signal path. A network topology consisting of a single cable terminated with resistors to which all network devices are attached.

Bus, data: The main bus inside a microcomputer, used for transferring data between the CPU and peripherals.

Bus, network: The main network cable or line that connects network stations.

Bus master: This controller I/O board is an intelligent device which performs data transfer while the CPU services other requests.

Byte: A byte represents a binary character, and usually consists of 8 bits.

Cache buffer: An area in the RAM of a NetWare file server into which portions of last requested datafiles are temporarily stored. Data requests from network stations can then access data from the file server's memory rather than from the disk. This increases the speed of network operations, since data in memory can be accessed up to 100 times faster than data on the file server drive. See also Directory caching and Disk caching.

Carrier detect: An RS232C interface modem signal that indicates the modem is receiving a signal from another modem.

Carrier Sense Multiple Access (CSMA): This is a "contention network access scheme." A workstation monitors the network and transmits any time the cable appears to be clear (no other workstation's carrier signal is sensed).

C/C: See Cluster controller.

CCITT (Consultative Committee on International Telephone and Telegraph): A committee established under the United Nations within the ITU (International Telecommunications Union) to advise and recommend worldwide standards.

CD-ROM (Compact Disc-Read Only Memory): Normally a 4.72" plastic disc developed by Phillips and Sony to store digital information in microscopic pits which can be read by a laser beam. Visually the same as the audio compact disc except that it contains computer data instead of audio data. Extremely large volumes of data can be stored onto these discs which can later be searched to locate and retrieve any desired information upon demand.

Channel: A data communication path, either physical or logical, or both that allows data transmission to travel from between locations. See also Disk channel.

Character: A unit of information that is usually composed of 6, 7, or 8 bits. IBM PC-compatible microcomputers use an extended ASCII character set.

Check bit: One nondata bit added to a character transmitted that enables the terminal to check each character it processes. Also referred to as a Parity bit.

Checksum: A number provided with a group of data bits during transmission, for checking the accuracy of the data received.

Chip: A wafer of silicon imprinted with various integrated circuits required for specific functions. An integrated circuit.

Clear To Send (CTS): An RS232C interface modem signal between the modem and a controller used to operate over a communications line.

Clock, external: A clocking or timing signal from another device. Some modems can provide external clocking. See also Clocking.

Clocking: Synchronizing the timing of communications information between a sender and receiver.

Cluster controller C/C: The main function of the cluster controller is to allow the attachment of "dumb" terminals. Terminals are attached to the cluster controller using a BNC connector. Cluster controllers attach to the Front End Processor (FEP) through an RS232 port, or they can be directly attached to the host (Channel attached).

CMOS RAM: Microcomputer system configurations are stored in a type of random access memory. This configuration information includes: number and type(s) of drives, date and time, as well as information on the size and type of memory. The CMOS RAM is normally battery maintained and is not directly available to the computer's operating system.

Coaxial cable (Coax): Cable consisting of two conductors (wires) where the center conductor carries the signal and the outer tubular braided conductor, provides the ground and shielding against electrical interference.

Collision: When multiple workstations simultaneously transmit onto a common communications channel, they collide, resulting in a garbled or corrupted data transmission.

Command: An instruction, entered by a user at the keyboard, that tells the computer what and how to perform a specified task.

Communication buffers: Specified areas in the file server RAM or bridge RAM that are used to temporarily hold packets arriving from the various stations until they can be processed and sent to their destination. Also referred to as "routing buffers."

COMn: A serial communications port. See also Serial port.

Configuration, hardware: The specific type of hardware installed in or attached to the file server or workstations such as drives, network interface boards, memory boards, printers attached, and so on.

Configuration, software: An install or setup procedure that configures software programs to run on the microcomputer's specified hardware, operating system, peripherals, and so on.

Connection number: A number assigned dynamically to all stations that attach to a file server. This number can be found by executing the WHOAMI or USERLIST NetWare commands.

Console: This term is used to describe the file server monitor and keyboard. Commands entered at the file server are called "Console Commands." These commands include functions for printer and disk drive control, "DOWN" the file server, "SEND" messages, and accessing file server information.

Contention: A common access method used by multiple topologies which shares a network cable based on first come, first served.

Controller address: Jumpers and dip switches are used to physically set a number on a hard drive controller board known as the address. This number is specified during NETGEN to enable the operating system to locate the controller on a disk channel.

Controller (board): This device enables a CPU to communicate with a peripheral (drive, network interface card or NIC, tape drive, etc.). This device regulates and manages input/output (I/O) of its attached device.

Control Unit Terminal (CUT): This is a type of terminal which is not "intelligent." It can only display text.

Coprocessor: A optionally installed microprocessor designed to handle specific tasks, thereby reducing the workload on the CPU. For example, a math coprocessor. See also Disk Coprocessor Board (DCB).

CPU (Central Processing Unit): The microprocessor (chip or chip set) that provides the processing capability (intelligence) to enable a computer to operate. It controls all activity within a computer system, receives information, processes it, and then sends it where required, for example, to the file server hard drive.

Crash (crashed): A commonly used slang term that refers to hardware and/or software that has stopped or quit running.

CRC (Cyclic Redundancy Check): This is common method of error checking a received message for accuracy. Bits are calculated and added to a message block by the sender then recalculated and matched by the receiver to detect errors.

Cross talk: Emissions passing between cable elements or multiple cables create signal interference.

CSMA/CD (Carrier Sense Multiple Access with Collision Detection): A network access scheme that is based on contention with the addition of a method of recovery in the event of a collision. When a collision is detected, transmitting stations cease transmission and wait a random interval before retransmitting. See also Contention.

Current directory: The DOS directory you are working in, also referred to as default directory.

Current drive: See Default drive.

CUT: See Control Unit Terminal.

Cylinder (hard drive): This term refers to data storage areas on a hard drive, each with distinct boundaries. Generally, the more cylinders a hard drive has, the higher its storage capacity.

Database: A collection of data organized and stored in files by a user or network users, through use of a application program.

Database Management System (DBMS): A application program designed to create, organize, store, and retrieve machine readable information in a database.

Data Communications Equipment (DCE): Any hardware installed which provides all functions required to establish, maintain and terminate a connection, the signal conversion and control between the data terminal equipment and the common carrier's line. A modem is a DCE.

Data integrity: The condition in which data is maintained in an uncorrupted and usable format.

Data Set Ready (DSR): An RS232C Interface control signal from DCE which indicates to the attached DTE that the modem is ready to receive data.

Data Terminal Equipment (DTE): Data processing equipment such as microcomputers, terminals, and printers.

Data Terminal Ready (DTR): An RS232C interface control signal from the data terminal indicating to the modem that the terminal is ready for transmission.

Data transfer rate: The average number of bits, characters, or blocks per time unit transferred from a sender to receiver.

Dedicated file server: Reserved for the single function of being a file server. A dedicated network file server, for example, cannot be used for any purpose other than network operations.

Default: The standard dictionary meaning of "failure to meet obligations" has been changed when this term is applied to computers. Here it refers to a value or set of values available to software programs, hard drives, and printers automatically. Software can typically be installed using "defaults" only. For example, a word processor may specify defaults of a 66 line page, tab settings at every ½," and a page size of 8½ x 11." While NetWare will operate using defaults, this is not recommended.

Default drive: The DOS drive designation that a microcomputer is currently using. The drive prompt (A:>, C:>, F:>, etc.) identifies the default drive letter (workstation or network).

Default server: The file server on which your default drive is located. Any NetWare commands you enter will be directed to the default server unless you specify otherwise.

Delimiter: A symbol or character that signals the start or end of a command parameter. For example, in the command CHKVOL F: M:, the blank space is the delimiter between F: and M: to mark the two distinct parameters. Delimiters can include the comma (,), the period (.), the slash (/), the backslash (\), the hyphen (-), and the colon (:).

DEModulation: The process of converting an analog signal back to its original digital form.

Destination: The workstation, drive, directory, file, printer, and so on, where you are sending data.

Device driver: A software module or program under the control of the CPU, that translates and controls any input/output to a device. For example, for each type of hard drive accessible by the file server, a corresponding device driver is normally linked with the operating system.

DFT: See Distributed Functional Terminal.

Diagnostics: Programs or user logic to test computer hardware and software to determine whether they are operating correctly.

Digital: A discretely variable signal (typically the binary conditions On or Off) or characteristic such as a pulse, as opposed to an infinitely variable analog signal or characteristic such as time, temperature, or movie video. Baseband topologies use digital transmissions.

Digitizing: The process of transforming two dimensional text or graphics into a digital format.

Direct connect: In LANs, the process of attaching a workstation to the network cable without an intervening hub or multiplexer. A NIC is used to accomplish direct connect, dependant on the topology.

Direct memory access: See DMA.

Directory caching: NetWare's method of decreasing the time it takes to locate a file on the file server hard drive. The file allocation table and directory entries are retained and updated in the file server's RAM. A file's location can then be read from the file server RAM, which can be 100 times faster than reading from the file server hard drive.

Directory entries (volume): In a NetWare volume, information stored in the volume's directory table, usually a directory name or filename. A directory's trustee list takes up one or more directory entries, depending on how large the list is. The maximum number of directory entries on a volume is specified in NETGEN during installation.

Directory entry table: A table kept current by NetWare containing information about each file and directory such as the name, creation date, size, date and time of each update, file attributes, trustees, and so on. This table is written to the file server hard drive, while a copy remains resident in file server RAM for enhanced access time.

Directory hashing: NetWare's indexing of a file's physical location on the file server hard drive so that files can be located more efficiently, and in less time. With directory hashing, NetWare enables a computer to search through only a few directory entries, in contrast to the DOS method of searching through all entries sequentially.

Directory name: A user-assigned name that both identifies a directory and identifies its position within the directory structure. In NetWare, the full directory name lists the file server name, the volume label, and any subdirectories leading down to the directory you need to access. Also referred to as the directory path.

Directory rights: Restrictions at a directory level that regulates any trustee activity within it. Directory rights are specified on a single directory basis and do NOT flow down through the directory structure. See also Maximum Rights Mask.

Directory structure: In both DOS and NetWare, the different levels of directories (parent and sub) organized to form a hierarchy or tree structure. Directories contain files, grouping them together conveniently. A list of these files can be displayed when the NetWare directory command, NDIR, or the DOS directory command, DIR is used. See also Directory name.

Disable: To turn off, to render inactive, to prevent certain interrupts from occurring in a piece of hardware such as a network interface card.

Disk: A magnetically encoded storage medium in the form of a circular platter. For example, two types of disks are used with modern microcomputers, hard and floppy. Hard drives use a metallic base and are usually installed within a computer or disk subsystem. Floppy disks (called diskettes) use a polyester base and are always removable. See also Disk drive.

Disk cache block: A block of data written into a cache buffer during a drive read. See also Disk caching and Cache buffer.

Disk caching: As files are requested, they are read into the file server's memory. This means that the latest requested files are always maintained in memory, where access can be up to 100 times faster than from disk.

Disk channel: The transmission route for data, between the CPU and storage systems (hard drive or tape). A disk channel can be any data bus added by a disk coprocessor board, or an internal disk drive in a NetWare file server. Multiple disk channels contribute to data integrity and can improve the file server's efficiency in handling data I/O. See also Disk coprocessor board and Disk duplexing.

Disk controller: A card or board installed in the microcomputer that controls the method by which the data is written to and read from the drive.

Disk coprocessor board (DCB): An optional CPU board that acts as an intelligent interface between the file server CPU and the disk controller. The DCB handles hard drive I/O, thus increasing the file server's performance. A Disk coprocessor board and any attached disk subsystems make up a complete disk channel.

Disk drive: A storage device that allows users to write, read, and delete data, regulated by a disk controller. A disk drive can be internal (built into the microcomputer) or external (attached as a peripheral to the microcomputer).

Disk duplexing: An SFT NetWare method of protecting data in which the same data is written simultaneously to two hard drives on separate channels (controllers). If one channel (controller) fails, the data integrity on the other channel remains intact. When drives are duplexed, read requests are sent to whichever drive in the pair can respond faster with the requested data, thus increasing the file server's efficiency. When multiple read requests occur simultaneously, the requests are split between channels and can be processed faster. See also Disk mirroring.

Disk interface board: An add-on board that acts as an interface between the CPU and the disk controller. See also Disk coprocessor board.

Disk mirroring: Data is copied to two separate hard drives (on the same channel), a feature of System Fault Tolerance (SFT) NetWare. Should one drive fail, the data on the other drive (a mirror copy) is still intact. Mirroring uses the same controller (channel), a factor which limits the amount of data protection provided by this feature. A failure of the drive controller would affect access to both drives and data integrity could be adversely effected. See also Disk duplexing.

Disk Operating System (DOS): An operating system that consists of a collection of software programs that instructs a microcomputer how to transfer information to and from peripheral input/output devices.

Disk subsystem: Attached to a file server, this external unit contains a hard drive or drives. The disk subsystem gives the file server more hard drive storage capacity than can physically fit inside the file server.

Distributed Functional Terminal (DFT): This is an "intelligent" terminal that is used for some controller processing and can support up to five Logical Units (LUs) over one coax connection.

DMA (Direct Memory Access): This is a high-speed method of transferring data directly into the file server's RAM from a peripheral device (e.g., hard drive). The file server CPU passes requests to a special integrated circuit (chip) which controls the reading and writing of memory, independent of the file server CPU. This enables the file server CPU to perform other tasks and can positively influence overall file server performance.

DOS text file: A file made up of ASCII characters.

Download: Data received from another computer. Conversely, data sent to a host computer is called an upload.

Download/upload: The transfer of data between computers usually via modem. Transferring data from a host to a remote computer is downloading, from a remote computer to a host is uploading.

Down time: In a NetWare system with UPS monitoring, the "down time" is the number of minutes between the time the UPS begins supplying power to the file server and the time the operating system DOWN's the file server. See also UPS.

Drive: A physical data storage device that can be accessed such as a floppy drive, hard drive, or tape drive. A drive at a workstation is called a local drive. See also Disk drive.

Drive letter: A letter that can represents a logical drive which can be either a local drive or a network drive. A short cut or convenience for referring to a specific directory located on a network hard drive.

Drive mapping: See Map.

Driver: See Device driver.

Dumb terminal: A video screen and keyboard with no local CPU that cannot perform error detection or use a protocol. Usually attached to a mini-computer or a mainframe.

Duplexing: See Disk duplexing.

Duplex transmission: Two way transmission which permits simultaneous transmission in both directions. Also full duplex, as contrasted with half duplex.

Dynamic memory: Memory that requires constant rewriting or refreshing with continuous electrical current. An example is dynamic RAM. All data in RAM is lost when the power supply is turned off.

Dynamic resource configuration: NetWare 386 monitors the amount of memory available, and reallocates resources to optimize performance.

Effective rights: The rights a user can actually use in a given directory. Two contributing factors to effective rights are trustee rights granted to a particular user and any directory rights specified in the directory's maximum rights mask. Directory rights always take precedence over trustee rights, therefore any trustee right not specifically denied in the maximum rights mask is an effective right.

EIA (Electronic Industries Association): A standards organization specializing in the electrical and functional characteristics of interface equipment.

EIA Interface: A standardized set of signal characteristics and hardware protocols such as time or duration, voltage, and current that is specified by the Electronic Industries Association.

EIA RS232C: A widely accepted standard which is the interface between a modem and line controller for voice grade communication lines.

EISA (Enhanced Industry Standard Architecture): The Industry Standard Architecture (ISA) extended to a 32 bit architecture, also compatible with ISA boards.

Email (electronic mail): This term refers to the exchange of messages and/or data between users, on a LAN, on a BBS or commercial information utility.

Embedded SCSI: A hard drive that uses a SCSI interface and has the controller board built into the hard drive case.

Emulation: The duplication or mimicking of some or all the functions of one device in another device. For example, an microcomputer can emulate a dumb terminal for communicating with a host or mainframe computer.

Enable: To turn on, to restore a feature that has been disabled. To place in a state that will allow specified interrupts to occur in a device (such as a network interface card). Interrupts are usually enabled with a jumper or dip switch.

Error detection with retransmission: An communication error handling technique where the receiver can detect errors, then requests retransmission of the message or portion from the sender.

Error rate: A direct relationship of the number of bits, elements, characters, or blocks incorrectly received to the total number transmitted.

ESDI (Enhanced Small Device Interface): A fixed disk controller used for high speed access to large capacity hard drives.

Ethernet: Xerox originally developed this local area network protocol for mini computer communications.

Expansion slot: A space within a microcomputer where add-on boards or cards can be plugged into to the data bus.

Extended memory: In a personal computer running DOS, memory above the 1 MB address range is extended memory. Very little application software can use this memory directly, most require special drivers or remapping the extended memory as expanded. Extended memory in the file server can be used directly by NetWare.

External bridge: See Bridge.

FAT: See File Allocation Table.

Fault tolerance: See SFT.

Fiber optics: The process of modulating a visible or light signal to carry information through glass or plastic fibers.

File: A collection of data stored as one unit and given a filename. A file may contain many a program or data. A file can be saved to the drive, and then retrieved later to be run, viewed, or modified.

Filespec: One of several variables that can appear in a command format in NetWare manuals. Filespec represents the identification of a complete directory path includes the filename.

File Allocation Table (FAT): An index on a drive that records the actual physical drive location of all portions of a file.

File attributes: With NetWare, files can be "flagged" with any of a variety of attributes that govern the way a file can be accessed or viewed. Files are usually flagged Shareable, Read/Write. The "Shareable" flag indicates that multiple users may simultaneously access the file "Read/Write" indicates that users can read the file, and can "Write" to it.

File server (dedicated and nondedicated): This is the computer with NetWare installed as the operating system. The NetWare file server controls system access and all security configurations. A dedicated file server acts only as a file server, while a nondedicated one acts as both a file server and a workstation.

File sharing: A feature of networks that allows multiple users simultaneous access to the same file. See also File attributes.

Firmware: A program that resides in ROM and is not erased when the computer is turned off. It is usually treated as a hardware unit. See also ROM.

Flags: See File attributes.

Floppy disk drive: A drive that accesses a floppy disk. See also Disk drive.

Floppy disk(ette): Removable magnetic storage media. See also Disk.

Foreground task: A job or task that is has priority status and is executed by the CPU before background, or subordinate tasks are executed. See also Background task.

Form: Referred to in NetWare printer commands, the form number can be used to designate legal paper, letterhead, bond paper, labels, or continuous feed paper.

Format: A logical or physical arrangement of the tracks and sectors on a floppy disk or a hard drive. To be usable, a disk or drive must be formatted so that the tracks and sectors are compatible with the disk driver and operating system in use.

Frequency Modulation (FM): A form of modulation in which the frequency of a carrier wave is varied according to the value of the modulating signal.

Front End Processor (FEP): This is a device that controls remote networks and cluster controllers. It is the processor that attaches to a mainframe. It is an intelligent machine that contains anywhere from 16 to 32 RS232 ports. Its main function is to offload the processing from the host mainframe and allow the connection of cluster controllers.

Full DupleX (FDX): A circuit capable of transmitting simultaneously two ways. Sometimes referred to as duplex.

Gateway: A device that allows communication between two dissimilar networks or protocols using industry standard protocols such as BISYNC, X.25, or SNA. A gateway includes both hardware and software with its own CPU and memory and may perform both protocol and bandwidth conversion.

Gaussian noise: Noise where the amplitude of the signal is characterized by the Gaussian distribution. Also referred to as white noise, ambient noise, or hiss.

Gigabyte: Usually a measurement of data storage equal to 1000 megabytes.

Group access: A method of granting identical trustee rights to multiple users at the same time so they can all access the same directories. Instead of repetitively assigning each separate user the identical rights, the supervisor can create a group with the required rights then make each user a member of that group, and in this way, every user in the group has the same trustee rights.

Half DupleX (HDX): A circuit designed for transmission in either direction at a time but NOT both directions simultaneously.

Handshaking: An exchange of predetermined signals between two data sets (modems) establishing the connection and also during the data transmission. A handshake method (such as XON/XOFF) is an important part of a complete transmission protocol. A serial (asynchronous) transmission protocol usually includes the baud rate, handshaking (if any), parity setting, number of data bits, and number of stop bits.

Hard copy: A tangible paper printout or copy rather than simply a screen display.

Hard drive: A high-capacity magnetic storage device that allows users to read, write, or delete data. Hard drives may be network drives, or they may be local drives physically attached to a workstation. See also Disk drive.

Hardware: Physical equipment including all of the electronic and mechanical components of a network such as microcomputers, network interface cards, hard drives, hubs, cables, and so on.

Hardware interface: Physical hardware used to electrically connect the controllers to matching devices.

Hashing: See Directory hashing.

Hayes compatible: Modems that claim to use the commands originated by Hayes Microcomputer Products. While not required for serial communications, it is an defacto industry standard and most communication software programs support the Hayes command set.

HDLC: See High Level Data Link Control.

Head: The mechanism in a drive that reads and writes data to a magnetic media. When a hard drive is operating, the drive heads float on a cushion of air just above the surface of the rotating platters while they access the disk.

Header: Control information prefixing a message text, for example, source and destination address, priority, or type of message. Also called Heading or Leader.

Hexadecimal: This numeric notation system (base 16) is used to specify addresses in RAM.

Hierarchy: Refers to a directory structure made up of different levels and the entire structure is organized in a branching or tree format.

High Level Data Link Control (HDLC): A communications protocol that transmits certain commands that are not available in SDLC. X.25 networks use HDLC for transmission.

Home directory: Also referred to as a user's private directory. This directory is usually created by the network supervisor for each network user. The supervisor should also establish a drive mapping to locate the user in their own directory when they LOGIN.

Host: This term is often applied to mainframes, minicomputers, and file servers when they provide services to another computer. For example, a network workstation taken over and controlled by a remote microcomputer is referred to as the host.

Host-to-terminal: A central CPU (the host) serves multiple dumb terminals in this network scheme. Also known as centralized processing or a master/slave scheme.

Hot fix: During the NetWare installation, a small section of the hard drive is reserved for use by the "Hot Fix" feature. This area is used if NetWare performs a read-after-write verification, and finds that the data cannot be read reliably. The data is then transferred to the "hot fix" area, and the defective block address is added to the bad block table.

Hub: This device, used on certain network topologies splits or amplifies network transmission signals, allowing the network to be grow. See also Active hub and Passive hub.

Hz (hertz): A unit of measure of frequency, this represents the number of cycles per second. One hertz equals one cycle per second.

Identifier: Specific words used in a NetWare login script command to represent variable information. When an identifier appears in the login script, the current value for the information is supplied by NetWare. Examples are HOUR, DAY_OF_WEEK, LOGIN_NAME, STATION.

IEEE (Institute of Electrical and Electronic Engineers): This organization is one of many, who attempt to establish industry standards. The IEEE 802 committee has defined and published numerous documents on local area network standards.

Initialize: During the NetWare installation process, refers to dividing a file server hard drive into one or more volumes and setting up the NetWare directory entry and file allocation tables on each one. This also removes all existing data from a storage medium. See also Format.

Interface: Enabling two devices to communicate. Used to refer to the design of hardware and software which allows connection and communication between network components.

Interference: Undesired effects on communications channels or cabling which are a result of noise and other signals.

Internal bridge: See Bridge.

International Standards Organization (ISO): An international agency that develops standards for information exchange.

Internetwork (internet): Two or more networks connected by internal or external bridge(s). Users on an internet can transparently use the resources (files, printers, hard drives, etc.) of all connected networks if they have security access.

Internetwork packet exchange: See IPX.

Interrupt: This signal generated by application software program(s) can break into the execution of a program and suspend it with a new command. An interrupt will eventually allow the program to proceed from the point of the break in (or interrupt request). This interruption is done to allow another request to be processed, utilizing the computers resources. Any or all of the computer's resources may be appropriated by another request during the suspension time.

I/O (input/output): The process of moving data, as in the transmitting of data from a disk to a printer for printing, or from disk storage to display on a workstation screen.

I/O port: Data is communicated between the CPU and peripherals with this circuit.

IPX (Internetwork Packet Exchange): A protocol that allows the exchange of message packets between users on an internet. With IPX, applications running on a NetWare workstation can communicate directly with other workstations or devices on the internet. IPX is based on Xerox Corporation's Internetwork Packet Protocol.

ISO protocols: International Standards Organization's (ISO) Open System Interconnection (OSI) model. These are guidelines for network communication and design, divided into seven distinct layers.

Jitter: A type of line distortion noticeable at high speeds which is caused by the variation of a signal from its reference timing positions which can be the cause of data transmission errors.

Jumper block: A group of jumper pins used to make hardware configuration settings or changes to a board. See also Interrupt.

KB or K (kilobytes): A unit of measure for RAM or hard drive storage capacity, (2^{10} = 1024 bytes).

Kilo Bits Per Second (KBPS): A data rate equal of 1000 bps.

LAN (Local Area Network): See Local Area Network (LAN).

LAN driver: A specialized driver that must be linked to the NetWare operating system or shell to allow communication with a specific type of network interface card. See also Drivers.

Laser (Light Amplification by Stimulated Emission of Radar): A device which passes a beam of light through a special crystal so as to produce an extremely narrow coherent beam of vastly increased power. Stronger laser beams are used write information onto CD ROM discs by burning microscopic pits into the surfaces of the discs. Weaker laser beams are required to read the discs.

Laser card: A credit card sized plastic card that can contain 2 to 10 megabytes of non erasable data.

Latency: The time interval or waiting time between a station access request to a transmission channel and completion of the request.

Line drivers: Line drivers are DCE's that "drive" a digital signal directly through a transmission path. The device may amplify, reshape, or code the digital signal.

Line speed: The maximum data rate that can be reliably transmitted over a line under ideal conditions. Varies with capability of the hardware and line used in bits per second (bps).

Local Area Network (LAN): A computer-based communications system usually limited by geographic area. The term network is used to include any combination of hosts, terminals, microcomputers, and other attached devices.

Local drive: A drive that is physically attached to a workstation but is not accessible by NetWare from the file server. A local drive is normally accessible only by the workstation to which it is physically attached.

Lock: A method used to prevent multiple users from accessing data simultaneously. Such advisory locks such as with a semaphore warn the user that a file is in use but do not prevent its access. Most operating systems such as NetWare provides hard locks, which cannot be overridden. See also Record locking.

Logical: Conceptual, not physical. As an example, the directory information accessible by users implies is only a logical arrangement of files and directories. The actual segments of the files may be scattered all over the drive, but the logic of the operating system allows them to be presented in an orderly manner for the user's convenience.

Log in: To gain access to a system or network. Logging in to a NetWare network involves executing a login script and establishing yourself as a user with specified rights.

Login/logout: The entry of a login name and a password of activating or deactivating a workstation as a network entity. Login procedure for a local area network requires the starting (booting) of a network user program, often followed by keyboard .

Login script: A set of instructions that directs your workstation to perform specific actions when you log in or sign on to the network. The network supervisor should create a system-wide login script which is executed by all users as they login. Your individual login script executes after the system login script. When you attach to any additional file servers you do not execute a second set of login scripts.

LPT1: A printer port of a microcomputer. See also Parallel port.

Map or mapping: The process of assigning a logical drive letter to a chosen directory path (on a specified volume and file server). This is can be accomplished with the MAP command line utility or through SESSION menu utility.

Maximum rights mask: This is the same thing as directory rights. Directory rights are used as an extra security measure. When you create a directory all eight rights are assigned to it automatically. These work together with the trustee rights to determine what a user can do in a given directory, which creates the effective rights mask. Restricting a directory right will prevent any user except for SUPERVISOR (or equivalent) to override of the denied right, even though other users may have those trustee rights.

MB: See Megabyte.

Mbps: Megabits per second is a rate or data flow of approximately 1,000,000 bits per second.

Megabyte: A term for 1,048,576 bytes (2 to the 20th power), or approximately one million bytes. Usually referred to when discussing memory or drive capacity.

MegaHertz (Mhz): A segment of analog frequency equal to 10(6) hertz, one million cycles per second. Referred to when comparing CPU clock speeds. See also Hz.

Memory: An essential component of a computer's central processing unit. Memory is the work space where programs and/or data are executed or manipulated. See also Random Access Memory (RAM) and Read Only Memory (ROM).

Menu driven: Any software operated by selecting from a list of restricted operating options that are displayed in a menu. Considered to be more "user friendly" than COMMAND line operation.

Message packet: Network communication is accomplished in units called message packets. These packets contain data to be transferred, service requests, the information on how the request and the data should be handled, and the source and destination.

MHz: See Megahertz.

Microprocessor: See CPU (Central Processing Unit).

Mirroring: See Disk mirroring.

Modem (MOdulator/DEModulator): A signal conversion device to convert digital signals from a DTE to analog signals or tones for transmission over a telephone line. The receiver, another modem converts the analog back to digital and passes them to a DTE.

Monitor: A computer display or screen.

MS-DOS: MicroSoft Disk Operating System. See also Disk Operating System.

Motherboard: The "main circuit board" of a computer system, into which add-on boards or cards can be plugged into, increasing the available functions of the system. An example of an add-on card is a NIC (network interface card).

Multiple access: A condition in which multiple users can simultaneously open/access the same file. Sometimes referred to as concurrent access.

Multiplexer: This is a device that mixes low speed lines to combine their individual data transmission volumes. This allows the transmissions to occur on one high speed line. Also referred to as a MUX, this device may be a microprocessor.

Multipoint: Networks that are connected to a multiple of other networks create one virtual wide area network, and are referred to as multipoint. Usually public or private data networks are used to make this connection.

Multiplexing: Simultaneous support of multiple data transmissions on a single medium (cable or line).

Multiserver network: This is a single network which utilizes two or more file servers operating on it accessible by any attached user, who has the appropriate security rights. A multiserver network is NOT the same as an internet(work).

Multitasking: The ability to handle multiple jobs by a single CPU. On a nondedicated NetWare file server, multitasking refers to the server running in the foreground as a local workstation while all the network tasks are operating in the background.

Multiuser: A system in which multiple users share a single CPU's resources. Usually, in a mini or mainframe environment, multiuser indicates a host-to-terminal system, whereas in the LAN environment this indicates a peer-to-peer system.

MUX: See Multiplexer.

NetBIOS: An IBM developed emulator program that allows workstations to run multiuser application software on networks that support NetBIOS calls.

NetWare: A registered trademark used to describe the Novel network operating system and related products sold by Novell, Inc.

NetWare operating system: The operating system developed by Novell, Inc. The NetWare operating system is loaded into the file server when the file server is booted. It controls all system resources and the way information is processed on the entire network or internetwork.

NetWare shell/requestor: Special NetWare program(s) that are loaded and stay resident in the memory of each workstation. It is called a shell because it surrounds DOS and intercepts the workstation's network requests, rerouting them if required to a file server. Shells/requestors are available for different versions of DOS, OS/2 and Macintoshes so that all may connect to the same NetWare network.

Network address: During the installation of NetWare, using the NETGEN utility, a unique identifier number is assigned to each separate network attached to an internet, called the network address. In case of a file server operating more than one network (multiple NICs in the server), a unique address must be given to each additional network.

Network bus: See Bus.

Network drive: A physical drive attached to and/or controlled by the file server.

Network interface card (NIC): An add-on circuit board (card) that permits the connection of a workstation to a network cable. NICs can include, a transmitter, encoder/decoder circuitry, memory buffer, and a coprocessor.

Network operator: A user with special privileges on the network. An example is a print queue operator who is allowed to manage printer queues, changing or deleting print jobs in the queue.

NLM (NetWare Loadable Module): NetWare 386 feature). A program that can be dynamically loaded/linked and unloaded into the file server memory.

Node: Any attached network station.

Node address: See Station address.

Noise: Random electrical signals or magnetic disturbances, which can degrade the performance of any communication channel.

Nondedicated file server: A nondedicated file server functions as both a workstation and a file server, on the LAN. This must be requested during the installation of NetWare.

Null modem: A modem eliminator designed to directly connect two DTE's (data terminal equipment). It also performs any necessary signal conversions and may provide clocking.

Object: A defined entity on the network and thus accessible from the file server. Users, groups, file servers, print servers, archive servers, and so on. are classified as object types and are defined in the file server's bindery files.

Open System Interconnection (OSI): A model of seven layers defining local area network guidelines.

Operating system: A specialized software program that manages the hardware/software interfaces in a computer. See also NetWare operating system and Disk Operating System (DOS).

Overwrite: To write data to a storage device over existing data, destroying the original data.

Packet: A group of bits that are treated as a unit for communications and routing purposes. See also Message packets.

Packet switching: Transmitting packetized data across a shared medium (cable or line). This is a common transmission method on local area networks.

PAL (Programmable Array Logic): A programmable chip used to combine logic functions on a circuit board.

Parallel port: Commonly used as a printer interface. This port-type allows data to be transmitted a byte at a time, all 8 bits moving in parallel. See also LPT1.

Parameter: Value(s) restricting or determining the specific form of a command. Parameters with more than one value, are called a variable.

Parent directory: Any directory immediately above a subdirectory. SYS:PUBLIC is the parent directory of the subdirectory SYS:PUBLIC/MSDOS.

Parity: A common error checking method applied to characters or blocks of transmitted data. Eight bits of each transmitted character are totalled and a parity bit added make it total an odd number for odd parity or an even number for even parity. Most communications software requests that the data be retransmitted if there is a parity error.

Parity error: See Parity.

Parity check: See Parity.

Partition: Either a portion, or all of a hard drive can be allocated to a operating system (NetWare, DOS, OS/2, etc), creating a drive partition.

Passive hub: Some network topologies utilize this hardware device to split transmission signals. A passive hub does not amplify the signal. See also Active hub.

Password: A group of characters that is part of the security features used to confirm a users identity.

Path: A designation of a complete directory path starting from the drive and volume to the directory or subdirectory level not including the filename.

PDN: See Public Data Networks.

Peer-to-peer: A network communications scheme between devices with local processing power.

Peripheral: This term refers to any physical device such as a printer, modem, or a hard drive, that is physically connected to, and controlled by a computer.

Point-to-point: Data is transferred in a point-to-point environment from one location directly to another without the requirement of switches.

Polling: The status of attached devices or ports is regularly checked by this (polling) system, for requests which are then accepted and executed.

Port: If referring to hardware, it is a component that allows a CPU to communicate with a peripheral device. See also Parallel port and Serial port. Also refers to moving and/or translating data or programs environment to another.

Print device: A printer or other peripheral device used to create hard copy of data.

Print function: Any printer command that determines print job characteristic, for example the style of typeface.

Print job configuration: All characteristics that determine how a job is printed. This may include the mode, the form number, the number of copies, and a particular printer or queue that will be used.

Print mode: The of a group of print functions are combined. Some of the factors possible included are the style, size, bolding, and orientation of the typeface. The network supervisor uses the PRINTDEF utility to design and save various print modes, allowing users to easily select the desired combination of print functions.

Print server: The process that takes any print jobs from the print queue and sends them to the specified printer.

Prompt: Any character or message (from software) that appears on the display screen requiring a response from the user. "D:>" and "Enter your password :" are two possible prompts.

Property: One of the descriptive features of an object, defined in the file server's bindery files.

Protocol: Usually, a set of procedures or conventions for determining how and when to format and communicate data between two or more computers including any error handling. In a local area network, major protocols cover both the hardware level (Token Ring, Ethernet, Arcnet, etc.), and transport level (XNS, TCP/IP, etc.) See also XON/XOFF, and Parity.

Public access: This refers to the fact that all users have access rights to open, read, and search files in a particular directory.

Public data network (PDN): This is a system that is used to transport data to a remote location. These can also be called value added networks. Public data networks can connect to information services. These can be both public or private data services. Public data networks often use packet switching systems such as X.25.

Queue: "A waiting line" in which multiple jobs can be stored, pending processing or execution. A common queue in NetWare is a print spooler, which holds all data sent to network printers. The print spooler sends the data to the printer as fast as the printer can process it.

Random Access Memory (RAM): A type of temporary memory storage in which each byte of information has a particular address, independent of all other bytes, and can be accessed quickly in any order.

Read: To retrieve any data from a storage device (drive or memory).

Read-after-write verification: NetWare reads back any data written to a file server hard drive and compares it to the original data kept in file server RAM. If both sets of data match, the data is released from RAM. If not, the blocks physical location is marked as "bad," and NetWare's Hot Fix redirects the data to a redirection area located elsewhere on the drive. See also Bad block table, Hot fix, and Redirection area.

Read-only: A type of file attribute or FLAG that protects both program and datafiles. If a file is flagged Read-Only, a user can only read the file but cannot modify it. See also File attributes.

Read Only Memory (ROM): See ROM (Read Only Memory).

Read/Write: A file attribute or FLAG that permits a user to open and/or modify a files contents.

Record: A collection of logically related data that is usually one unit within a datafile. Example: first name, last name, address, and phone #.

Record locking: An important feature of multiuser operating systems/application programs that prevents multiple users from gaining simultaneous access to the same record in a shared file, thus ensuring data integrity. See also Lock.

Redirection area: A percentage of the file server hard drive space set aside during NetWare installation (with NETGEN) for Hot Fix. The redirection area is set up as a table for data blocks "redirected" from any bad physical blocks identified on the file server hard drive.

Redundancy: Within a protocol any portion of the total characters or data that could be eliminated without any actual loss of information.

Redundancy check: A programmed check based on the systematic insertion of characters or data used specifically for checking purposes.

Remote reset: A common network feature that enables any workstation to boot (load DOS and the network shell) from the network, without requiring a local workstation drive.

Remote workstation: A personal computer that is not physically attached to the LAN, but is connected to the LAN by a bridge. A remote workstation may be either a stand-alone microcomputer or a workstation on another network.

Request To Send (RTS): An RS232C control line between a modem and DTE initiating the data transmission sequence on a communications line. See also RS232C.

Resident program: A program that is loaded into workstation memory and remains there until the system is powered down or until it is reset (booted). See also TSR.

Resource: A term used by the NetWare installation program NETGEN. Refers to any device, feature, circuit board, or built-in circuitry that utilizes one or more of the following ways to communicate with the file server's CPU: interrupts, DMA lines, memory addresses (RAM or ROM), or Input Output (I/O) addresses.

Resource set: A term used by the NetWare installation program NETGEN. It collection of related resources has been assigned an identifying name. For example, if you choose the IBM Model 80 resource set, it will include definitions of all microchannel hardware available on the Model 80. See also Resource.

Response time: Any time interval the system requires to react to a given request, usually measured from the workstations. For example, the time between typing DIR at the F: > prompt and displaying the resultant directory listing.

Restore: To copy data from a backup storage device or archive copy onto to the file server hard drive.

Retry: The retransmission of a block of data a specified number of times.

Rights: Rights are a set of privileges which can be assigned to users or groups in a specified directory. It is these privileges that determine what these objects can do in the directory, combined with directory rights.

RJ11C: The standard 4-pin modular phone jack used with a single line telephone system.

RJ45: The standard 8-pin modular phone jack used with multiline systems.

ROM (Read Only Memory): This refers to permanent memory built into a chip. Often designated as "firmware," a ROM is a memory chip with data permanently embedded within its circuits. ROM data cannot be erased or modified. Data in a ROM can be quickly and randomly accessed. See also Random Access Memory (RAM).

Root directory: This directory is the highest directory in a "tree" directory structure. This directory is the "root" with all directories created below it. The root is the main directory on a volume, all other directories and subdirectories are below it.

Routing: Assigning the communications path by which a data packet or phone call can reach its destination.

Routing buffers: A portion of memory reserved during NETGEN in a file servers or bridge computer's RAM. Routing buffers temporarily store and queue the message packets to be processed when the file servers or bridge computers CPU or bus is busy. See also Buffer.

RS: Recommended Standard, that is, RS232C.

RS232C: A common hardware protocol for interfacing microcomputer system components. On a microcomputer, an RS232C is a serial port to a modem or a printer.

Screen buffer: A high memory area in RAM that contains the screen characters and attributes.

Scroll: To move the screen display or portion up, down, left, or right.

SCSI (Small Computer System Interface): Pronounced "Scuzzy." A common computer industry hardware and software standard that sets guidelines for connecting and communication between peripheral storage devices and their controllers to a CPU.

Search drive: A logical drive letter assigned to any network directory where the operating system will automatically search for an file if the file is not in the current (default) directory.

Sectors: Physical locations on a disk platter. Each track on the disk is divided into multiple sectors like a pie.

Security: Control of users access to directories and files on a NetWare network. Four levels are, login name and password, trustee rights, directory rights, and file attributes or FLAGS. See also Password, Rights and File attributes.

Security equivalence: User(s) or group(s) can easily be assigned the same (or equivalent) rights as another user. This function can only be used by the network SUPERVISOR (or equivalent).

Serialization: A method of software copy protection. In NetWare, each file server's operating system has a unique serial number and some application software or VAPs are locked to that unique serial number.

Serial port: A port through which each bit in a byte (character) is sent sequentially, one at a time. At the destination, the bits of data are reassembled into 8 bit bytes (characters). On microcomputers, the COMx ports are asynchronous serial ports. See also RS232C and Asynchronous.

Server console: See Console.

Session: In the SNA environment, this term is used to refer to a connection between two stations.

SFT (System Fault Tolerance): This NetWare feature increases data integrity by utilizing several levels of hardware and software options for this task. See also Disk duplexing, Disk mirroring, Hot fix, and TTS.

Shell: See NetWare shell.

Simplex (circuit): A circuit permitting transmission in one specific direction only.

SNA/SDLC (Systems Network Architecture/Synchronous Data Link Control): A protocol commonly used for communications between an IBM host computer and peripherals. SDLC is a full duplexed transmission system. It contains the following frames: a flag, address field, control field, data field, frame check sequence, and ending flag. These fields direct the communication to the appropriate destinations and provide error checking.

Software: Parts of a computer system that are intangible and not physical. Computer programs are referred to as software.

Spooler: Software or hardware that will take data being sent to a peripheral and store that data into temporary storage. The spooler releases data to the peripheral as the data can be processed.

SPX (Sequenced Packet Exchange): This is a NetWare protocol which allows two network workstations to communicate. Internetwork Packet Exchange (IPX) is utilized by SPX, however, the delivery is guaranteed by SPX.

Star: A LAN topology in which workstation cables radiate from a central point, one per cable.

Start bit: The control bit sent to indicate the start of a asynchronous transmission of a group of data bits.

Station address: A unique number (decimal or hexadecimal format) assigned (depending on NIC) to each station on a network, called the station address. This address is also referred to as either the "physical node address" or "node address."

Station number: See Connection number.

Stop bit: The control bit sent to indicate end of a asynchronous transmission of a group of data bits.

Storage: A device or medium (floppy diskette, hard drive, magnetic tape, cd rom, etc.) that receives and holds files (programs and/or data) for retrieval. Storage may be permanent or temporary.

Streaming tape backup: A method of tape backup in which data is recorded sequentially on a the tape as it "streams" past the recording head.

Subdirectory: Any directory below another directory in the directory structure. For example, SYS:PUBLIC/MSDOS is a subdirectory of SYS:PUBLIC.

Supervisor: This can either refer to the person responsible for the operation of a network, or the user SUPERVISOR. The network supervisor usually installs and maintains both hardware and software on the network. The user SUPERVISOR is a special username that is created during installation. The user SUPERVISOR automatically has all rights (which cannot be revoked) in all file server volumes and directories. Users or groups may be granted a equivalence to the SUPERVISOR. See also Security equivalence.

Switch block: A set of switches mounted in a block. In some microcomputers, switch blocks are used to control system configuration such as type of monitor, amount of RAM, and number of drives. NICs often use switch blocks to set any required addresses (such as station, IRQ, base I/O, and base memory location).

Synchronization: A process of maintaining the correct timing for communicating data between a transmitter and receiver.

Synchronous: A regulated time interval between successive data blocks of bits. All synchronous equipment communicates in blocks of bits instead of in a series.

Synchronous modem: A modem which uses a clocking signal to perform bit synchronization with the incoming blocks of bits.

System Fault Tolerance: See SFT.

Telecommunications: Transmission of data between separate locations over communication lines.

Terminal: A "user interface" device lacking any built-in processing capability. Terminals normally have only a keyboard and a display, and attach to and are dependant on a host computer for any processing or data storage.

Terminal emulation: This is software that gives a microcomputer the appearance of a mini or mainframe terminal. This is used when attaching to a host.

Terminate and stay resident (TSR): A program that is loaded into memory, executes a specific function, and does NOT release the memory space occupied by the program on exiting. The services of a TSR program are usually available after the program has been exited.

Terminating resistor (terminator): A grounding resistor placed at the end of a bus, line, or cable, preventing signals from being reflected or echoed.

Token/token passing: A token passing topology can be have any or all of the following token types, data token, synchronize-minor token, major/activity token, and release token. These are special recognizable packet configurations. This is a network access scheme in which these special packets or tokens are circulated around a network. Any workstation wanting to transmit, captures the token and when the workstation completes its transmission, it releases the token.

Topology: This term refers to the physical layout of network components (cable, stations, bridges, gateways, hubs, and so on). These can be a star, ring, or bus with various combinations. On a star, all workstations connect directly to a file server or hub. On a ring network, the file server and workstations are cabled in a ring, and a workstation's packets may have to pass through multiple workstation's NICs before reaching their destination. On a bus, the file server and all workstations share a central cable (called a trunk or bus) which they are connected too.

Tracks: These are locations on the physical disk platters, usually in the form of concentric circles. Tracks are divided into sectors to form the primary units of disk storage.

Traffic: Often used as a rough description of cable utilization volume (such as heavy, light, etc.)

Transaction: Any task is completed as a result of a set of operations (or transactions).

Transaction Tracking System: See TTS.

Transceiver: A transmit and receive device that converts digital information to and from a signal through a communication medium (cable or line).

Transient program: A program that is read or loaded into RAM, performs a specific function, and exits, releasing the memory space occupied by the program. See also Terminate and stay resident (TSR).

Transmission speed: The rate data elements sent per unit of time, usually expressed as bits, characters, or words. Common usage is bits per second (bps).

Transmit: To send signals or messages from source to destination through a communication medium such as coaxial cable, twisted-pair cable, phone line, fiber optic cable, microwave, and so on.

Transparent: Refers to hardware and/or software operations not normally noticeable to the user.

Trustee rights: The rights granted to a user or group allowing access to files (programs or data) located in a specified directory or subdirectory. See also Rights.

Trustee: A user with trustee rights.

TSR: See Terminate and Stay Resident.

TTS (Transaction Tracking System): A NetWare data protection system if the workstation or file server fails in the middle of a transaction. The transaction is "backed out" and the data is restored to its last completed state if there is a failure. See also Backing out.

Twin AX: This is a shielded coax cable, which receives its name from the two center conducting leads it contains. It is used in the IBM 5250 environment.

Twisted pair: A two wire cable type composed of two braided wires.

Upload/download: The transfer of data between computers usually via modem. Transferring data from a host to a remote computer is downloading, and from a remote computer to a host it is uploading.

UPS (uninterruptible power supply): A backup power system, often incorporating a battery which has been designed to provide continuous power in the event of a power interruption of a limited duration.

User: Any person who has a valid username/password on a file server.

Utility: Any program that performs one or more basic system management tasks, hardware, or software diagnostic.

V.: Numbers are CCITT modem recommendations.

V.24: List of definitions for interchange circuits between DTEs and DCEs. See also Data Terminal Equipment (DTE), Data Communications Equipment (DCE), and RS232C.

Validation (data): Checking data for correctness, or conformance with applicable rules, standards, or conventions.

Validity checking: A technique used to check the accuracy of data after a transmission.

Value-added process (VAP): An application that runs "on top" of the NetWare operating system in the file server (in much the same way application software runs on top of DOS).

VAPs tie in closely with NetWare so that products such as print or database servers can provide their services to all attached workstations without interfering with the operation of the network.

Virtual circuit: Used with X.25 networks, these circuits use a scheme of packet switching that gives the appearance of one dedicated line.

Virtual console utility: A utility program such as FCONSOLE that allows a workstation to perform as a file server console, to monitor and control some aspects of any file server activity.

Voiceband: A section of the available bandwidth for audio transmission, generally 300 to 3300 Hz. Also referred to as voice grade (VG).

Volume: This refers to a "logical" portion of the storage space on the file server hard drive. A volume root (similar to the DOS root directory) is the highest level in NetWare's directory structure or tree. By default, NETGEN creates one volume called SYS:. During installation (NETGEN) the hard drive can be divided into one or more volumes of predetermined storage size. Within these volumes users with the required rights can create and access directories and subdirectories as required.

Wait state: A set period of time when the CPU does nothing, it simply waits. A wait state is employed when you need to slow down higher speed devices to reliably communicate with other circuitry or devices operating at lower speeds.

Wait time: Referring to a NetWare UPS monitoring system, the "wait time" is the number of seconds the UPS will wait before signalling the file server that the normal power supply is off. When the main power supply fails NetWare informs all operational workstations to log out and then DOWNs the file server. See also UPS.

Warm boot: The process of resetting or booting computer while the power stays on. See also Boot.

Wide Area Network Interface Module (WNIM): An workstation interface card that physically routes LAN-to-remote, LAN-to WAN (wide area network), or remote-to-LAN asynchronous communications.

Wildcard character: A character recognized by some software as a universal replacement for one or more characters in filenames. NetWare recognizes the * and ? wildcard characters.

Word: A logical unit of information, can be 8 bits, 16 bits, or 32 bits, depending on hardware capabilities. Requested data is moved in a "word" across an interface or bus.

Workstation: Any microcomputer that is connected to a network.

Workstation number: See Connection number.

WORM (Write Once Read Many): This is a commercially available laser disc system where you can write to a blank disc. It is not compatible with CD ROM.

Write: To record or store data on a device.

X.25: A CCITT recommended protocol that defines the structure, contents, and sequencing procedures for data transmission between data terminal equipment, data communications equipment, and a public data network (usually packet switched).

XON/XOFF protocol: This communications protocol is used to establish and control the flow of communication between two devices such as a computer and a printer. Sometimes called "handshaking" this process is software driven in the computer/printer example to prevent data from being sent faster than the printer can process it.

APPENDICES

A.1 FILE EXTENSIONS

In this chapter

Common file extensions, the software program, and a brief description of the file usually found with this file extension.

Most files created by application software programs have file extensions. In many cases the file extension will tell you what kind of file it is. This list of some common file extensions in use is provided for easy reference when doing "housekeeping" on the network, to make it easier to identify files prior to deletion or archiving. This list is by no means complete, though examples have been given to outline file extension naming conventions.

> **NOTE:** Some word processors such as WordPerfect, or line editors such as Edlin or Q-Edit do not have a required file extension for datafiles, and a file extension can be added or even left blank as required.

File Extension	Program	Description
$$$	DOS	"Pipe" file created using the | redirection flag at the command line
$$$	(various programs)	Temporary work file, used by a program and usually deleted before the program is finished. If you have a file with a $$$ or a TMP extension, check it out-something may have gone wrong.
@@@	CodeviewDisk	

ACT	Bitcom	Account datafile, communications account
AIO	APL	Format file, for Application Programming Language (APL) file transfer
APL	APL	Format file, for Application Programming Language (APL) work space
APP	SQL Windows	Application file, Structured Query Language (SQL) Windows
ASC	(Various programs)	American Standard Computer Information Interchange (ASCII) text file (recognized by DOS), does not include control characters, typically added by most wordprocessing software
ASM	MASM	Macro Assembler source code file
AUX	PDox Pro	PDox Pro program file, which profiles Paradox database run time
BAK	(Various programs)	Backup file, usually an older version of a datafile
BAS	Basic	Basic program code file, not necessarily in ASCII
BAT	DOS	Disk Operating System (DOS) batch file, used for a set of commands to be executed by DOS, for example AUTOEXEC.BAT. Check your DOS manual for details
BIN	(Various programs)	Binary file, not an ASCII format, contains 8-bit information
BK1	WordPerfect	A Backup file created by WordPerfect when the program is not properly exited
BK!	WordPerfect	A timed backup file optionally created by the program

BMP	MS Windows	A datafile required for Windows bitmap structure
C	C Compilers	Source code file for programs written in the "C" language
CAL	Super Calc	Spreadsheet datafile
CFG	(various programs)	Usually a configuration file, presenting choices for various machines and environments in which the software will run
CHK	DOS	File of data recovered using the CHKDSK/F option
CMD	DBase	File containing DBase programs (Command file)
CMP	MS Word	Spell Check dictionary compare file
CNF	(various programs)	Usually a configuration file, presenting choices for various machines and environments in which the software will run
COB	Cobol	Source code for a program written in the COBOL language
COD	Fortran	Compiled code file, FORTRAN program
COM	DOS	Command file, usually an executable program file in memory image format. To activate the program in a DOS environment, use the letters of the file name.
CRF	MASM	Cross reference file produced by a Macro Assembler compiler
CTX	MS Word	On-line tutorial files (course text file)
CUR	MS Windows	Windows cursor datafile
DB	Paradox	Paradox datafile (tables)

DBF	DBase	DBase database file
DBS	SQL Windows	SQL Windows database file
DBT	DBase	DBase Text database datafile
DEF	(various programs)	Definition file
DEV	(various programs)	Device driver file, used by config.sys to install drivers (See CONCEPTS, Chpt.3 Software, Sec. 3.1 Basics)
DGS	PC DOS	Diagnostic file
DIC	(various programs)	Dictionary file, part of spell check-various word processors
DIF	(various programs)	Data Interchange Format (DIF) file, used for data interchange between application software programs
DIR	(various programs)	Directory file
DOC	(various programs)	Document file
DRV	(various programs)	Device driver file, for example MOUSE.DRV would be for a mouse
EPS	(various programs)	Encapsulated PostScript file in PostScript language
EXE	(various programs)	Executable program file, for example, the main WordPerfect program file is WP.EXE. To activate the program in a DOS environment, use the letters of the file name.
FMT	DBase	Format file, for screen display
F#	Paradox	Form file, information required to define forms for data presentation

FNT	(various programs)	Font file, used by word processors, desktop publishing, and other programs to define "fonts" for text
FON	Windows	Font file
FOR	Fortran	Source code file for a program written in the FORTRAN language
FRM	DBase	Form file with formatting information for DBase reports generated from database information
H	C Compiler	Header file, with source code for a program written in C language
HEX	Debug	Hexadecimal file
HLP	(various programs)	Help file, usually electronic program documentation for users
ICO	MS Windows	Icon file, with the data required to create an Icon
IDX	(various programs)	Index file, usually indexing information for a database
IMG	MS Windows	Image file
IMP	Pascal	Implementation file
INC	(various programs)	Include file
INI	(various programs)	Initialization file, used by MS Windows, and MS Word
INT	Pascal	Interface file
JOR	SQL Windows	Journal file
LAY	Superkey	Layout file, for keyboard information

LBL	DBase	Label file, mailing labels, etc.
LEX	WordPerfect	Spell check file, dictionary
LIB	(various programs)	Library file, usually a compiled program in any of a variety of formats
LOD	(various programs)	Load file, for example, used by the Ventura desktop publishing package to import text from various word processors
LST	MASM	Assembled Source code listing file, for Macro Assembler
MAC	(various programs)	Macro file, usually created from the keyboard, listing a key sequence which can be replayed exactly as required
ME	(various programs)	Information file, for example a file called READ.ME, can usually be viewed using "type read.me" at the DOS prompt line
MEM	DBase	Memory file
MNU	NetWare	Menu file, with information for customized user menus
NDX	DBase	Index file, with database indexing data
NET	Paradox	Shareable network file, used to track users, and files in use
OVD	Paradox	Overlay file
OVL	(various programs)	Overlay file
OVR	(various programs)	Overlay file
OV#	(various programs)	Overlay file
PAS	Pascal	Source code file for programs written in the PASCAL language

PCX	Paintbrush	Picture file
PCC	Paintbrush	Picture file (cutouts)
PFM	MS Windows	Metric printer font file
PGM	(various programs)	Overlay file in most cases
PIC	(various programs)	Picture file (graphics)
PIX	(various programs)	One or several pictures in a single file
PIF	MS Windows	Program Information File, for example, WordPerfect has PIF files for Windows memory loading requirements.
PRD	MS Word	Printer definition file, for printer communication
PRF	VisiCalc	Print format file
PRG	DBase	Program file
PRN	(various programs)	Print file, can indicate the format
PUB	Pagemaker	Publication file, for page layout
PX	Paradox	Primary Index file
RC	MS Windows	Resource Script file, listing resource definitions
R#	Paradox	Report file, each one is numbered and contains definitions of customized data output (reports)
SC	Paradox	Script file, created using the paradox PAL language, scripts are "played" when required
SCN	Microsoft	Screen file of on-line tutorials
SET	(various programs)	Setting file, in Wordperfect, it integrates the three initials users type in at start up, saved into

		a file containing formatting, fonts, screen display options, etc.
SOB	Microsoft	On-line tutorial file
SOM	Paradox	Sort file
SQL	SQL Windows	Datafile
STY	(various programs)	Style file. In Ventura styles contain setting for page layout, special text "tags" fonts graphics, etc. Sty files also used by WordPerfect in a similar way, however editing is more difficult.
SUP	WordPerfect	Supplemental spell check file, added to the default path during spell check, can be edited the same as a document, or combined with the main dictionary.
SYM	MS Windows	Symbolic definitions for debugging
SYN	(various programs)	Synonym file, has thesaurus program information
SYS	(various programs)	Device driver file
TIF	(various programs)	Tag Image File Format (TIF) used to exchange graphic files
TMP	(various programs)	Temporary work file, used by a program and usually deleted before the program is finished. If you have a file with a TMP, or a $$$ extension, check it out-something may be wrong if programs are not exiting correctly.
TXT	(various programs)	Text file, often in ASCII format
VAL	Paradox	Validity check file
VC	VisiCalc	Spreadsheet datafile
WK1	Lotus 1-2-3	Spreadsheet datafile (ver. 2.X)

WKS	Lotus 1-2-3	Spreadsheet datafile (ver. 1.0)
WRI	MS Windows	Write document file
X#	Paradox	Index file
XLC	MS Excel	Chart file
XLS	MS Excel	Spreadsheet file
Y#	Paradox	Index file
Z#	Paradox	Index file

A.2 CHECKLIST FOR A WORKING SYSTEM

In this chapter

Checklist for Installing NetWare, NetWare utilities in UPPERCASE LETTERS, command line utilities in lowercase

These are the steps in setting up a NetWare system. This list is provided as a checklist, the keystrokes and Utilities are listed as sub headings of the step. The NetWare Utilities required to perform each operation are listed in UPPERCASE LETTERS, while the command line operations are in lowercase. This checklist is provided as an overview, and does not detail each operation. For a detailed description of the operation of NetWare's Utilities listed, see the reference section.

1. Design Directory Structure on Paper.

2. Design Security Structure on Paper.

3. Create Directories.

- MD
- FILER

4. Install Application Software.

5. Flag all necessary files, that is, shareable, read only, and so on.

    - FlAG
    - FILER

6. Create Templates for Optional Account/Balance Restrictions.

    - SYSCON (SUPERVISOR OPTIONS)

7. Create Users.

    - SYSCON (USER INFORMATION)

8. Create Groups.

    - SYSCON (GROUP INFORMATION)

9. Assign Members to Groups.

    - SYSCON (USER or GROUP INFORMATION)

10. Assign Trustee Rights to all Groups.

    - SYSCON (GROUP INFORMATION-TRUSTEE DIRECTORY ASSIGNMENTS)

11. Assign Individual Trustee Rights.

    - SYSCON (USER INFORMATION-TRUSTEE DIRECTORY ASSIGNMENTS)

12. Assign Any Individual Optional Login/Password, Time, or Station Restrictions, and Give Users a Password.

    - SYSCON (USER INFORMATION-ACCOUNT RESTRICTIONS)

13. OPTIONAL: Set up any Required Console Operators.

    - SYSCON (SUPERVISOR OPTIONS-FILE SERVER CONSOLE OPERATORS)

14. OPTIONAL: Establish Intruder Detection.

    - SYSCON (SUPERVISOR OPTIONS-INTRUDER DETECTION/LOCKOUT)

15. OPTIONAL: Set up Accounting.

    - SYSCON (ACCOUNTING)

NOTE: Remember to give users an account balance.

- SYSCON (USER INFORMATION-ACCOUNT BALANCE, UNLIMITED CREDIT)

16. Create System Login Script.

    - SYSCON (SUPERVISOR OPTIONS-SYSTEM LOGIN SCRIPT)

17. Create Individual Login Scripts.

    - SYSCON (USER INFORMATION-LOGIN SCRIPT)

18. **TEST IT!** Login as each one of the users you have created in step 7, and make changes as required.

19. Set up Printers.

    - PRINTDEF (Optional)
    - PRINTCON (Optional)
    - PCONSOLE (Optional)

20. **TEST IT!**

21. Create any Menus and Supporting Batch Files Users will need.

22. **TEST THEM!**

23. OPTIONAL: Set up Uninterrupted Power Supply (UPS) configuration (config.) file.

A.3 DOCUMENTATION

In this chapter

Documenting a Network, why and how. A suggested documentation style

---

A.3.1 Why Document a Network?

System documentation is considered a requirement for mainframes and minis. Systems analysts have discovered that it is absolutely indispensable for

- system maintenance,
- installing software upgrades,
- training new personnel.

Whereas documentation is regarded as essential for both mainframes and minis, Networks do not seem to be as important, for at first glance, a LAN appears to be just microcomputers. The reality is that modern networks, utilizing the distributing processing of microcomputers have more computing capabilities than minis did even a few years ago.

Computing once the exclusive territory of mainframes and minis is fast being taken over by microcomputers. There is a much greater choice of application programs for micros, all at a fraction of the cost for a comparable minibased program. This cost saving is true even for multiuser software packages common on LANs.

Only a few years ago a mini with a 28 megabyte disk drive was considered the latest technology. Today file servers with a single drive capacity of over 500 megabytes are not uncommon. Large file server drives now make it possible for database applications to process and store vast amounts of data, many times larger than what was considered to be a major database only a few years ago.

Clearly the technology has changed, unfortunately the need for documentation has managed to get forgotten in the headlong advance of technology.

Unfortunately the need for documentation is only first recognized when a new system manager takes over a network, finding that nobody has any idea what is on the system, where datafiles and applications are located, or what many applications are used for and who is using them.

In many cases, without documentation it can be difficult and extremely costly to determine even the most basic information, here are a few examples

- How are the physical, logical, and search drives set up and how do they operate system wide and per user?
- What are the subdirectories in each volume, and what do they contain?
- What are the volumes, drive storage used/available?
- When was the file server installed, and what version of NetWare is it running?
- What versions of all software on the system?
- How do various software packages communicate?
- What network workstation utilities are available, and where are they located?
- How often are backups done, and where are they stored?
- Are there unnecessary or outdated directories, datafiles and/or software packages?
- what size/capacity is the file server, is SFT enabled, are the drives mirrored or duplexed?

Good documentation should be able to answer these and many more questions easily. The answers should be on paper, not in the mind of one individual who has unfortunately left the company.

A.3.2 A Suggested Documentation Style

While there are endless possibilities for documentation, this text offers a simple documentation formula, which if followed should provide most of the answers you will require. It has been designed by the authors utilizing their combined expertise to provide good documentation at a reasonable cost. A complete system documented by two of the authors while developing this style was done in less than a week, which included time for revisions. This did not include the time to prepare a wiring (topology) map which was already available. Ideally, documentation should be completed by one person who knows the system intimately, usually the Manager of Information Services (MIS) and a technical writer familiar with NetWare. Obviously each situation is different, and the time has been offered only as a guideline for an MIS contemplating system documentation.

The documentation should be done in four sections

- management,
- system,
- user,
- support.

A.3.4 Management Documentation

This section has been designed to give management a "snapshot" of the system, without getting into much technical detail. It focuses on management concerns such as physical descriptions, wiring (topology), as well as backup and maintenance procedures. If possible a quick map of the topology and workstation locations should be supplied. Any unusual technical expressions should be explained in a definitions list at the end of this section.

These are the suggested sections

Network Operating System: Include the NetWare version, and the installation date if that information is available.

File Server(s): Document the physical description of your file server hardware. Indicate if the server is dedicated or nondedicated, and include the model number(s) and installation date(s). Indicate the size of the memory, and the hard drives, mirrored or duplexed.

Document any internal or external bridges on your LAN. In general terms, describe the bridging used, and the interface card options chosen for that bridging.

A.3.5 Physical Wiring (Topology)

Indicate the network topology, and explain any hubs backbones, and so on, that have been utilized, and how additions and reassignments can be best accomplished.

A.3.6 Network Backup

Backup Storage Provisions

Explain any special storage provisions such as fireproof vaults, and the rating (insurance use) and any other backup storage locations such as the off site backups. Document the location of the backup log.

Daily Backup (complete system): Clearly outline what medium is used, and if these are done every weekday, or seven days a week, how they are labeled, and where are they stored. When do these backups rotate, in other words is there only one for each day which gets used over and over once a week. A rotational daily backup is usually recommended providing the other recommendations listed are followed. This is not a hard and fast rule, however. The management section does not need to explain the software used, put this information in the system documentation. Clearly indicate where these backups are kept.

Weekly Backup (complete system): Document what actually happens. If weekly backups are not done, suggest that five backups (or more if required) be used on a rotational basis to ensure that a full month's backup is available at all times. Clearly indicate where these backups are stored.

Audit Backup (complete system): Document what actually happens. If audit backups are not done, suggest that permanent monthly (or more if required) audit backups be maintained. If tapes, lock the backups, or if floppies, attach write protect tabs. These should be run after month end and after year end processing. Clearly indicate where these backups are stored.

A.3.7 Network System Maintenance

A single sentence should indicate how often system maintenance is done, and by whom. Refer the reader to the system documentation for further details.

A.3.8 Local Hard Drives

Document all local hard drives, and indicate the size in megabytes, the backup medium (disks or tape), how often this is done, and where the backups are stored. Identify clearly the person responsible for this backup.

Local Hard Drive Maintenance

Outline how this is done, and by whom.

Definitions

Explain any unusual words used, or refer to the Glossary contained in this book. Management does not always know terms such as System Fault Tolerance (SFT), nor in most cases do they need to know more than the overview. This can be achieved through the use of the Glossary.

Attachments

Note any attachments such as the Wiring (Topology) map, and any sample forms such as a backup log mentioned in the documentation.

A.3.9 System Documentation

General Overview

Explain that this section provides a road map of the network system and like a road map it provides an overview of the system layout. Ideally detailed information for versions, installation dates, and updates of individual software packages listed in one location. The actual files in each directory should not be listed, but rather the directory names should indicate the contents.

File Server Name, and Volume Name(s)

List the names as required, indicating the size (in megabytes) of each volume, and its logical drive designation.

First Volume (SYS: -created by NetWare during installation): Four subdirectories of the volume SYS: are created automatically by NetWare during installation, they are, LOGIN, MAIL, PUBLIC, AND SYSTEM. Document these four, and any additional directories you create, as follows

<LOGIN>

This directory, one of four created by NetWare during the operating system installation can be accessed prior to Login. Therefore, by definition there is no security for this directory. It contains two files:

LOGIN.EXE-allows the user to Login to the system,
SLIST.EXE-provides a list of all available file servers to which a user can login to.

<MAIL>

This directory is one of four created by NetWare during the initial operating system installation. As users on the system are created, NetWare sets up a subdirectory with each User's ID number. Note if a custom login script has been written for each user to configure the system, interface for individual user requirements.

<PUBLIC>

This directory is one of four created by NetWare during the initial operating system installation. Document what is installed here, however this directory should contain all of the required NetWare utilities, shareable batch files, and other shareable DOS utilities. Ideally, versions of MSDOS should be contained in appropriately named subdirectories which are then mapped as search drives to suit workstation hardware requirements during the Login process by the System Login Script (NET$LOG.DAT) usually created by the supervisor.

<SYSTEM>

This directory is one of four created by NetWare during the initial operating system installation. It should contain NetWare system utilities used for maintenance including a system security diagnostic program (SECURITY).

<DIRECTORY_NAME>

Indicate the contents of each additional directory you have created, and explain what the files are used for, and if necessary how they communicate with other software located in other directories.

Second Volume: Additional volumes are created if required, during installation. If your system contains additional volumes, document them.

<DIRECTORY_NAME>

Indicate the contents of each directory, and explain what the files are used for, and if necessary how they communicate with other software located in other directories.

User Documentation

Document as required any custom software developed for Users. This can be a long process, and should not be embarked upon without considering the time and costs involved. There are many good books on the preparation of good user documentation, and reference to these is recommended.

Naturally, it is recommended that you do not document application software for which some form of documentation is currently available, this is completely unnecessary and extremely expensive.

Support Documentation

This documentation is a daily tool for supporting all software on the network, and as such it has been fully described in another section (See Part 2 REFERENCE, Chpt. 19 System Management, Sec. 19.4 Documentation.)

INDEX

A

B

C

D

E

F

G

H

I

L

M

N

O

P

T

U

V

W

X